FRANCES
A CHELSEA (

FRANCES FAVIELL (1905-1959

Faviell Lucas, painter and author. She studied at the Slade School of Art in London under the aegis of Leon Underwood. In 1930 she married a Hungarian academic and travelled with him to India where she lived for some time at the ashram of Rabindranath Tagore, and visiting Nagaland. She then lived in Japan and China until having to flee from Shanghai during the Japanese invasion. She met her second husband Richard Parker in 1939 and married him in 1940.

She became a Red Cross volunteer in Chelsea during the Phoney War. Due to its proximity to the Royal Hospital and major bridges over the Thames Chelsea was one of the most heavily bombed areas of London. She and other members of the Chelsea artists' community were often in the heart of the action, witnessing or involved in fascinating and horrific events throughout the Blitz. Her experiences of the time were later recounted in the memoir *A Chelsea Concerto* (1959).

After the war, in 1946, she went with her son, John, to Berlin where Richard had been posted as a senior civil servant in the post-war British Administration (the CCG). It was here that she befriended the Altmann Family, which prompted her first book *The Dancing Bear* (1954), a memoir of the Occupation seen through the eyes of both occupier and occupied. She later wrote three novels, *A House on the Rhine* (1955), *Thalia* (1957), and *The Fledgeling* (1958). These are now all available as Furrowed Middlebrow books.

BY FRANCES FAVIELL

FICTION

A House on the Rhine (1955)
Thalia (1957)
The Fledgeling (1958)

MEMOIR

The Dancing Bear (1954)
A Chelsea Concerto (1959)

FRANCES FAVIELL

A CHELSEA CONCERTO

With a foreword
by Virginia Nicholson

DEAN STREET PRESS
A Furrowed Middlebrow Book

A Furrowed Middlebrow Book
FM4

Published by Dean Street Press 2016

Copyright © 1959 Frances Faviell
Introduction copyright © 2016 Virginia Nicholson

All Rights Reserved

The right of Frances Faviell to be identified as the Author
of the Work has been asserted by her estate in accordance
with the Copyright, Designs and Patents Act 1988.

Cover by DSP

First published in 1959 by Cassell & Company Ltd.

The lines from A. P. Herbert's poem 'Let's be Gay'
on page 207 appeared in his book *Let's be Gay*
and are reprinted by kind permission of Sir Alan Herbert
and the publishers, Methuen & Co. Ltd.

ISBN 978 1 911413 77 6

www.deanstreetpress.co.uk

For
My son, John

FOREWORD TO THE NEW EDITION

I FIRST CAME across Frances Faviell's memoir of the Blitz when embarking on research for a book of my own about women's wartime experiences. A couple of the standard histories referred me to *A Chelsea Concerto* (1959), so I borrowed a copy from the London Library. This was the beginning of a two-year quest to trace its author, and to pursue every possible avenue in trying to retell her story.

What was it about the book that so possessed me? There is a huge genre of what might be termed "Blitz-Lit", telling the story of that extreme period endured by (largely) Londoners, between autumn 1940 and spring 1941, when the Luftwaffe attacked their city nightly, and in which more than 40,000 civilians were killed in seventy-one major air raids. But among all the available diaries and memoirs (and I read many of them), Faviell's Chelsea story was the star.

There are books where we want to find out what happens, and *A Chelsea Concerto* is certainly one of those. But more than that, I found – every time I turned to it – that I relished its author's company. I wanted to be with her; I wanted to experience the Blitz through her eyes and sensibility. The book had been out of print for years and, with difficulty, I acquired a second hand copy.

Frances Faviell was not her real name. She was born Olivia Faviell Lucas in 1905 and studied painting at the Slade School under the famous Henry Tonks. Little is known about her first marriage to a Hungarian painter named Karoy Fabri, but after they parted Frances continued to paint under the name Olivia Fabri. In 1940 she was engaged to a government official named Richard Parker, whom she married that autumn; their son, John, was born in an air raid in September 1941. Her chosen borough, Chelsea, was rich in artists and writers, and she relished their company. She was well-travelled, attractive, a talented linguist and artistic.

Faviell paints as vibrantly with words as she must have with colours. In early September 1940, the sky above the Thames is 'gay and alive with silver balloons...like drunken fish.' A few days later, the sirens alert London to its first bombardment, and Frances watches the East End burning from the roof of her building in Cheyne Walk: 'Presently, instead of darkness following the sunset it remained light – a curious yellow-orange light almost like sunrise.' With an artist's eye, she records the tracery of searchlight patterns, the beauty of fires caused by incendiary bombs falling 'like fireflies', and the blood-red taint of the sky above London after the appalling raid of 29 December: 'the kind of sky in which Turner would have delighted.'

But Faviell's powers of observation are not limited to the picturesque. For the social historian like me, her noticing glance has a compelling authenticity. A lull in the bombing brings women out to have their hair permed – '...during the Blitz...no one fancied being caught in a raid when fastened securely to the waving machine.'

Likewise, she picks up on the wartime propensity for firemen and rescue workers to call each other by nicknames – 'Smasher, Crasher, Tapper, Dibs, and similar ones...It gave some sort of equality to the heterogeneous mixture of people all working together in the common cause.' Elsewhere, she notes the tendency for guests to arrive at a Christmas party equipped with pyjamas and toothbrush, prepared to stay the night in an air raid shelter should the need arise. In the shelters, too, Frances's maternal heart is stirred at the 'infinitely moving' sight of mothers, in the most primitive of circumstances, helping their children prepare for sleep, tucking them up with a cuddly toy. And we are there with her.

Emotions like this are easy to share – but Frances's humane readiness to allow vibrant responses to surface is unusual in the stiff-upper-lip literature of the time, and it is this above all which makes her such a rare companion. When Frances tells us she feels 'real craven fear', we are terrified with her. Her patriotism is real too, as is her choked emotion at the spectacle of the little boats limping up the Thames, after rescuing the British Expeditionary Force from Dunkirk. We are with her too during the strains, stresses and cheerful democracy of the First Aid Post, and we share her engulfing fury and despair at the burning of her city, and the pointless loss of life. Compassion underlies her narrative. The cast of characters who inhabit Faviell's Chelsea – painters and writers, refugees and VADs, The Giant, Penty, Kathleen, Mr and Mrs Ferebee, Granny from Paradise Walk and many others, some lovable, some exasperating, but all real – are a microcosm of London's suffering millions. Their personal adversities were repeated across our capital, and across our nation.

Underlying the particulars of daily life in wartime Chelsea is a love story. Richard Parker is not at the forefront of Frances's tale, but he is never far away. During the Battle of Britain Frances and Richard watch a twisting diving dogfight in the sky above Hendon. Suddenly, she recognises that she is witnessing 'the real thing... WAR. I was glad Richard was with me...I thought then – nothing matters if you are with the person you want to be with.' As in the best of stories, it becomes vital to the reader that their happiness should survive the horrors that will befall it.

On this front, the reader may need a strong stomach. Frances Faviell's account brings the atrocities of war into ghastly close-up. Working as a nurse at a First Aid Post brought her up against horrific injuries; it was often her task to reassemble bodies dismembered by blast, in preparation for identification. But as we read, we know that not even this can prepare her for the experience of a direct hit on her own home. If you want to know what it feels like to be bombed, look no further. If for nothing else, the penultimate chapter of *A Chelsea Concerto* should find a prominent place in the anthologies of war.

Post-war, Frances picked up the artistic social life that she left behind in 1939. With time and peace of mind to give to painting, she resumed her work as a miniaturist and portraitist, and acquired a name as a published writer. But the war memories persisted. Though she found it painful and difficult, Frances embarked on her book about the Chelsea Blitz, finding it both liberating and cathartic. But *A Chelsea Concerto* was to be her last literary venture. In 1959 Frances Faviell confronted an unwinnable war, for at fifty-four she was dying of an untreatable cancer.

Her book was forgotten, by all except historians. Unpicking Faviell's own story from her memoir, in order to re-tell it in a larger context, and discovering what happened to her in the years leading up to her death, was to prove challenging. But a prolonged search finally led me to Frances's son, John Parker. It was a relief to meet him, to fill in the gaps in my knowledge, and to discover that many of my instincts about his mother were correct.

Now, at last, John's efforts are bringing *A Chelsea Concerto* to a new audience, and his mother's jewel of Blitz-lit will live again.

Virginia Nicholson
November 2015

ACKNOWLEDGEMENTS

ALTHOUGH this account of the Blitz and its prelude is as correct and authentic as I could make it, it is necessarily restricted by being a personal experience and is in no way intended either as a documentary or a history. It has been extremely difficult to obtain the details as there are as yet no collated records of the Blitz; and for this reason I have confined my book to those incidents in which I either participated, witnessed, or which were vouched for by those working in my own group of Civil Defence.

As with each painter the same model presents a different aspect, so to each of us a shattering experience such as those eight months has necessarily left widely divergent memories coloured by that aspect of the Blitz which affected us each personally. Should this book give the impression that only a small circle was involved I would remind readers that in the Civil Defence Services we were all strictly confined to our own particular area or post unless specially seconded in emergencies to others. That large and magnificent band of ordinary civilians, artisans, housewives, business men, artists, authors, and people of every walk of life are now scattered. Many are dead – others prefer not to remember those tragic but stirring days – and for me the writing of this account has been painful as well as difficult. If I have inadvertently been incorrect on any point I apologize and beg the indulgence of all those concerned as I do for the omission of all those wonderful fellow workers with whom I have lost touch. To the many people who have helped me with information and with the checking of dates and times of events and incidents I am deeply grateful and herewith record my thanks.

Through the good offices of Captain Councillor Cecil Townsend of the Royal Hospital and Chelsea Town Hall I was not only able to get in touch with many former friends from the days of the Blitz but also to obtain valuable help from Mr F E Wenham, Civil Defence Instructor, Mr Jack Eldridge, assistant to the Town Clerk in Civil Defence, and Mr Ronald Buse, his assistant.

Miss Doris Eldridge, of the Chelsea Municipal Library, was most kind in helping me trace records and reports of events and in hunting up sources of information. The Editor and staff of the *West London Press* were both interested and very helpful; and I am indebted to their paper as well as to *The Times* for much help, as also to the *Daily Telegraph* and to the *Manchester Guardian* for corroboration of events and checking of dates. The Imperial War Museum's staff were extremely helpful. I owe an enormous debt to Miss Jo Oakman, fellow painter and former ARP warden, who most generously allowed me access to her private records of the Blitz and who checked and re-checked various incidents with me. Mr and Mrs George Evans and Miss Hilda Reid, former ARP wardens in the area in which I worked, have been most gracious in giving me details from their own personal diaries of the Blitz and in helping me with their own recollections of events. Dr Graham Kerr allowed me the use of her own diary of the first part of the Blitz and Mr Graham Kerr, former ARP warden, helped me with personal memories, as did the Misses Iredale-Smith, who were wardens for our own street.

Lady Compton, my former Red Cross Commandant, has been extremely kind with much help on many points, and to her and my fellow VADs, especially Peggy Dowdall, I owe special thanks, as I do to Dr Lendal Tweed. To Suzanne, Elizabeth, and Denise Fitzgerald I am as much indebted for their help with dates and events as I am for their unfailing kindness to us during and after the Blitz. Mrs Margerie Scott, author and broadcaster, sent me much help on various points from her present home in Canada and to Sir Ernest Rock Carling I owe thanks both for constant encouragement and for the checking of events.

Mrs May Sargent helped me with details of her relatives the Marshmans, and the Registrar of Births, Marriages, and Deaths in Chelsea gave me valuable help in corroborating dates.

My final and perhaps most hesitant thanks are due to Edmund Blunden, who urged me to persevere and complete this book when I was about to abandon it as hopeless.

Map of CHELSEA

PROLOGUE

LAST NIGHT there was a concert in aid of the Red Cross in the beautiful chapel of the Royal Hospital, Chelsea. A lovely still, mellow evening and the gardens and building itself looked inexpressibly peaceful and ageless as the audience strolled in them during the interval and watched the barges passing on the Thames. I walked there too, and chatted with some of the old Pensioners sitting in the late sun on the benches under the cloisters, under those Latin words which describe them so touchingly as 'broken by age and the wars'.

From there I could see children and dogs playing in that piece of ground near the river belonging to the hospital and open to the public – the place where I once walked and played with my little Dachshund Vicki, known to many as 'Miss Hitler', and where I met and made many friends. And suddenly, as I stood there, they all came crowding back again – the grey ghost faces, the wail of the sirens, the sound of gunfire, the crash and reverberation of bombs, the drone of planes and the crackle of flames. Back they all came... Kathleen, Anne, Cecil, Larry, Catherine and the baby, Grannie and the horse, Beauty, the East Enders, the refugees...

Why just now? Why? I don't walk in this part of Chelsea as frequently as I used to do, so much has happened since then. But sometimes on an evening such as this I stroll along the Thames and up Swan Walk and so come to what used to be my home, No. 33, Cheyne Place. It is all rebuilt now, a small elegant, modern house. It used to be much taller and the first floor had three windows from which I could look down Swan Walk to the river, and above this was the flat where Kathleen, Anne, and Penty lived. Farther down the river the Old Church, destroyed the same night as my home, is almost rebuilt and Queen Elizabeth the Queen Mother will attend its consecration.

Chelsea has a proud record of her citizens in the days of the Germans' Blitz on London. They acquitted themselves magnificently in the Battle of the Bombs, emerging at the end of the war with a splendid list of decorations and awards for their gallantry under fire. The little borough was the third most heavily bombed in London. Of her war-time population no less than 2,099 were bomb casualties, 534 of these being fatal. This meant roughly that one in every fourteen persons in Chelsea was killed or injured. Her citizens, many of them distinguished in the world of art and letters, many of them ordinary, unpretentious workers at everyday jobs, joined together in a unanimously determined effort and worked magnificently in Civil Defence to battle with the bombs.

It seems only yesterday that I too, like these pretty young nurses selling programmes, wore that uniform of the Red Cross. And the ghosts will not recede or leave me in peace. Pushing, jostling, thrusting away their grey forms they blossom before my eyes from the muted cobwebby hues of memory to those of warm, pulsating life. They will not recede; insistent and determined they force me to take up my pen and go back with them to the summer of 1939...

Chelsea
June 1956-March 1958

PART I

REHEARSAL

CHAPTER ONE

WE WERE HAVING a grand-scale Civil Defence exercise in Chelsea. It was June 19th, 1939. We all thought the idea very silly – we'd had one scare the previous year – and now it all seemed childish. We'd filled sand-bags, dug trenches, fitted thousands of gas-masks, only to throw them all away in an excess of relief when Chamberlain returned from Godesburg with a respite from Hitler. The scare of war had largely died away because the public had decided that it should die away. There would be no war – and the forlorn abandoned gas-masks on rubbish heaps, and the bursting sand-bags seeping over pavements and streets, were witnesses to the public's decision.

And now, almost a year later, here we were in Chelsea having this full-scale exercise in our little borough. Mrs Freeth, my housekeeper, and I had both been given our parts to play. I was to be a casualty, she was to take shelter on a piece of pavement marked with white-painted lines to indicate that here (when built) would be the air-raid shelter for our area. I was living at No. 33, Cheyne Place in the Royal Hospital Road. In this exercise this was in District Sloane under Major H A Christie. Our group warden was Mr Paul de Laszlo. Air-raid wardens had called and instructed us in the parts we were to play – we had been thoroughly drilled.

The exercise was timed for twelve noon, and Mr Harold Scott [later Sir Harold Scott], the Commissioner for Police, had ordered that all traffic should be stopped for fifteen minutes – it was said that he himself would be present. Friends who had trained with me in first aid and who were acting as wardens appeared for the first time in uniforms. They caused a lot of ribald comment. Brown overalls with ARW in yellow on the breast pocket brought jeers from many onlookers. The uniforms, mass produced, did not fit – and some of the women's seats were on a level with their knees. I felt sorry for some of my friends with trim, neat figures having to appear in public in them.

The sirens wailed – the anguished lament of a soul in torment – and we all took up our positions with combined grumbling and that fear of ridicule ingrained in us all. It did seem ridiculous to have to lie flat on a piece of marked pavement pretending to be a casualty, but it seemed to me that to do so was the easiest way out of an argument as to whether I was to be in the First Aid Post or in the Control Report Centre in the Town Hall, I having taken the training for both. Mrs Freeth, worried about some special dish in the oven, thought it a ridiculous way of wasting a morning. She had Vicki, my Dachshund, in her arms, being determined that if the dog couldn't stand there with her in the allotted space she wouldn't stand there either. It was a point on which our warden was not prepared to argue. Whether dogs or cats would be allowed in shelters he was unable to say, but to Mrs Freeth's argument that as the shelter wasn't yet built Vicki had just as much right to stand on the pavement as she had there was no answer. The rumour went round that many distinguished visitors had arrived to see our exercise, including Sir John Anderson, the Home Secretary, Sir John Gowers, the Regional Commissioner, and Mr Harold Scott. Everyone was on his or her mettle!

At the given signal I lay down on the pavement awaiting the attention of my fellow VADs in the Mobile Unit. I lay there staring up at a poster, which after the interminable wait for the exercise to begin I knew by heart.

'Although we differ in many aspects of policy, we unite in urging you to volunteer for training – to protect yourselves and your neighbours.' It was issued jointly by the Chairmen and leaders of Chelsea Communist Party, Chelsea Conservative and Unionist Party, Chelsea Labour Party and Trades Council, and Chelsea Municipal Reform Party.

Its impressive message that in unity lies strength was marred by a large swastika painted on it, and looking up at it made me chuckle happily.

The Oswald Mosley Party had been going round at night in their black shirts daubing posters with Hitler's emblem. I had seen this particular one being done a few nights previously when out on Vicki's nightly exercise. The young Blackshirt had been bent, absorbed in his task, with his pot of paint unattended on the pavement. I ran suddenly and quietly across the road with Vicki and kicked the pot adroitly so that not only *did* its contents upset all over the pavement but great splashes of it went over the dauber. Apologizing profusely for my dog's carelessness in tipping over his paint, I left him swearing at me. 'There's a copper coming – hurry up!' I shouted. He was still swearing – there was nothing political about his language. There were actually two policemen approaching, and the young

Blackshirt vanished, leaving the upturned paint pot behind. From the windows of my studio a few minutes later, I watched them halt on their beat to examine the mess on the pavement and the freshly painted swastika on the poster. Then out came their note-books.

The Blackshirts sometimes held meetings at the top of Chelsea Manor Street near the coffee-stall. I loved to stop and heckle them. Their manners reminded me of their fellow Brownshirts in Germany. It was safer to be accompanied by a male when attacking them, Mosley's followers, like Hitler's, having scant respect for the fair sex.

I lay now on the pavement and looked up at the swastika and made up my mind to paint it over with white paint. I would go and buy a cheap pot of white paint for the purpose. I wasn't unusually patriotic but I had seen what the swastika meant and did in Germany. I could just see Mrs Freeth and Vicki standing patiently in the imaginary air-raid shelter. Vicki was frantic because I was lying on the pavement, which she thought suspicious to say the least of it. The First Aid Party arrived. My leg (broken in two places) was strapped. My wounds were bandaged with many giggles and much chaffing, and I was taken in charge to await an imaginary ambulance. Vicki's struggles became so frantic when she saw me being tied up that Mrs Freeth called out that she had better take her home. 'Stay where you are, the raid is still on!' shouted an authoritative warden. Mrs Freeth and Vicki stayed. Ambulance bells clanged, whistles blew, fire engines raced, rattles sounded – it was absolutely maddening not to be able to see what was happening. Only one eye was left free of bandages and my lowly position made visibility poor. The flurry of violent activity went on in the deathly silence of the trafficless streets. Comments, some jocose, some ribald, some angry, were being freely exchanged all round us. 'Lot of tommy-rot, won't be no air raids here. All this silly playacting!' I heard fellow-casualties grumbling. Those in the imaginary shelters echoed their comments. They had voiced the thoughts of many who believed what they wanted to believe. There would be no air raids on England! It was unthinkable. Old Granny from Paradise Row left her allotted place and started away determinedly in the direction of her home. 'Raid's still on, come back!' shouted a warden at her. 'Call of nature, can't do nothing about that, raid or no raid,' she retorted, and marched resolutely away. At last the continuous flute-like voice of the All Clear sirens sounded. The exercise was over! With relief and more grumbling we could all go home.

Next day we read in the Press that it had been an unqualified success. Every section and service of the ARP had worked perfectly. Chelsea was praised everywhere, and other boroughs had learned from her foresight. The unstinted praise of the much scorned wardens made up somewhat for their frequent unwelcome visits to the homes of residents to obtain lists and particulars of their occupants. We resented this intrusion into the privacy of our homes – an Englishman's home was supposed to be his castle!

In the sunshine, warm at mid-day, and very lovely in June, my upstairs neighbour, Kathleen Marshman, and I walked back to Cheyne Place. Kathleen was a widow, whose elder daughter Anne worked in the City. Upstairs in the flat with the Sealyham dogs was her younger daughter, Penty, playing records, her favourite ones being those of George Formby. Penty, of a happy disposition, and easily amused, was mentally retarded and would never be able to earn her living. I was trying to teach her to paint simple designs on lamp shades and trays, so that, at least, she could earn some pocket money. She showed distinct ability and interest in this. Kathleen and I had a drink after our exhausting experiences (she had also been a casualty) and we had a good laugh about it all.

Our opposite neighbour, Elliot Hodgkin, the painter, was also returning from the exercise. He was training with me in first-aid, and although disabled in one arm was, to my chagrin, much quicker and defter at splints and bandages than I was. From the windows of my studio I used to watch him at work on the opposite side of the street. He often painted right in the window, as I did. He was already well known for his exquisite flower pieces.

Kathleen had to rush off back to her work with the Disabled Servicemen's Handicrafts. I was doing some designs for the hand-block printed fabrics for which they were becoming known, and she was delighted with them when I showed them to her. 'You don't think there'll really be a war, do you?' she asked anxiously, as her work was for the maimed wrecks of men left by the 1914-18 war – and I could understand her horror of another. But when I looked at the Green Cat I was not sure and I did not reply.

The Green Cat was eighteen inches high, and sat on a lacquer stand. Made of translucent green celadon, he was incredibly beautiful. He was not just a cat – he was CAT. But I could never look at him without remembering my hurried departure from Peking in July 1937 when the Japanese were advancing on the city, and for the first time I had seen refugees. Long struggling lines of weary trudging figures with their babies strapped on their backs and small children clinging to their thighs. I had reached Peking with great difficulty and only with the help of Chinese friends, and had just acquired the Green Cat for which I had exchanged my Leica camera, when we were ordered to leave immediately for the Settlement of Hong Kong. The journey was a nightmare because of the Cat. The little Chinese, Ah Lee, who had sold him to me had warned me that he was the *Guardian of the Home.* As long as he was treated with deference and respect my home would remain safe and prosperous. With great trouble and annoyance to others, I had got him home intact – and he was my most beautiful and treasured possession. Was he going to prove a Guardian of my Home? I looked at him sitting there in the studio window and I thought of all those fleeing pathetic refugees. It had happened in China – it had happened in Spain. Hadn't the doctor lecturing to us on first-aid told us about it? Gruesome and vivid as were the details he had given us they had stuck in my memory. Some of his phrases would not leave it. 'You won't find sterile bandages and boiling water at hand when the casualties occur. Casualties don't choose their place of annihilation – the bombs choose them – anywhere – anytime. You must be prepared for anything.' And later in his lecture he had warned us about filth. 'Don't back away from dirt and filth – you'll see plenty. Blood and tissues and spilled guts are not pretty, ladies and gentlemen – and they SMELL. You'll have to get used to that. If you come upon a casualty with half his stomach laid open and his guts hanging out thrust your hands unhesitatingly into the wound and pack them back, hold your fists there to keep them in position if you have nothing else. The mess and smell may revolt you, *but that man needs his guts* – keep them in for him until medical help arrives.' Had I not seen all those refugees – many of them bandaged and maimed – those words might not have been imprinted so indelibly, word for word, in my memory.

I looked now from the window, down Swan Walk to the Thames, and conjured up a picture of the Royal Hospital Road as it would look if the recent exercise had been real, and if the circumstances which the doctor from the Spanish Civil War had described, applied here. I could see it – with the fires blazing, the buildings falling, the guns barking, and the planes droning above. It was horrible. But it was only in my imagination, which had always been too vivid. I shuddered – and shook myself back to reality. Everything was just as usual. The sun was shining, the river reflecting its light. The trees in the little Hans Sloane Physics Garden were full of noisy birds and some of them were in flower. That little garden had been there since 1673, I reminded myself, and the house on the corner of Swan Walk even longer. In the Royal Hospital Road people were walking to and from their lunch and their work. This was Chelsea – not Spain or China. 'Come and have your lunch – it's late,' called Mrs Freeth. 'That blessed exercise has taken all the morning.'

It was hot and still and sultry that summer and each day seemed more tense and heavy than the last. It was difficult to concentrate on painting although I was at work on several portraits. Two of these were of young girls from South Africa who had been in London for the Season and had been presented at one of the Presentation parties. They were lovely and delightful girls and the sittings had been a great pleasure to me. They were, however, becoming apprehensive and nervous as letters urging them to cut short their Season and return to the Cape began coming by every mail. It was essential that I got the portraits finished in case they had to leave suddenly.

My friends Leon and Mary Underwood came to see the portraits and Leon gave me some valuable help, as he invariably did. I have always had a great admiration for Leon, as sculptor, painter, writer and as a man, while as a teacher he is, I think, unsurpassed. He has that rare gift of inspiring in his pupils immense enthusiasm and, what is more, some of his own determination and inflexibility of purpose to achieve any given aim. I am fortunate indeed in having had the privilege of being in and out of his studio since I was in my teens. Leon, always unflinchingly honest, had no self-illusions about war. There *would* be one. He was certain about that. He had gone through the 1914-18 one. His son, Garth, would be of the age for immediate call-up for this next one. I think I learned how to look a thing in the face and not avoid it from him.

Leon loved cats, and admired my Green Cat immensely. I envied him his complete concentration on whatever he was doing. War or no war, he urged me to finish the portraits.

At last on August 24th the Emergency Powers Bill was passed through all its stages and became law. Lord Halifax broadcast the same evening. The Executive by this Act received powers to take further measures necessary to secure public safety in the event of war. M Daladier made a statement about Danzig on the 26th, saying that France was determined to uphold Poland's independence.

By now we all knew that war was inevitable, and on the Sunday, the 27th, another very hot, sultry day, streams of cars were already leaving London. People had begun buying up commodities in the shops. The streets of Chelsea, especially around the Duke of York's Barracks, seemed full of khaki, soldiers were milling round everywhere. My two lovely young South Africans came round in a great state. Both had received cables ordering them to return at once. But the whole shipping future was in the balance – thousands, like them, having suddenly decided to go home, it was impossible to get on any boat. They were in despair, but there was little I could do to help them. Many families were already sending their children out of London, carloads could be seen, toys, perambulators, dogs, cats and birds all piled in with them or balanced on top of them. It gave me a strange feeling to see this – and the hot, still, brooding weather seemed so like that we had had during Munich, but the strain of that period was now intensified. I had finished one portrait and it had been crated in readiness for when a boat could be found. The other one was still not to my satisfaction – somehow the joy I had felt in creating it had all dissolved.

In August we had a full-scale night exercise in Civil Defence. Again a mock air raid was in process over Chelsea. It was certainly less conspicuous for the actors and actresses than it had been in bright sunlight. On the other hand it was more dangerous in the black-out. Naturally there was some confusion and a few unfortunate incidents and much laughter. I was not a casualty this time, but a relief telephonist in the Control Room or Report Centre in the Town Hall, deep in the basement and well reinforced and sand-bagged. We had been trained by Mr T S Cane, the Borough Surveyor, in receiving and dealing with messages. There was a map in Control which showed at all times the distribution and position of all Civil Defence Services. To us it seemed a lovely game of make-believe, rather like halma, each Service in their separate corners awaiting their moves. Mr Cane had been a severe teacher, unrelenting about clarity, speed, and the legibility of handwriting. Alas, mine was so illegible that I had to print very carefully. I have never been able to read my own handwriting except immediately after it is written. As I was only to be a *volunteer* relief he passed me in spite of this, as I came up to his standard on speed and my reactions were apparently adequate. Several of the women full-time telephonists were excellent at the job, amongst these two young Scottish girls, Sheila and Chris, with whom I had become very friendly. During the training exercises we had had a lot of fun together. They were all on the night exercise now.

It was exciting down there in that sand-bagged room as the mock messages from the wardens for help, for fire services, ambulances, stretcher and heavy rescue parties to be sent to various streets and squares in Chelsea came over the lines. We had been thoroughly grounded in the names of all Chelsea's streets, terraces, squares and gardens, walks and avenues. Mr Cane was very strict about this, explaining to us that the saving of lives could depend on our knowledge of the correct position on the Civil Defence plan of each and every place in the neighbourhood. I remember his scathing remarks to me when I did not know in which district was Ixworth Place. Thanks to him I am well acquainted with the whereabouts of every Chelsea address. It had all seemed so silly when we had just been practising imaginary incidents and writing imaginary messages, but it was quite exciting when the messages actually came from the wardens during the big black-out exercise: although few of us really thought that we would ever have to receive them in an actual air raid.

CHAPTER TWO

I HAD A number of German and Austrian refugee friends in London and they kept on telephoning in consternation as the news grew more and more disquieting. To them it was incredible that we had not heeded the growing threat from the country from which they had been forced to flee. One of these friends, Ruth, who had been divorced under the Third Reich's new bill on Aryan-Jewish marriages, and had fled to Britain with her small daughter, Carla, was absolutely frantic. The situation was rapidly unhinging her mind. She was still suffering from the shock of the recent 'purges' in Germany when her entire family had disappeared into concentration camps, and with the Press and radio concentrating on the possibility of war now she was becoming rapidly worse. She not only telephoned several times a day, but she wrote me long letters every day as well. I began to dread the thick familiar envelopes with the violet ink, and to try to ignore the telephone. Her worst fear now was that if we went to war she, as a German refugee, would be sent to a concentration camp.

It was useless to assure her that they did not exist in Britain. She said she knew that they did – that in the 1914-18 war Germans had all been behind barbed wire – an island camp in the wildest part of the British Isles – an island somewhere. Nothing would calm or reassure her. She kept telling me that by continuing to see certain other refugees I was putting her and Carla in danger. Some of the refugees were spies for the Nazis, she insisted. She was incoherent, muddled, and hysterical, and although I was desperately sorry for her I found her very trying.

At the end of the week Neville Chamberlain returned from Scotland and presided over a full meeting of the Cabinet which resulted in the immediate call-up of certain personnel of the Army, Navy, Air Force, and ARP, and the Civil Nursing Reserve.

I wondered if it were coincidence that all the German girls employed as household helps by my friends had returned to Germany on the pretext of summer holidays, and that several German acquaintances had also gone *to the Baltic*. The Baltic could also be Germany. Ruth was violently excited by this. 'They've all been recalled,' she insisted, and 'Ask any German you know-either they are on holiday in Germany or in the Baltic.'

How did Ruth know these things? But she did know them. I presumed that there was a refugee drum system here as there was all over the East. 'There is going to be war,' she cried, absolutely distraught, 'and I have nowhere to go – I cannot go back to Germany where I'd be thrown into a concentration camp – but if I stay here they will intern me just the same – *in a camp* – you must help me. You MUST.'

There were thousands like her and it was impossible to reassure them. What I found difficult to understand was the hysterical fear of Ruth and her fellow refugees. Surely nothing which could happen to them in the future could be worse than what had already happened? I found it difficult to put myself in her place – because I didn't want to have to think of such horrors. I had, while in Germany, attended a Nuremberg Hitler Rally and it was without exception my most terrifying experience hitherto. In the fierce light of thousands of flood lights and arc lamps a huge solid mass of hypnotized humanity had literally petrified me with its emanation of leashed power ready to explode at the slightest wish of the Führer.

On Thursday, August 31st, Mr Elliot, the Minister of Health, had made an announcement about the decision of the Government to evacuate school children and younger children accompanied by mothers, expectant mothers, blind, and crippled people. The newspapers carried the heart-breaking little lists of necessities for those to be evacuated. School children were to be taken by their teachers to homes in safer districts where they would be housed by people who had already offered to receive them and look after them. Parents were urged strongly to allow their children to go and were to be told where their children were as soon as they had reached their new homes.

Thousands of children had been registered during the Munich scare – now some 500,000 school-children from nearly a thousand LCC schools were actually evacuated. With the hundreds of *other* volunteers I went to Charing Cross to help this huge undertaking.

The move caused a certain air of panic among the parents whose children were to attend school next day with their little cases ready for unknown destinations; many of them would be away from their parents for the first time in their young lives.

The teachers, many of them young girls, were wonderful in their patience in dealing with anxious mothers and agitated fathers, and here I had a glimpse of the magnificent work of the WVS, who seemed able to cope with anything from little Doris's diarrhoea to 'our Tommy's' inability to sleep by himself. They dealt with lost children, lost luggage, forgotten packets of food, took children to lavatories, and performed a thousand and one tasks with amazing efficiency and cheerfulness.

A little boy in my group had come quite alone –no parents were seeing him off. He sat quiet and round-eyed in the train when at last we got them all into their seats. Then I saw large tears trickling down his cheeks. I thought he was crying for his parents, but he had eaten his packet of food for the journey as his mother had not given him any breakfast. The other children were all proudly displaying theirs. 'What shall I do? Mine's all eaten!' he asked, weeping. The WVS coped with this too – they had thought of everything. Weeping children, wailing children, laughing children, and bravely smiling white-faced children– the stations were full of them everywhere and the Southern Railway had notices at Charing Cross telling the general public of certain trains which had had to be cancelled because of the huge-scale evacuation and asking the public not to travel unless their journeys were absolutely essential.

It was strange to stand in the station when train after trainload of children had disappeared – and the sudden silence after their shouts and chatter had a poignancy which was shattering. Here we stood, waving good-bye to thousand upon thousand of London's future citizens, and to me there was something more ominous in this than in any of the growing tension abroad. I went back to Chelsea feeling miserable. A few children played in the streets, for the schools were temporarily closed to those who had not been evacuated, and the unnatural stillness was noticeable everywhere.

At night from sunset to sunrise there was now a complete black-out which it was the duty of the air-raid wardens and the police to enforce. Black-out curtains were being run up everywhere – dark rugs and cloths hung temporarily over windows. I found Mrs Freeth re-hanging the long studio windows with my lovely Indian ones which had been lined with heavy black. She was pasting black paper round the edges of the window frames and sticking the glass all over with cellophane tape. On my painting table lay the latest Government leaflet *What to do in an Air Raid*. Mrs Freeth had twin sons of fifteen, Jackie and Ronnie. She also had a married daughter and a grown-up son, but her diminutive prettiness, her lovely marmalade-coloured hair, made it difficult to believe that she was already a grandmother.

It was September 1st, warm, sunny, and lovely, when it was announced on the radio that German troops had invaded Poland at 5.30 that morning. The same day Danzig, the pivot of all previous controversies with Poland, was proclaimed united with the Reich by Herr Forster, Nazi leader of Danzig from whose buildings the swastika now flew.

We heard that Poland was resisting valiantly, and I listened to President Moscicki's stirring proclamation to the country to resist the invaders. It seemed extraordinary that one could listen over the air on a perfect summer day to such world-shaking events. It must have been strange in the 1914-18 war to have had no radio and to have had to rely entirely on couriers and war correspondents' despatches for news. Now, with the previous year's tension reaching a dramatic climax, people would await the BBC's news bulletins with such eagerness and apprehension that for many the days seemed to be marked only by the intervals between them.

We knew that no answer had been received from Germany to Britain's and France's ultimatum that their troops quit Poland, and those who secretly hoped for some dramatic last-minute dash by an envoy stating that the terms of the ultimatum had been complied with realized the death of such wishful thinking with Neville Chamberlain's broadcast to the nation on Sunday morning, September 3rd, at eleven-fifteen, that we were at war with Germany. Scarcely had his voice died away from this short dramatic announcement when an even more dramatic event startled the listeners – the sounding of an unmistakable air-raid 'Alert' warning at eleven-thirty.

I had been listening to Mr Chamberlain in the studio with some friends and my upstairs neighbours, the Marshmans, and Mrs Freeth, and the air-raid siren sent everyone scurrying about to the half-finished or the temporary shelters to which they had been allotted. We looked out of the windows into the streets, which were still lost in the usual Sabbath quiet. So unexpected was the air-raid warning that there appeared to be no wardens out yet.

Our landlord owned a Rolls Royce which he kept in a garage at the back of No. 33. Over it was a flat for his chauffeur and family. The entrance to the garage was through an archway of ferro-concrete and the entrance to my two-floored flat was under this archway, one side of which formed a wall of the entrance hall and dining-room. The huge studio above this ran right across the whole frontage and the archway. When we had been filling sand-bags during the Munich scare of the previous year the landlord had provided enough sand-bags for the archway to be closed at each end and had reinforced it so that it made a splendid shelter for us tenants. When the scare died away, however, he wanted the use of his Rolls Royce, as he was an old man and could not get about. So all the sand-bags were taken away, and he built a shelter for us at the back of the house in the small courtyard there. It was to this shelter we sent our friends when at last air-raid wardens appeared shouting in the streets for everyone to take cover.

It seemed quite unreal to all of us – for the cloudless blue sky showed nothing untoward and the silence of that Sunday morning was only shattered by the orders of the wardens. Most people thought it was a joke or some kind of hoax – actually it was a mistaken warning given for an unidentified lone plane which turned out to be a friendly one – but we did not know this until later. By the time we had all made up our minds what to do and I had decided to report to the First Aid Post, the All Clear was warbling and everyone had come out of the shelters and was gathering in small groups to discuss the events of the morning. I saw neighbours who never spoke to one another chatting excitedly, and when we listened to that first All Clear warbling note I don't suppose any of us had an inkling of how eagerly or with what relief its advent was to be welcomed in the days ahead.

That afternoon I went with a friend for a long walk in Battersea Park. The sky was gay and alive with silver balloons going up slowly and awkwardly like drunken fish. Chelsea boasted two, to be affectionately known as Flossie and Blossom, though why both should have been feminine was a mystery unless it was that they were operated by men.

Blossom's site was only a few hundred yards from 33, Cheyne Place, on the cricket grounds of Burton Court. Flossie was tethered in the grounds of the Royal Hospital.

Looking across London and right up the Thames towards Westminster as far on all sides as the eye could see, I counted over eighty members of this glittering silver barrage intended to protect us from low-flying enemy planes. But the scene was so peaceful, the gardens in the park so lovely, and the people walking by the river so unperturbed and ordinary with their perambulators and dogs, that it was impossible to realize that these silver roach in the sky were there because we were at war. War seemed too remote and archaic a word to contemplate.

In the park by the river we met my Norwegian friend, Asta Lange, with her dog, Peer Gynt. Peer Gynt was a terrier whose ancestry was cloaked in mystery. Black and white, he was as intelligent as his mistress, whose acquaintance I had made through his admiration for my small Dachshund. Asta was excited about the news, and as we all walked, we talked about Norway and its threat from Hitler, for Asta had no illusions as to Hitler's talk of *Lebensraum*. *Lebensraum*, she said, meant Norway and Denmark. 'He will need food – especially dairy produce for his jackbooted armies. You just see if I am not right.' Asta was small and not young in years, but she was an ageless lovely person whom one would trust in any kind of emergency. She had something tough and indefinable about her, a resilience to life and its problems which attracted me to her just as Vicki was attracted to her tough, wiry little terrier. She lived near me in Cheyne Gardens and we often met in the grounds of the Royal Hospital, a favourite playground for dogs and children.

The thought uppermost in everyone's mind now was – what difference is the war going to make to *me*? How is it going to affect *me*? Kathleen Marshman was worrying about that. Working for the Disabled Soldiers' and Sailors' Industries, she was wondering how long such an organization would be able to carry on. The widow of a naval officer, she knew only too well what war could mean. She knew that it wouldn't be long before supplies of materials would make things difficult, and that a fresh war could ruin the livelihoods which the disabled victims of the last one had so painstakingly built up for themselves and their families, and she could not help being depressed. Only a few weeks previously the Queen had visited an exhibition and sale of the men's work which Kathleen had helped to arrange at Claridges. The girls who sold the beautiful work had included many of the season's most lovely debutantes, Kathleen's daughter, Anne, and the two attractive young girls from South Africa whose portraits I was painting.

As a result of the Queen's interest, business was still brisk, and there were enough orders to keep the men busy for some time ahead. But now? What would happen now? Kathleen Marshman was one of those people who possessed the rare gift of making every occasion seem like a party. She made each guest feel that he or she was the one person present in whom she was interested. Extremely generous and hospitable, she loved company, and her flat, like mine, was always overflowing with guests. Her elder daughter, Anne, was a pretty blonde girl who seemed rather quiet and melancholy, but this I discovered was due to a recent love affair which had gone awry. She was naturally vivacious and gay and extremely unselfish. Her protective love for her younger sister, Penty, who could never be like other girls, was most touching when one considered that for an attractive girl like Anne with many young men friends the presence of this retarded sister must sometimes have made things awkward.

Anne was passionately fond of dancing and at this time was learning tap dancing. I used to hear her practising in the kitchen above my bedroom and sometimes she would come down to dance in my big studio, which had a parquet floor, and she would make me try all the latest steps which she was mastering. I had been friendly with this family since moving in to No. 33 but now that war had been declared we all instinctively became much closer. Kathleen Marshman had had a sad life in many ways, and her greatest worry now was her little daughter, Penty.

CHAPTER THREE

THE FIRST WEEKS of the war were curiously quiet as was the weather, still, warm, and sunny, and a strange brooding spell hung over us all. The RAF, however, were by no means quiet. They were making their first raids on Wilhelmshaven and Kiel and getting direct hits on the German battleships there. They were also dropping pamphlets on the Germans. The Royal Navy had begun an intensive blockade of Germany, and our British merchant shipping was being attacked by German U-boats.

On the 5th we were startled by the news of the torpedoing of the transatlantic liner, *Athenia*. Bound for New York, she had been sunk without warning when 250 miles off Donegal on September 4th. Amongst the 1,400 passengers on board were 300 Americans. Most of the passengers had been picked up by British destroyers but 128 had been drowned.

I think the news of the sinking of the *Athenia* really brought home to us the actuality of war – the victims of this brutal attack were, like us, civilians. Its effect on my young sitters from South Africa who were waiting for passages to Cape Town was unnerving. I was thankful when at last I saw them off on a boat-train in a blacked-out station bound for an unknown ship whose name they would only know once they were actually on board. It was a sad ending to their first visit to Britain and to their first season in London, but whereas we were nearing winter with the fear and horror of war looming over us, they were sailing into the sun to land where air raids, at least, would be unlikely. I watched their fresh, lovely young faces at the train window until it disappeared. Something vividly alive and care-free went with them, and, left standing on that dreary blacked-out station, I experienced the same feeling of emptiness that the train-loads of hand-waving children had given me. Meg's portrait was not completed – it was still on the easel in the studio. I went back after seeing them off and stood looking at it. In the pale pink presentation dress in which she had made her curtsey to the King and Queen she seemed now a tragic reminder of the end of summer. A summer which for her had been a gay succession of parties, dances, theatres, ballets, and operas to many of which I had accompanied her.

Many friends, both men and women, were called at once into the Services and there was a spate of hectic good-bye parties before they went. The night life was as yet uninterrupted, and getting to places in the black-out was fun. Ivor Novello's *The Dancing Years* was playing to packed houses and was the good-bye choice of many romantic young men and women. *Me and My Girl*, with its 'Lambeth Walk', had passed its thousandth performance and was still drawing large audiences. I went several times to this with parties. A painter friend called up in the Artists' Rifles took me to a wonderful performance of *The Importance of Being Earnest*, at the Globe. Its cast included John Gielgud, Edith Evans, Gwen Ffrangcon-Davies, Peggy Ashcroft, Jack Hawkins, and Margaret Rutherford. I found this play of Wilde's so fascinating that I began rereading all his works, including the fairy tales. They would remain in my mind all through the long rather dull hours at the First Aid Post, known as FAP, and seemed to me to have much more real importance than the bandaging at which I was not at all deft at first. Elliot Hodgkin, with whom I was often paired for these practices, used to tease me unmercifully about this. It irked me that a man should be so much better with bandages than I was.

In Calcutta I had worked for a time in the General Hospital because I had wanted to get more knowledge of the Indian people. But I had been allowed to do very little because I was European and the menial jobs had to be done by 'untouchables'. The European sisters in the hospital had had no use for me because I was untrained, and it was from the Eurasian nurses that I had learned the little that I knew about nursing. From Dr Rudolf Treu, in whose home I was staying at the time, I learned to read X-ray plates, for he had been one of India's most renowned radiologists, and he also taught me to give injections, for which he said I had a real gift.

Now, as well as the constant practices at the FAP in splints and bandages, and the first essential aid to the injured, we were being sent to various hospitals to get our necessary nursing experience. I was sent, first, to a hospital for women in the Marylebone Road. There was no question there about my not getting the menial jobs – they were about all I did get, and the day on which I emptied eighty-four bedpans without vomiting was quite an event. But even at this it seemed I was not too deft and had several unfortunate incidents.

I have always loved people and the patients fascinated me. One of them, Mrs M–, was a very fat woman and she had been very ill after a serious operation. Her husband being a flower-seller, her bed was always surrounded by the most choice and costly flowers and was the envy of all the other patients in the ward. But Mrs M–, who was on a milk diet, did not even notice them. She had a craving for some shrimps and the only thing which interested her was how to get them. 'Here, nursie dear,' she said to me coaxingly one evening, 'I'll give you all these bloody blooms if you'll bring me a few shrimps – just half a dozen, love. I've asked Albert again and again. Every time he comes in here with these bleeding flowers I say I don't want blooms but shrimps. But he's afraid of Sister. *You aren't, are you, love?*'

I was – I was petrified of her. Every time she approached I became fumble-fisted. Mrs M– continued to plead with me. She must have the shrimps, nothing else would do, as to the flowers she hated them. 'Make me feel like a bleeding corpse already,' she complained. The poor little husband, a perky Cockney, was in the depths of gloom at her attitude. She would not speak to him.

'Tell 'er I *daren't* bring the shrimps, nurse,' he begged. 'She don't believe me.'

Later, outside the ward, I came upon him weeping unashamedly. 'Sister says she's very bad,' he sobbed. 'She's never bin ill in all our married life. Nurse, don't you think she could have the shrimps – if she's got to go – why shouldn't she have what she wants?'

I knew perfectly well that she should not have anything but the diet prescribed by the doctors, but if she were going to die as her husband said, why shouldn't she have them? Condemned men, in fiction and in fact, are allowed to choose their last meal. I could not bear his pleading eyes – like those of a retriever dog. 'It's up to you,' I told him. 'If you bring them while I'm there I shall pretend I've only one good eye and that one, like Nelson's, will be on the other side. But there's always Sister – she has two excellent eyes.'

'I'll bring them to-night if I can get 'em. It'll give me something to do finding 'em for 'er.' He had brightened perceptibly as he hurried off.

Nurses are supposed to keep out of sight during visiting hours, but when Albert was leaving that evening he gave me a look which was unmistakable.

I lay awake all night worrying about Mrs M– and her shrimps. Supposing when I arrived at the hospital next morning she had died in agony? I should have helped kill her – but, on the other hand, if she were dying anyway, she would at least have had the shrimps which she craved. But when I crept nervously into the ward on duty next morning Mrs M– was propped up in bed as usual. 'I'm better, love,' she called, 'thanks to your nursing. Hear that, Sister? It was *her* that done the trick. She's the one!' and she winked knowingly and broadly at me. 'I don't know what has done it,' said Sister, 'but you *are* better.'

'So you got them?' I said later.

'Can you take away the shells?' she whispered, thrusting a fishy-smelling brown paper into my hands. I put it in the pocket of my apron but it looked conspicuous, and I was obliged to sidle out of the ward with the bulge hidden by a towel draped over my arm, praying that Sister would not call me. Mrs M– continued to improve, and Albert brought me the most wonderful flowers. When I told a friend, Mr Rock Carling, the surgeon [now Sir Ernest Rock Carling], about the shrimps, he was very amused and said that *the surgeon was always in the wrong* – if the patient had died from the shrimps the surgeon would have been blamed for an unsuccessful operation, and had she died without having had them the husband would have blamed him for depriving her of her last wish, while now that she was recovering the surgeon got no credit for her recovery – it all went to the shrimps!

Here I had my first experience of a death-bed. One patient was screened off in the ward, and I knew from the nurses and other patients that she was dying. Sister told me to sit by her and swab her mouth occasionally and moisten her lips. She was quite young and she was not dying easily. I found it so agonizing to have to watch her, that when Sister returned, she found me in tears. 'If you are to be of any use as a nurse you'll have to learn self-control. Never show any emotion at all. It's far better for the patient that you are detached, impersonal, and concerned only with your job.'

'But she's dying,' I said, 'and she's not much older than I am.'

'Then help her to die *comfortably* – that's your concern,' she retorted. And so I sat there for hours watching this grey-faced young woman dying all alone in a crowded hospital ward, and for the first time I really began to think about life and death.

I liked that Sister; strict and severe, she nevertheless taught me some sort of discipline in the short time I worked under her, and I have been grateful to her ever since.

At St Luke's Hospital, Chelsea, where I was later sent as a relief, I had very different work given me. Sister Griffiths [now Matron of St Luke's] was sorry for the VADs! She knew that they usually got all the dirty jobs and she allowed me to help with the flowers and the food, and make myself generally useful in the ward. She taught me how to give blanket-baths and how to arrange pillows to give the maximum comfort and support in the various cases. I liked this hospital very much. Being in Chelsea and so near my home I was able to put in much longer hours than the scheduled ones. I did not get at all tired from standing all day, being accustomed to standing at my easel. I loved nursing, and resolved to try to get accepted for training to become a State Registered nurse.

It was fun to exchange experiences with all the other VADs at the FAP. The ones we considered the luckiest were those who had been sent to the Children's Hospital adjoining the FAP, the Victoria. Miss White, the lady almoner, was delightful to us all. Most children's hospitals had evacuated from London, and the Victoria had not all its beds in use so that it was always busy with small out-patients.

Getting home in the black-out was always an adventure. Sometimes I would bump into a party of revellers, their voices and laughter being the only warning of their imminent approach, and too late I would come up against a body abruptly, apologize, as they did, exchange good-nights and a little chaff, and continue on my Stygian way with a glow of warmth when those encountered had been charming enough to offer to see me home. The darkness and the sand-bagged entrances to houses were kind to lovers. Mrs Freeth was indignant one evening when she came upon a couple in what she called a compromising situation in my area amongst the sand-bags. But the man was in khaki and so she excused him, she said.

Two young Germans came round from the Town Hall taking a kind of census of the occupants of every house. We thought this a bit much – but they were refugees and pathetically anxious to do their bit for the country which had given them asylum. The girl was fair and charming and told me that she wanted to get into one of the women's Services. The young man said that if he could not be accepted for the army he would try to get into munitions or the Fire Service. I felt sorry for the anomaly of their position. Like Ruth they were frightened and insecure. Ruth herself was rapidly becoming more and more desperate and Mrs Freeth more and more adept at putting her off on the telephone.

On September 4th aliens who stayed in England had to report to the police, and I accompanied Ruth there because she was quite hysterical. People were already beginning to look askance at all their German or Austrian friends and several boys in the street had shouted 'German sausage' at poor Vicki. I was amused to read in *The Times* during September an impassioned plea for the Dachshund who had been singled out in the 1914-18 war as being symbolically Teutonic. The Great Queen, after whom my Victoria had been named, had loved them and had had some sent to her after her marriage. The Mr Murray who made this plea rightly pointed out that both the Great Dane and the Alsatian were far more German in origin than the comical and obstinate but lovable Dachshund.

All this time the bombardment of Warsaw was continuing without respite, and listening to the anguish of that city as relayed on the radio gave some grim reality to the now endless practices in heavy rescue for which we nurses often acted as casualties. We were lowered into deep awkward pits dug for the purpose, in order that the rescue parties could have some practice in getting bodies out. Sometimes the task was very difficult and quite painful; worse still, our rescuers would sometimes get called away or interested in some moot point of procedure and we would be left in these insalubrious holes for what seemed an endless time. Sometimes we would call out as if we were trapped, which indeed we were, for we could not possibly have got out unaided. We hated these deep-hole practices, getting cold and bored and often extremely dirty.

On the 19th the news of the loss of the *Courageous* was published. She had been attacked on the night of Sunday the 7th – soon after the *Athenia*. Only 681 out of 1,260 of those she carried survived, and of these one was a boy bugler of only fifteen. I found this shocking – few of us had any idea that such young boys – mere children – would be allowed on warships. We were given the news by Mr Winston Churchill, First Lord of the Admiralty, in his review of the war at sea. I had been brought up near Plymouth, and my mother still lived there. She wrote me of two young friends whom she had known since childhood, who had lost their lives in the *Courageous*. Her letter was sad, saying that she was re-living all the days of the 1914-18 war and seeing again the terrible casualty lists. She reminded me of all the uncles and cousins who had given their lives then. 'What was the use?' she wrote. 'All it has produced is another war with the Germans.'

The reports on the siege of Warsaw were among the most terrible things to which I had ever listened. More so because I could listen in my beautiful room surrounded by comfort and with a good meal waiting downstairs in the dining-room. But I could not eat. There was, during all this time, a strange tense sensation in my inside which prevented me from swallowing. I looked round at the Peking horses surrounding the Green Cat. Ah Lee had said that the Cat would not be at home without objects from his own country round him.

In Warsaw they were eating horses. *Eating horses.* Here, in England, I was still able to ride them – going frequently to Putney for an hour's hacking in between the shifts at the FAP. So horrific was the news from Warsaw that people in the streets of London reflected it in the gloom of their faces. So appalling and harrowing were the sufferings of the brave Polish people that it was difficult to listen to the broadcasts without weeping. For us there were the make-believe raids – the mock bombing, for them the actuality – the real death.

And so that momentous September came to an end with the fall of Warsaw, the introduction of Sir John Simon's War Budget with its shock of the income tax being raised from 5s. 6d. to 7s. 6d. in the £ and with 'Registration Night'. On this night all housewives had to fill in the forms already distributed with the names and particulars of all people spending the night of the 29th under their roof. This was, we were told, for the purpose of identity cards and ration cards with which we were all to be issued. A lot of people with unorthodox relationships resented this very much.

Mr Ferebee, who had the small grocer's shop opposite No. 33, had warned us all of forthcoming shortages. I don't think that any of us believed him. His well-stocked shop which seemed to have everything one could possibly want made it seem unlikely that the shelves could ever be empty. But he had experienced the 1914-18 war, as had Kathleen, and they knew. Quite early in October, which opened with a National Day of Prayer ordered by the King, woollen goods began to disappear from the shops. People were thinking of the oncoming winter when fuel would be scarce and when factories now making civilian garments would all be employed on uniforms, and were buying frantically.

Under a new order no paper was to be thrown away. There was to be a special paper salvage for industry where it would be urgently needed for pulping to make cardboard for packing essential war materials. Petrol restrictions had come in with the declaration of war and all over the country the horse was said to be coming to the fore again, and the newspapers had photographs of old family traps and governess carts brought out from dusty stables, and the bicycle came into its own. The streets were more and more full of uniformed men and women, as were all the stations, where posters enjoined us to avoid unnecessary travel because the trains were needed for the troops. Many young friends had left for France with their regiments. Some of the theatres had begun to close, although the public demand was for them to remain open. The black-out gave new and fascinating aspects of the Thames against which the outlines of buildings and the whole skyline were imprinted without the former blur of light from the great city. In the day we enjoyed freedom from traffic jams – the streets had suddenly become a joy for walking and cycling, and I now cycled with Vicki perched in a basket on the front.

Tension between Finland and the Soviet was rapidly growing – just as it had grown between Poland and Germany. Towns in Finland were already being evacuated and ARP precautions taken all over the country.

On the 16th the loss of the *Royal Oak* was announced baldly – with no details. She had apparently been sunk on the 14th with the loss of over 800 men and 24 officers. It was with a greater shock than this that we learned from Mr Churchill on the 18th, in his naval review, that the ship had actually been sunk when at anchor at Scapa Flow. The skill and daring of the Germans who had carried out this raid were emphasized by Mr Churchill, who warned the country what kind of enemy we were up against.

The idea that the Germans could actually sink one of our ships in our own waters in our own harbour was somehow utterly shocking to us all. I don't know why. After all, the radio constantly told us of the direct hits which the RAF had been scoring for the past few weeks on ships in German harbours. Why then should it have upset us so much? Because it did. The thought that the Germans could enter our harbours and sink our ships at anchor there had the same incredibility as the thought that any stranger in the form of an air-raid warden could enter our homes without invitation. Our country, like our homes, was inviolate. But it *had* happened – and right at the beginning of the war.

Kathleen, whose life had been spent in naval circles, and I, who had been brought up with Plymouth as the nearest town, were equally shocked. Old Granny from Paradise Row was standing looking at some barges in the Thames the day after this news. 'I reckon someone ought to be guarding all these ships,' she said anxiously. 'There's no one even looking at them,' and her old eyes scanned the depths of the river as if she expected to see a German U-boat surfacing at any minute. Kathleen decided after this to send her younger daughter, Penty, to friends in the country. She was an added anxiety to both Kathleen and Anne now that we were at war.

In the middle of October the National Gallery Concerts started. All the paintings had been removed from their familiar places and the galleries denuded of their treasures made piquant and unusual concert rooms. I went to one of the very first of these at which Jelly d'Aranyi played, and sat on the floor amongst every type of listener. It was a surprise to find so many tough-looking Servicemen perched on fragile gilt chairs completely absorbed in the music. The larger green canvas chairs seemed occupied by those unable to relax and many should have changed their seats! The floor was popular for all of us who could not find a seat, and so entrancing was the music offered us that no one cared about its hardness.

After the fall of Warsaw fresh ARP exercises were being carried out all over the country with renewed vigour. In Chelsea we had several more intensive ones, and were all instructed that we must attend the gas lecture course. The Government informed us that steel air-raid shelters were now available for purchase at the price of £7 each, this including delivery but not erection. Known as the Anderson shelters, after their sponsor, Sir John Anderson, they were soon being erected in many back and front gardens in Chelsea where they could be covered with earth and camouflage. On Sundays now it was common to see groups of men helping their neighbours to 'put up the Anderson'. After the *Royal Oak* we were no longer so sure that the Germans would never invade our skies.

CHAPTER FOUR

ONE OF THE MOST striking changes that the declaration of war caused was in the circle of one's friends. A curtain of censorship cut off all those abroad, telephone communication with the Continent had been cut at the outbreak – and their letters, already censored, appeared unreal and disjointed. In one's immediate circle some assumed a veiled, suspicious, a queer hostile questioning attitude to any of their friends who had any vestige of foreign blood in them. 'You're not wholly British. I don't really know what your true feelings are, where your real sympathies lie, so it behoves me to be careful. I shan't tell you anything,' was their attitude. This was very marked in those working in Government departments – and soon almost all of them were either in the Services or in some Ministry. Thus the host of foreigners, many of whom had lived all their lives in Britain, now found themselves regarded as 'aliens', and treated with wary guardedness by those who had known them all their lives.

Some British friends apparently could not face war, and just left the country very unobtrusively with no good-byes, writing afterwards that they were in America or Canada as the case might be. Those who did this proved conclusively that we can never know any of our friends. We may think so, as I did, but an emergency often proves otherwise. Germans, Austrians, Czechs were all working with the rest of us in Chelsea at the outbreak of war. They all wanted to do their bit. In the excellent canteen for Civil Defence workers in the Chelsea Town Hall, I met a charming Dutch woman, the widow of a titled German refugee. She was suffering both from loneliness from the recent death of her husband, and from a sense of isolation at the activities of the British all round her at their war work. She was working in the canteen as a waitress, and served me when I was doing my shifts in the Control Room there. I had lived in Holland and spoke Dutch, and we became friends at once. She was known as Jennie, as her Dutch name was difficult to pronounce. In spite of the brutal treatment of her former husband, who had had Jewish blood, Jennie, widely travelled and widely read, had remained amazingly well balanced, in contrast to Ruth, who was almost insane on the subject of the Nazis.

Jennie had lived away from Holland for some time, and had few relatives there, so she had decided to stay in England, the country which had given her and her husband political asylum. She very soon became a frequent visitor to 33, Cheyne Place. My lovely Indian friend, Kumari, had enrolled as a VAD, and her brother, Indi, was trying to get into the RAF. Almost everyone was immediately involved in some kind of war-work – because for the past year, since Munich, they had all been associated with some organization connected with such an event.

It was difficult to concentrate on painting with so many political upheavals, but after October things seemed to settle down, and life, except when we were sent as reliefs to some hospital, was somewhat dull in contrast to that of those serving men and women who had already gone overseas. Social life was becoming rapidly less, but there were still dinners, lunches, and cocktail parties, and there were a great many weddings. I could see Elliot Hodgkin at work every day in his studio on the opposite side of the Royal Hospital Road. His concentration filled me with admiration. I was trying to paint a little boy who constantly tried to stick pins into poor Vicki. I disliked him so much that it was impossible to get anything but a very unpleasant aspect of him, which, of course, his mother did not appreciate. I was glad when she decided to evacuate from her Chelsea house and the sittings came to an end.

The Green Cat brought me many callers. He was visible from the road which he faced. One day, soon after I had moved into the place, a gentleman had called and asked Mrs Freeth if the owner would allow him to come in and look at the cat in the window. He had, she said, an unpronounceable name. The gentleman was elderly, came up, and apologizing for his intrusion pleaded his interest in the cat. He asked me if he might examine it, and where I had found it. I told him about Ah Lee in Peking and of my having wanted to possess the cat so much that I had exchanged my Leica camera for it. He asked me if I wanted to sell the figure. I said I would never part with it – it gave me so much pleasure. He congratulated me on my taste and said he shared my feelings for it. 'I will give you my card,' he said smiling, 'in case you ever change your mind.' He put the card on a table, and looked at several pieces of porcelain which I had brought back from China and Japan. He told me about them all, and recommended several books on Chinese art for me to read.

He was a fascinating person and I enjoyed talking to him enormously. After he had left I looked at the card on the table. The name was George Eumorfopoulos. Leon Underwood, who knew him well, was very amused when I told him this story.

One day in October another visitor rang the bell and asked to see the cat. This was Miss Ethel Walker, ARA, the painter, who lived farther along the river in Cheyne Walk. She knew me quite well, but she had never visited me before. When Mrs Freeth brought her to the studio she seemed astonished to find that the cat belonged to me. She admired it enormously, she said. But she did not admire my work. Unasked, she went round examining every canvas in the studio. She asked me where I had studied and if I wanted to be a portrait painter. 'This is quite horrible,' she said, looking at the portrait of the little boy. 'You'd better come to my studio and I'll teach you. You'd better come tomorrow morning.'

I was delighted, and being free the following morning I presented myself at her house on the Embankment, which had a lovely view of the river. Miss Walker painted in a room on the first floor. She seemed very old indeed and had two very old dogs, rough-haired terriers called David and The Angel. I had taken Vicki with me and this did not at all please her. 'I don't like those little German dogs,' she said when I rang her bell, and her two dogs greeted us with a terrific protest. 'And nor do they! What do you want?'

'You told me to come,' I said, disconcerted. 'Yesterday in my studio you told me you would give me a lesson.'

'Oh well,' she said, as if she had completely forgotten it, 'the model hasn't turned up, but you can come up and see some of my work. Pick up that sausage creature or I won't be responsible for my *dogs*!'

I followed her up the stairs to her painting room. It had huge bay windows and a magnificent view of the Thames. The room was full of canvases. She painted her sitters against the light, which seemed to me to be terribly difficult. But she had some kind of strange power of making the very air between her and her model scintillate. 'I can tell you what is wrong with your work,' she said abruptly. 'You put in your backgrounds *after* you've painted part of the head – isn't that so? What is the use of painting a head against nothing? Afterwards when you get the tone of the background in, you have to change all the tones of the face – isn't that so?' It was no use trying to tell her that I attempted to keep everything going at once. 'If the model turns up tomorrow you can paint her here with me, and watch me at work,' she said finally.

For the next few days I changed my shifts at the FAP so that I could go and work in her studio. The model was a lovely Eurasian but I found it difficult to paint her against the window with the Thames behind her.

'Don't come here in that ugly uniform,' said Miss Walker, watching me put on the navy blue long coat and the squat round cap of the VAD. 'It doesn't suit you. You'd better get out of the Red Cross and work hard at your painting – you certainly need to.'

I did not see her again for some weeks and then one afternoon I was returning from a lunch party and I bumped into her on the Embankment. 'What a pretty hat! What a *very* pretty hat!' she exclaimed. 'I should like to paint you in it. Who are you, my dear?'

'But Miss Walker,' I said, disconcerted again, 'you know me very well. I live in Cheyne Place in the Royal Hospital Road – you know the big windows with the Green Cat in them.'

'Oh yes,' she said laughing, 'but you always wear that hideous uniform. Naturally I didn't recognize you in that delicious hat. Yes, you must sit for me-when will you come?'

We arranged the sittings, which went very well until Vicki chewed up the frivolous little hat.

Next day I went to the sitting without the hat. Miss Walker was furious. When I explained what Vicki had done she was very angry. 'You must get another hat – exactly the same,' she said. 'It's the *hat* which attracted me – it's the hat which is the key-note of the painting. Get another one.'

I went to the shop where I had bought it, and told them what had happened. Had they another? The hat was a model, I was told, there was not another. Could they make me one? I got the answer we were all soon to get accustomed to. *In war-time, madam? That would be difficult.* But surely they could find one like it? They could not. They searched and telephoned in vain.

A few days later the shop found a hat which was almost the same – the flowers were white, not violet, but they would change them for me. The hat came – it was so like the former one that only an expert could have known the difference. Miss Walker said grudgingly that it wasn't the same but it would do, and the sittings continued. Her comment on Vicki's behaviour was that nothing else was to be expected from a *German* dog!

I bought the portrait when it was completed. I did not see myself in it, but I liked it as a painting. At this time I also bought a delightful little canvas of a nude by Lord Methuen, and a drawing by Augustus John. Ethel Walker gave me several drawings. Leon had given me some beautiful examples of his woodcuts and engravings, and I now bought a small painting of his Mexican period which I loved. I had earned a lot of money in India painting portraits of people who were very exacting in their demand for ten fingers and ten toes, every jewel in their jewel box and every decoration and medal imaginable. To be able to buy some other painters' work was a tremendous pleasure and compensated somewhat for having had to do so much that was tedious and uncongenial.

First-aid lectures, gas lectures, nursing lectures filled up the weeks before Christmas, and these were interspersed with short shifts in hospitals getting experience and in endless practising of bandaging and splinting imaginary casualties. The practices went on – the being lowered into deep holes so that the rescue squads could practise getting trapped people out. There were concerts in the ARP showing off local talent, and there were visitors to the FAP who came to be shown round. On the 24th Mrs Neville Chamberlain came to visit us. We had a great turn out of the Chelsea Red Cross personnel for her.

Sister-in-charge had inspected all our aprons – day and night staff – Dr Symes, Chelsea's Medical Officer for Civil Defence, was there. Dr Graham Kerr received the visitor with Betty Compton, who was Commandant-in-charge. Betty was far too young and pretty to have such an onerous-sounding name. She looked most impressive in her red dress and apron in spite of her youth. She and Ruth Malcolm were delightful Commandants, invariably supporting and upholding their VADs in the inevitable ups-and-downs which attended our hospital debuts. Sister-in-charge at this inspection was a former King's nurse.

Mrs Chamberlain asked a great many questions, and showed a great interest in everything. She asked the purpose of a small chain hanging from a fire-extinguisher and before anyone could stop her had caught hold of it. Unfortunately a shower of sand was released by the chain – and the result was a welcome break from the stiff atmosphere as her hat received most of it!

The autumn had been long and sunny, a continuation of the wonderful weather since the outbreak of war, but now it suddenly became bitterly cold. I found my cotton nurse's dress a bit chilly, but our cloaks were lined with vermilion red which at least gave the impression of warmth. The Germans were massing behind the Siegfried Line, and this gave rise to many skits and sketches in the current revues and musicals.

Suddenly all our lovely silver balloons disappeared for a few days, which caused much speculation, but at the beginning of November they all reappeared. Alas, their bright silver had become a dirty green. They were still pretty, but nothing like as lovely as when they had been silver roach. They were not all easy to get up – and our one in Burton Court gave a lot of trouble as she floated vertically with great elephants' ears sticking out.

Guy Fawkes day was quiet, no fireworks being allowed in the black-out. I felt sorry for the children – but some had packets of indoor sparklers to console them – and those who wanted bonfires had them in the afternoon before darkness fell. The stamping out of these before black-out by wardens added to their usual duties.

All visitors to my home at this period had to submit to acting as a casualty for practice, and we had several parties among the VADs for this purpose. In the Town Hall Control Room as telephonists we had constant practice not only in the receiving of warnings and taking messages, but also in the position of the places from which they were purported to have come.

Several friends from India were coming home to join up, others had returned there quickly fearing that they would otherwise be unable to do so. Life at this time resembled a transit camp – for the most unexpected people would appear and ask for a bed for a night while on their way to some destination or other, known or more often unknown. Hitler was making some ominous comments on Norway, Denmark, and Belgium. 'Small nations,' he announced, 'have to adapt themselves to their larger neighbours at least in the economic spheres.' This was followed by the usual *Lebensraum* talk. This had become a joke amongst us all – at the FAP, if we were crowded in the bandaging practices, we would ask each other for a little *Lebensraum*.

Christmas was quiet and many families were united with their children again, for in the absence of any air raids thousands had returned to their homes. There were parties and celebrations in the Civil Defence, in the FAP, in the wardens' posts, the AFS – and Christmas trees in many of them. The King broadcast from Sandringham. He spoke first to the children who were separated from their parents. I always admired the King's determination to overcome his trouble with public speaking – because my own father had suffered from exactly the same disability, and I knew what he must be enduring. His last words were typical of the *man*, as distinct from the King, and in the simplicity and sincerity of their delivery left no doubt of their speaker's own faith. 'I would like to say to you: "I said to the man who stood at the Gate of the Year, 'Give me a light that I may tread safely into the Unknown.' And he replied, 'Go out into the darkness and put your hand into the Hand of God. That shall be better to you than light, and safer than a known way.'" I can still hear the voice of King George as he quoted those words. They carried more weight for me than many long sermons from the pulpit.

CHAPTER FIVE

IT WAS AN UNEASY spring with the ever-widening field of tension growing in intensity on all fronts. Chelsea presented a strange face to those who had known it in its normal aspect. The shelters which had now materialized, the sad look of mourning caused by the black-out, the uniformed citizens, the balloons, sand-bags, trenches, the barbed wire, and perhaps most of all the lovely gardens of the Royal Hospital, which like all other gardens had, by Government order, been dug in allotments for the growing of vegetables. I used to stand in Royal Avenue with its sand-bags and its wardens' post and wonder what Charles II and Nell Gwynne would have thought of it now. The thousands of Anderson shelters, already considered, like the gas-masks, as obsolete by the public, were hidden under vegetation in many gardens now. Some of them had made splendid marrow beds the previous autumn, and now were sown with radishes, carrots, and lettuces. Others grew rambler roses over them. The wardens' posts had their own cultivated plots and very fine some of them were. Kathleen and I considered what we could grow on the roof of No 33, and were coaxing lettuce and mustard and cress seeds. During the summer we had sown some splendid tomatoes in window-boxes, and were planning to extend them this coming summer. Food was already becoming a major problem, and every small item helped. We were all hunting out ancient bicycles and attaching large baskets to them and using them as our only means of transport.

Although German behaviour in the torpedoing of Swedish, Norwegian, Danish, and Dutch vessels threw a shadow of events to follow, of neutrality repudiated, no one was prepared for the shock which April 9th brought with its news that at 5 a.m. strong mechanized units had crossed the Schleswig-Holstein frontier near Flensburg, and occupied the whole of Denmark within a few hours without any organized resistance. Simultaneously German troops were landed from warships and transports at Copenhagen, Nyborg, Cjedser, and other places. By 8 a.m. Copenhagen, lovely peaceful Hans Andersen city where I had often painted and sketched near the statue of the little mermaid, was in German hands. Norway rejected Germany's ultimatum, determined to resist, and early on April 9th German troops landed at Bergen, Stavanger, Trondheim, and Narvik. The King and his Government left for Hamar, and Oslo was occupied the same afternoon. The Germans immediately took over the radio station.

I went round to Asta Lange as soon as we heard this. She was in a fury of shocked anger. The BBC was broadcasting to all Danish and Norwegian ships to put in at British ports where they would receive every assistance and comfort. We listened to this, and Peer Gynt sensed his mistress's distress and was miserable too. What could one say to a friend whose country had been so ruthlessly invaded and looked as if it were doomed to follow in the wake of Poland, Finland, and Denmark? Supposing it were England, what would Asta have said to console me? But Asta, like her fellow-countrymen, was tough and brave. 'We shall fight,' she said. 'They won't find us as easy as the Danes.'

They didn't. The Norwegians were fighting magnificently and putting every possible obstacle in the path of the invaders, who were pushing in more troops to crush the intrepid little country. British troops were rushed to Norway on the 15th.

In May the phoney war, as we called the long, unnaturally calm interval when it appeared to the public that nothing was happening in spite of our being at war, came to an abrupt end, and the country was shaken to its foundations by the revolt, climax of a growing anger, of the Tory Party against its own leader, Neville Chamberlain. Excitement was intense. There was no other topic of discussion anywhere – the unprecedented overthrow of a leader by his own party was shattering to the British idea of loyalty. But the revolt voiced the general public's dissatisfaction with the policy of inaction in the growing face of danger.

On May 13th a new Prime Minister paid his respects to the Commons, one who had a different idea of war from Chamberlain's bloodless one. During the phoney war we had been left in doubt and confusion as to Britain's policy. The new leader left us in no possible doubt. Winston Churchill knew absolutely which path Britain was to take. 'I have nothing to offer you but blood, toil, tears, and sweat,' he told us. This sounded more like the accepted idea of war – more like the doctor from the Spanish war who had lectured to us. 'You ask what is our policy? I will say it is to wage war by sea, land, and air with all our might.'

There were those who were horrified at this blunt statement, but these were not only the still-faithful Chamberlain followers, although he had many sympathizers, they were also the Fascists and the Communist elements. I myself had several pacifist friends amongst the painters I knew, and it was understandable that to an artist the idea of war was doubly repugnant. To most of us, sickened and outraged, and at the same time apprehensive where this relentless march of the Nazi armies would end, this new definite statement of positive action against them came as a welcome relief to a long period of unbearable suspense. 'You ask what is our aim?' asked the new leader Churchill. 'I'll answer it in one word, VICTORY.'

So assured and confident was the voice of the man who had taken over leadership of the country that a great wave of elation swept over us all.

'Blood, toil, tears, and sweat' appealed somehow to the mood of the public and the words themselves caught the public fancy. They were used constantly – in fun, in satire, but also in grim earnest, while the single word VICTORY gave the man in the street a simple definite aim, just as the genius who had used it meant it to.

Jennie had been telling us for a long time that there were many Nazis in Holland. Somehow it didn't fit in with my impression of the kindly, tolerant Dutch in whose country I had lived for more than two years. But on May 10th, with another more acute shock – for this time it was much nearer home – the Germans launched, without warning, a land and air attack on the Netherlands, Luxembourg, and Belgium, and also on French towns. The Belgian and Dutch troops put up a fierce resistance and fought determinedly in defence of their homelands and at the same time their Governments appealed desperately to Britain and France to come to their aid.

The next few days were ones of complete horror as we listened to the BBC's accounts of the bombing of undefended towns and of the slaughter of their innocent citizens – men, women, and children. Rotterdam, where I had painted many Dutch children and still had many friends, suffered a relentless, savage, and persistent air bombardment day and night, culminating in its complete obliteration on May 14th.

Sitting in Chelsea listening, looking at the Thames, it all seemed completely unreal. Rotterdam, The Hague, Amsterdam, Leiden, familiar homely towns with their flat, peaceful, sleeping landscapes, their canals and medieval buildings, all under the Nazi heel! It was so horrible that it was like some monstrous nightmare – from which we must surely waken. But there was no awakening except to worse news – the proclamation broadcast by General Winckelman that the *war* – he did not use the word invasion – had ended in the complete capitulation of Holland. By then Queen Wilhelmina and her daughter Juliana, with Prince Bernhard and the two young princesses, had already arrived in England and had been followed by their Cabinet. Refugees were arriving in every kind of vessel, trawlers, small fishing smacks, and every available craft, and both at Dutch and Belgian ports they had been ruthlessly bombed and machine-gunned.

Chelsea began preparing for refugees who were already fleeing from the Low Countries. We already had Czech, German, and Austrian refugees, but a great many people had evacuated from London and hundreds of large houses stood empty. I heard that interpreters were urgently needed and went to the Town Hall to offer my services. A charming young lady who was taking down particulars of volunteers told me that *Flemish*, which I wrote down as one of my languages, was of no use – they wanted *Belgian*!

In spite of this I was telephoned from Whitehall the next day and asked if I would be available at short notice to interpret Dutch and Flemish (almost identical). I had to collect all kinds of permits and passes, and be interviewed before being given them. No one tested my knowledge of the languages. That was taken on trust! All that mattered before I was given the passes was that I was a hundred per cent British, it seemed.

Dover was a restricted area under Defence of the Realm Regulations, and it presented a bleak, grim, barbed-wire aspect now, very different to the one to which, like many travellers, I had become accustomed, the white, sunny, welcoming cliffs and the castle, unchanging symbols of home. The journey itself, with the WVS, was a revelation in the thoroughness with which signposts and names of all places had been removed. It was lovely weather and the countryside had a fresh appeal after the rather grim one of London. But Dover seemed bleak, austere, and unfamiliar as we handed in our passes and received fresh ones.

The WVS and the Red Cross were already doing splendid work there. As the men, women, and children arrived in their fishing boats or motor launches, tired, dirty, terrified, and apprehensive of their reception, there were these splendid women to help them through their police screening, the Customs, and all the extra war-time red tape. The Customs sheds, in which with other returning travellers I had often waited for the inquisitive probing fingers of the Customs officers, were being used now for all kinds of purposes as well as these. The refugees were given hot drinks immediately and their most urgent needs attended to. Clothing and blankets were provided, beds for those who arrived too late to travel. There was no time to think or get upset – they streamed in and each new lot presented a fresh problem before they could be sent to the hostels which had been hastily provided for them.

I had seen refugees from China only from the distance of the trains and at the railway stations, and in Holland when fleeing from the Nazi aggression. The melee of human misery arriving first in Dover and later in London was close – a contact impossible to ignore, a contact with war – a warning as to the nearness of its approach.

'What will they do with us? Where are we going to live? Are we to stay in London? Do you have air raids here? How are we going to live without money?' And the ceaseless wail of anguish for those left behind. Almost every family had a member missing and were loath to leave the ports lest the loved ones should turn up in the many vessels constantly arriving. There was a preponderance of women, children, and older men. The young men had all been conscripted and their whereabouts were unknown to their womenfolk, who, frantic at the approach of the German armies rolling over everyone and everything like some monstrous juggernaut, had fled to the ports and begged for places in any vessel which could pack them in. 'How lucky you are to have the sea! We had nothing to save us on our frontiers,' they told us. They had been cold, seasick, terrified the whole way, cowering down in the boats from the pursuing German air force. 'Many boats went down!' they told us, 'and thousands of refugees are left behind – there are no more boats.'

The feeling most aroused in me was anger – furious anger. I know I cursed the Germans in their language and my own – but of what use was it except as an outlet for my torn, outraged feelings? One family had a little Spanish girl with them. This little orphan, Agatha, victim of the Spanish Civil War, had been adopted by a French family and was now for the second time in her short life without a country. There were families who were unhurt and volatile in their abuse of the Nazis – and there were others who, grey-faced and overcome with the horror of their country's fate, were silent in their suffering.

And now there was plenty to do in Chelsea, where a large number of the refugees were to be housed. St Mark's College was turned into a reception station and from there they were sent to Cheyne Hospital, the former children's hospital on the Embankment, now in charge of Adelaide Lubbock from FAP2. When I went there in answer to an urgent summons for an interpreter I found that the doctor with whom I was to work was Dr Alice Pennell, whose sister, Cornelia Sorabji, the famous Parsee barrister, I had met and made friends with in Bombay. Dr Alice, a well-known Chelsea figure in her lovely saris, was delightful to work with. She had a delicious sense of humour and a mind enriched by travel and study.

Nearly all the refugees were suffering from some wound, ailment, or shock and exhaustion. The men were mostly those who were either too old or physically unfit for military service.

In Cheyne Hospital I met another friend from India, Lady Benthall, whom I had last seen in Calcutta. She was established in her small office working for the refugees. Her son, Michael, whom I had also last seen in Calcutta, had been studying ballet, but was now going into the army. He did not mind in the least, but feared the effect of army boots on his feet. A ballet dancer's feet are his fortune and have to be treated with respect. Ruth Benthall, although fragile in appearance, was astonishingly efficient at her job. Nothing surprised or shocked her. I envied her her calm poise, and the detached dispassionate way in which she tackled some of the extraordinary problems arising from the sudden arrival of all these refugees. Nothing daunted her – she simply found a way to deal with it. It was strange to discuss Calcutta with its brilliant seasons of balls and racing and its endless round of pleasure. How far away it all seemed to us sitting there in that overcrowded hospital by the river.

It seemed years ago – a world vanished like that last season in London. I discovered that it was she who had asked for me to be attached to the refugees, because of my knowledge of languages, and had got permission for me to do so from my Commandant.

Cheyne Hospital for Children with its many windows looking onto the Thames was strange bereft of all its small patients, who had been evacuated to the country. I had known it well when the cots had been drawn up to the windows and the little convalescents would be out on the balconies watching the boats. It seemed horribly bare and aseptic for these homeless people – devoid of any comforts or cosiness such as is dear to the hearts of the Belgians. They were miserable – but we assured them that it was temporary and that they would soon be moved to houses where they could live more normal lives.

Local residents had given clothes, furniture, and kitchen equipment in answer to the borough's appeal for the refugees. The clothing was laid out on long tables in the dining-hall of Crosby Hall, used formerly for foreign university graduates. Elizabeth Fitzgerald, sister of Denise, with whom I worked in the Control Room, was helping here. It was rather like the scene at a jumble sale at a church bazaar – and the lofty arched roof of the ancient Crosby Hall heightened this impression. Some of the clothing donated as suitable for refugees was truly amazing. Top-hats, dress suits, ball gowns, fans, ancient rubber galoshes and extraordinary undergarments made it appear as if the residents of Chelsea wore perpetual fancy dress, whereas they had probably cleared out all their rubbish before leaving their houses. Elizabeth was in charge of some of the long tables of odd-looking garments. She, and a young man helping her, caused much amusement trying on the clothes. They found a Shetland wool nightgown which someone had obviously washed and stretched so much that it reached from one side of the hall to the other.

The choosing of clothes was a deadly serious business for each refugee or family. Hats did not come under the list of necessities at all, and the women fell upon the most unsuitable, frivolous hats with shrieks of delight, regardless of the fact that they had chosen nothing else, and not even looked at the piles of serviceable garments described as *equestrian hose*!

Some of them were openly contemptuous, saying critically that they had never seen such garments in their lives. Looking at them dispassionately it was difficult to believe that any humans had worn some of them!

Elizabeth, with infinite patience, kept holding up one extraordinary garment after another for their edification. She seemed to me to have the makings of the expert saleswoman as she pointed out the beauties of the goods and I translated for her into Flemish.

Some of us had volunteered to scrub out the houses intended for the refugees, and on this job I again met Elizabeth with her teenage brother, Paul, working hard. We were taken to the houses in a borough van complete with pails, soap, and brushes and told that we would be collected later. Sometimes we would wait and wait for the van which was to collect us, sent not because we were exhausted from our work, but to make sure that the cleaning materials and utensils were safely returned! It was dirty work – but we had fun. I had learned to scrub at the FAP where 'surgical cleanliness' was the standard which the Sister-in-charge enforced. Now, in these houses, empty since the previous September, and already thick with soot and dust, the knowledge was put to good use. Mrs Freeth, as always, insisted on coming to help, and together we did the best that we could. After working one whole long day Elizabeth and her brother, Paul, took me back with them to the Royal Hospital where their father, Maurice, was Secretary. Their mother, Suzanne, was already working hard helping the French-speaking refugees; she was partly Belgian and the family were bi-lingual in French and English.

The lovely Royal Hospital dating from 1684, familiar all over the world because of its scarlet-coated old Pensioners, and also perhaps because of the annual Flower Show there, has always fascinated me. Its history is enthralling, and the beauty of its buildings, designed by Wren, never fails to delight me. Some of the old Pensioners often came to my studio for beer on Sunday after their Church Parade and I had used several of them as models. They liked to sit still, and they liked earning a few shillings for doing so. I had often stood on the Embankment and looked at the lovely facade of the building from the river. Now, for the first time, I saw its interior and soon became a constant visitor there. The wing where the Fitzgeralds lived, on the left of the Governor's apartments, was lovely.

I first saw Suzanne that afternoon in the green Adam library which looked out across the grounds to the Thames. It is one of the most perfect rooms I have ever seen. Of a soft apple green, with its Adam panelling, and exquisitely proportioned fireplace, it made a fitting background for the charm of its hostess. I took an immediate and warm liking to Suzanne and Maurice Fitzgerald and their family. The eldest son, young Maurice, was already in the Middle East with his regiment.

I saw on this first visit something of the graciousness and charm of the building itself, for Maurice took me all over it, showing me the great hall, the dining-room, the chapel, and the strange little cubicles of each of the old Pensioners where his personal possessions were kept and where he might eat if he wished to do so alone. Everything was exactly as it had been when it was built. It was fascinating to stand there looking up at the inscription over the cloisters,

In Subsidium et Levamen emeritorum Senio Belloque Fractorum, condidit Carolus Secundus auxit Jacobus Secundus, perfecere Gulielmus et Maria, Rex et Regina, Anno Domini MDCXCII.

and imagine that from here, perhaps, Nell Gwynne had watched the realization of her dream in the building of a home for the old soldiers 'broken in the wars', as the words said. Here, perhaps, she had stood with Charles II, who had planned it to please her, and chosen the most renowned architect of the day to design it for her, and surely Christopher Wren surpassed himself in the setting and placing of this noble building.

The Royal Hospital had been bombed in the 1914-18 War by a zeppelin, and a tablet commemorated the event. The old soldiers regretted bitterly the fact that they were too old to fight again and many of them had tried to volunteer. I was introduced to one old man of over eighty with an impressive row of medals who had written to the Air Ministry when the War Office had turned him down. He had said that although he could not fly a plane because he had never learnt, he felt sure that he could sit in the tail and work the lever to release the bombs. The Air Ministry had replied with a perfectly charming letter in which they thanked him, saying that should they need him he could be sure that he would hear from them. He showed me this most proudly, and whoever composed it was a most understanding person.

The Hospital's chapel was a little gem, and in the late afternoon sun was full of a deep golden light. The whole place had a tranquillity and charm which was entrancing – not even the visible signs of war – the balloon, the sand-bags, the barbed wire entanglements, and the flower gardens being dug up as allotments for vegetables – could take that away. It seemed indeed a place where the old warriors could spend their last days in leisure and content although they indulged freely in the grumbling which is a soldier's privilege.

Suzanne and I belonged to a Committee of Women which had been formed to look after the refugees, and which met at Whistlers house in Cheyne Walk. I found it very difficult to pay attention to all the proposals and arguments put forward by the women as to the whys and wherefores of this and that plan. For me it was so exciting to be actually sitting in this historic house which itself was so beautiful that I could not avoid taking in every small detail. Here Whistler had lived and worked, painting his beloved Thames from his windows. I found myself imagining that small dapper figure at the windows or on the staircase and was lost in a reverie of his troublous life, his quarrels, his feuds, his battles, instead of listening to the squabbles of the committee. The house had been lent us for the meetings. It was decided that the women on the committee would each adopt a number of houses and become godmothers, or *'marraines'*, to the refugees in them. The houses allotted to me at this meeting were in Tedworth Square and Royal Avenue and the refugees destined for them were all Flemish-speaking ones.

I was to spend the greater part of my time with the refugees and be available on call for the FAP and the Control Room. Margerie Scott, who had been at FAP2 working with Dr Pennell, was now transferred to the Town Hall where she was to be rehousing manager not only for the refugees but also for possible bombed-out people. Margerie Scott, author and broadcaster, was already doing broadcasts on the North American Service about the refugees who had arrived in Chelsea.

King Leopold's capitulation to the Germans on May 28th caused a wave of fury amongst the Belgian refugees. It didn't seem to occur to them that there was little else he could have done, or that their own mass flight had done nothing to help. The news was the signal for an outbreak of the misery and dissatisfaction which these displaced people were feeling. I had to he called to Cheyne Hospital twice to help quell violent altercations which led to blows. Meanwhile the safety of our own troops was now a matter which tore at all of us. What if they were caught in a net and unable to leave Belgium now that it was to be occupied by the Nazis as Denmark and Holland had been?

CHAPTER SIX

WHILE THE FATE of France hung in the balance, many British families were enduring anguished suspense waiting for news of their sons and fathers. Mary Underwood was worried about Garth, from whom she had not heard recently. He was somewhere in France, and had been for the last six months or so. I had had several letters from him but apart from the fact that they were living in a vast forest there was no clue at all as to his whereabouts in France. Leon was doing camouflage work at Leamington Spa with a large group of artists recruited by the Government for this work. The days, warm and still, as they had been both at Munich and at the outbreak of war, continued in a sort of unspoken anguish of tension until we heard that British troops were being evacuated from Belgium.

My young friend, Sally Clapcott, whose father had been Mayor of Chelsea, had recently married a young officer. They had exactly three days together before he had to join the BEF. On the last day I had met them – scarcely more than children walking hand-in-hand round and round Sloane Square. They couldn't bear to say good-bye. I had seldom seen anything more moving than these two young people, recently so radiant at their marriage, now white and tense with the anguish of parting. I thought how lucky it was that the man I was going to marry was still in England.

On June 1st the newspapers had photographs of the BEF arriving back from the battlefields and with them were a number of French troops. But in families with a son, husband, or fiancé there was still unbearable suspense wondering if he would be amongst those coming back. Fresh batches of civilian refugees were arriving with the troops, and once more I was summoned to Dover to help with the Flemish- and Dutch-speaking ones.

This time the port presented an amazing scene. The harbour itself was so thick with ships that it would have been possible to walk across it passing from one vessel to another. The place was one seething mass of khaki. Troops were lying about utterly exhausted all over the place. The platforms on the station were a mass of sleeping khaki bodies which did not stir when the officials stepped over them. There were some French troops with them but they did not lie down or sleep. Tense and alert, they stood and watched the sky. The mass of ships in the harbour was a wonderful sight but an even more wonderful target. The civilians, many of whom had been wounded by bullets and shells, had only one idea – *to get under shelter*. They found it agonizing to have to stand at all in the open. Our own troops were so tired that they just slept anywhere, with no emotion except sheer exhaustion visible on their faces, turned up to the sky watched so fearfully by the foreigners.

I worked for a long gruelling day until relieved by another Flemish-speaking nurse late next evening, and this time the misery and wretchedness of displaced humanity was one of sheer stark horror. And yet I could not look at all the grey tired faces of our own troops without intense wonder and gratitude that they were home – that with the horror of bombing and machine-gunning which had accompanied them – the RAF covering them and fighting for their protection all the way – it was surely nothing short of a miracle that such numbers were safe on their own shores. The troops had learned not to talk – not so the civilians. They poured into our ears tales of Dorniers, Messerschmitts, and Heinkels attacking them and of hundreds of them being shot down into the sea by the RAF. And not all of our boys came home.

After my return to London Mary rang me up excitedly to say that she had heard from Garth and that he was in England and would soon be home. He had been torpedoed but was all right; his letter had been written in Plymouth.

Three days later Garth Underwood [now Professor of Biology at University College of the West Indies, Jamaica] walked into my studio. Gaunt and pale, he was otherwise unchanged. To me he was still the growing schoolboy who had so often, with his sister, Jean, spent Saturday afternoons and Sundays in the studio and played games with me and eaten quantities of buns.

Sitting, as he always did, almost astride rather than in a chair and munching the buns of which he was so fond, he told a terrible story of his experiences in getting out of France. He looked so young that in spite of his uniform it was difficult to believe that he was actually back from the horrors of war.

After a terrible journey from Brittany Garth's unit had reached the *Lancastria*, which was taking on the thousands of troops in the bay of St Nazaire, when a Heinkel had dropped four bombs on the ship. One bomb went down the funnel of the ship and blew the whistle, another had exploded in the bowels and caused a panic. There were over 5,000 troops on board and only 2,000 life jackets. The story of the ensuing stampede and sickening lack of any discipline or authority was one of the most appalling things to which I had ever listened.

Garth could swim, but not well, and he managed to reach a minesweeper which was about a mile away. There were any number of vessels in the bay but none of them appeared to be picking up survivors from the *Lancastria*, which, listing to starboard, was rapidly sinking with her decks overflowing with troops, many of whom could not swim. 'It was a lovely, still, sunny day which made the whole thing seem more unreal. As, at last, I approached the minesweeper the stern of the *Lancastria* disappeared and it seemed as if the ship had touched the bottom and rolled over on her side. She was still crowded with men – as many as could were still standing and they were singing "Roll Out the Barrel". As the waves came up they washed off the remaining men – there was as yet no indication of any boats being sent to pick up the survivors – and all those who could swim were making for various transports in the bay.' He told me the whole episode in detail and I wrote it down then and there. It is a terrible story and reflects little credit on those in authority.

Garth was a student of biology and had the scientist's eye for detailed fact so that he had missed nothing. He was interested in facts, not emotion – and even when facing death he had noticed all the little fish stunned by the explosion, and later when his transport was finally reaching Plymouth he had remembered that amphioxis were found off the Eddystone! Delivered in his flat, boyish way his appalling story made such an impact on me that for days I could think of nothing else but his last vision of the doomed *Lancastria* going down crowded with all those young troops standing on the listing deck still singing 'Roll Out the Barrel' until the waves swept them off.

At this same time Sally's young husband returned after having suffered horrible experiences when his ship had been torpedoed. More horrible to us was the knowledge that both these young men like thousands of others would have to return to their diminished units, and would undoubtedly be sent overseas again.

In Chelsea, apart from the food shortage, the black-out, the barbed wire everywhere, the sand-bags and the shelters, life did not appear, at least on the surface, to have changed very much. I sent Garth's story, as he had told it to me, to my mother in Plymouth. He had particularly praised the kindness of the Plymouth people who had received the half-naked survivors with wonderful warmness and generosity. When later it was announced that four-fifths of the BEF had been saved all I could think of was those young men on the *Lancastria*. I couldn't bear to hear 'Roll Out the Barrel' pounding out from the pubs and clubs at night.

During the anguished week-end of Dunkirk thousands of school-children were registered in Greater London for evacuation. The figure was something like 611,772. Thousands who had been evacuated at the outbreak of war had drifted back to London again. There had been no air raids, they had grown homesick and their parents longed for them and so they had unobtrusively returned. The Admiralty announced that 228 British naval vessels and 625 other craft took part in the withdrawal of the troops from Dunkirk, that 6 destroyers and 24 minor war vessels were lost, and that more than 335,000 men had been brought home from Dunkirk by June 5th. But *The Times*, a few days later, had long lists of missing officers in the casualty notices. In the afternoon of Sunday the 9th, when walking along the Embankment with my fiancé, Richard, and Anne, a fireman of the River Fire Brigade whom I knew from ARP practices shouted to me...'Some of them will be coming along soon, we're going to give them a rousing cheer.'

'Who?' I shouted back.

'The little boats,' he replied, 'and one of our fireboats is due back too.' The news had spread, for when we hurried along to Westminster Bridge a large crowd had gathered. And almost at once they came, those little dirty battered boats I'd seen like shrimps in Dover Harbour, their paint scraped and marked, and all down the river the river stations of the Fire Brigade gave them a tremendous cheer, as did the crowds gathered on all the bridges.

They came in little groups of two or three, led by a tug with eighteen motor launches in tow, a lovely brave sight. Even now it brings a choking sensation when I think how I'd seen them there exposed to the peril of air attack in that crowded Dover Harbour and then saw this unobtrusive, unheralded return to their own moorings after the dangers they had faced to bring our boys safely home. I said as much to Tom Baynes, whom I saw in Chelsea Reach cleaning up his boat next day. 'What d'you expect?' he said nonchalantly. 'Can't hang out the flags till the war's over. Like the boys, we didn't want cheers – all we wanted was to slip away home and sleep.'

CHAPTER SEVEN

June, usually the loveliest and gayest month of the summer, having begun grimly with Dunkirk, was to prove a fateful one this year. The evacuation of children went on again for six days. The stations were full of those same train-loads of young laughing or weeping faces being seen off with a gallant flutter of waving hands and handkerchiefs. But this time good-byes were more painful. Events had cast their shadows and many parents who had scoffed before were now apprehensive as to how far the onslaught of the Nazi armies would take them. If France gave in would they reach England? But it was unthinkable that France would not beat the Germans, hadn't she beaten them and driven them out of France in the last war? Hadn't she always been a strong military-minded nation?

The arrival of King Haakon of Norway with Crown Prince Olaf and the Norwegian Government as refugees did not dispel this fear. In the FAP argument and conflict of opinion would break out whenever we had nothing to do. We were all young and gave voice wildly about the rights and wrongs of nations and sometimes tempers got high. One of our sisters-in-charge was married to a Fascist, and her views, although absolutely loyal, were more tolerant and differed from some of ours. Our two Commandants, Betty and Ruth, would sometimes intervene and put an end to our disputes by giving us some task to do or test us on nursing and first-aid points. Dr Graham Kerr, young and keen, was giving us an intensive course of lectures on both nursing and first aid, and a gas course had to be attended at Carlyle Square. Almost everyone at the FAP had a fiancé, husband, brother, or boy-friend who had been immediately affected by the call-up. The Mobile Squads were formed of older and more experienced nurses. We had all chafed under the long delay and I was envied for my chance of working for the refugees. I was not so sure about this myself. At the quiet FAP there had been plenty of time for drawing and reading. Most of the girls knitted – but I did this very badly and preferred to draw. Now I found that there was never any time for anything except trying to alleviate the misery of the refugees by attempting to find some of the things they most needed. I was on my feet all day and no matter what I managed to produce it was never right. They were exacting – and any idea I had had that those to whom one gave were grateful was soon dissipated.

The houses allotted to the different families were sparsely furnished from bits and pieces given by those who didn't want them. They had a bareness and a grimness which chilled. Having been in many Flemish and Dutch houses and knowing their love of making them cosy with lace curtains, bright pictures, plants, and many ornaments, I went round collecting such objects from my friends. It was astonishing what 'horrors' they discovered in their attics and junk cupboards. China dogs, animals, flower pots painted in bright colours, old prints, Victorian pictures long thrust away, all of them, and yards of old-fashioned lace curtains, I seized on joyfully and took them to the bare houses for which I was responsible. I saw that the first urgent need was for those who spoke only Flemish – and there were many – to learn some English. Many English people speak French – but few Flemish. As the Government hoped that the men and many of the women refugees would soon be absorbed in the war drive for munitions it was imperative that they knew the rudiments of English.

Margerie Scott, who could always find everything, provided a blackboard and I found my facility for drawing extremely useful in the first lessons for adults – both men and women of all ages. They learned with difficulty – many of them could scarcely read and write in their own language, not because they had never learned how but because most of them were fisherfolk and they had had little need to do so. The children were another matter, they learned extraordinarily easily. I promised that the first child who could say a whole English sentence correctly to me, could come to the studio to tea. With them Vicki was a great favourite and the studio a tremendous attraction. I had taught her to stand upright on her hind legs and raise one paw in the Nazi salute when ordered to *Heil Hitler* and then to fall backwards motionless when ordered to 'Die for England'. She was quite famous for this performance which she much enjoyed giving and for which she received a piece of chocolate. One afternoon soon after this promise I returned home from the FAP to find almost the whole children's class waiting in the studio for the promised tea. Mrs Freeth had, as she told me, taken them at their word and let them all in. With much foresight she had run across the road to Mr Ferebee and bought some biscuits and a large cake. I tested the visitors out as to the sentence, all had a short one absolutely pat, except one small, shy child of eight. She was tongue-tied. 'Send her home. She doesn't know a sentence, Marraine. *Send her home!*' they shouted with the cruelty of childhood, but Mrs Freeth, who had been watching and listening, whispered to her to say after her, 'I love Vicki', and this she did, her small face scarlet with shyness and with Victoria clutched in her arms.

Mrs Freeth, who had never been outside England and who was in fact a real Cockney, soon proved that language is no barrier to friendship, nor is knowledge of other countries necessary in helping foreigners. She was quickly at home with all the families and knew their names, ages, and characters far better than I did. Whenever they came – and they always came – and rang the bell of my home Mrs Freeth dealt magnificently with them. If it was some household thing which they wanted to borrow she would take them into the kitchen and they could point to what they needed. When, however, it was a more personal matter – and they arrived in floods of noisy tears – she would give them a cup of tea and settle them in a chair or doing some small job with her until I arrived.

They had to be escorted to obtain identity cards and ration books and some of them to the police station for a kind of screening where an officer of the CID had to interrogate the men in particular. I was surprised at the patience and niceness of everyone at the police station, and at the apprehension of the refugees at even having to enter any place connected with the police. We sometimes had a good laugh when reading over the documents made in answer to questions put to them through me.

'Married?' asked the police officer to the man who had arrived alone. 'Yes, I see you are married. Is your wife here in England?'

'No,' with a vigorous shake of the head. 'She got left behind.'

'Oh,' said the officer, writing busily. 'That's a pity for you.'

'Not at all,' said the man simply. 'She had served her purpose. I can get a new one here.'

'Did she refuse to come with you then?'

Another vigorous shake of the head. 'No. I took good care not to give her the opportunity.'

One woman who was asked where her husband was, said furiously, 'How should I know? On the night we were to embark he must go off to the Café du Port to say good-bye to some floozie – well, I hope he's still saying good-bye to her – under the Germans! The dirty pig!'

Others who had been torn apart through no fault of theirs but by the ravages of war were suffering intense anguish, without news, or hope of any news of their loved ones. The tact and patience shown by the interrogating officers struck me as wonderful. They were quite young – and both of them expected to be called up very shortly. The older men would have to carry on – as they would in every profession and walk of life.

Almost all the refugees were suffering from some complaint and it was my job to take them to the out-patients' department of St Luke's Hospital. There was one middle-aged woman who came to tell me that she simply could not resist stealing from shops. A perfectly respectable married woman, her two sons and husband had escaped with her. 'I see something – a garment, a tea-spoon, a piece of china – and I *must* have it just as I had to have artichokes when I was expecting my sons. Yes, both times it was artichokes – and out of season too.' Shortly after telling me this she was in a chain store and saw a small saucepan. The urge came over her so strongly that she picked it up – then she turned round and bolted – and came to me. 'Marraine, you *must* take me to a doctor,' she begged.

I took her to St Luke's to a young and brilliant doctor there who was already interested in the refugees. He listened to my story with enjoyment. 'She needs psychiatric treatment probably,' he said laughing, 'but we just can't deal with it now in war-time. We're too short staffed everywhere. Tell her that I'll give her some pills – and that whenever she has this urge she is to think of *prison* and to take one. She is to carry them in her bag always.' Madame C was delighted. Some time later when I was again in the hospital with another batch of sufferers the young doctor asked me how the would-be shoplifter was. 'Fine,' I said, 'she says your pills are wonderful. She hasn't lifted a thing. She takes a pill and it works like a miracle. The police would like to know what those pills are, they know plenty of people who need them.'

'They're aspirin,' he said, laughing. 'It's more likely the thought of prison that does the trick.'

'No,' I assured him. 'It's the pills – she's convinced of it.'

The refugees ate in a canteen in the basement of a house in St Leonard's Terrace. Their rations were pooled and the women took it in strict rota to cook the midday-meal. This led to trouble very often. Some of the women were better at cooking than others and the men would grumble and say that they couldn't eat the food.

One elderly and remarkable woman, who had come alone, had undertaken to do the cooking for them all as she was too old for war work. Her name was Seraphine and she had a striking personality and could make any grumblers literally shake with fear. She had some extraordinary power over others. A number of the ladies on the committee had undertaken to help the refugee wives in buying food and arranging the menus. Suzanne, who was wonderfully practical, and accustomed to running a large household economically, was kept very busy with the constant problems arising from this communal cooking and eating.

We were invited to submit all these problems at the meetings which the committee held in Whistler's house which all the *Marraines* attended, presided over by Miss Eveleen Campbell Gray, the Lady Mayoress, and Margerie Scott. Some of the problems were difficult to overcome and endless argument would ensue.

I was still going to the Control Room as a relief when the regulars had their days off and the two young Scottish girls, Chris and Sheila, were frequent visitors to Cheyne Place, Mrs Freeth having completely adopted them as members of the household. A woman composer, Ellen Coleman, also worked in the Control Room, and she often invited me to her lovely house in Mulberry Walk where she would play in a beautiful music room opening on to a little garden. When I was particularly het up over the refugees, she would play me records of her compositions. One of our loveliest telephonists had married in May and we had all gone to the wedding. Her husband had been ordered to France immediately afterwards, as had Sally's, and like them they had only three days together. She had come back now, a tragic young widow. Her young husband had been one of those who did not come back from Dunkirk.

Italy's entry into the war was the signal in Soho for some ugly, revolting scenes, when the police began rounding up Italians, some of whom had been a lifetime in London working in their especial milieu of restaurateur. Ever since I had been an art student I had known the Calettas, whose restaurant in the King's Road was a favourite one with all of us. Madame Caletta's husband was one of those removed by the police. I don't know whether the Chelsea residents were more internationally minded than others, but there was only anger and sympathy when this happened. The Calettas were much liked and respected and it came as a shock to find that because of his Italian nationality a man who had given much employment and custom in Chelsea was suddenly regarded as an undesirable alien. I went to see Madame Caletta and found her dazed, but with none of the bitterness which one expected. She had not been interned – it was only the men whom the police regarded as a possible danger. In Glasgow there was violent anti-Italian feeling and there the Italian shops and cafés had their windows broken and their owners were stoned and abused. This was frightening, as were some of the incidents which Madame Caletta told me had happened to friends in London. The police, she said, had been correct and courteous – it was the people who had behaved with such unexpected violence. War, it seemed, brought out both the best and the worst in the population.

There was already constant quarrelling amongst the refugees and I began to become accustomed to a policeman ringing my bell to ask me to come and settle some quarrel or other. They had nothing to do, had none of their own possessions, none of their own cooking as they ate in the canteen, and bickering and quarrelling was the only outlet for their misery. There was a huge fisherman in one of the houses for which I was responsible who was extremely quarrelsome and who spread 'alarm and despondency', as we were constantly being warned not to do, by his gloomy prophecies about the outcome of the war. His wife was almost as big and raw-boned as he was, but their child was one of the most undersized delicate-looking children I had ever seen. It seemed as if the two tough, highly coloured fisherfolk had grudged any of their vitality and energy to this small daughter. When the news from France began to get more and more grave and the battle for Paris began, I had a lot of trouble with this man, whom I had nicknamed The Giant. As well as being enormous, with magnificent muscles from pulling in the nets, he was a bully and would terrify the smaller men with his threats.

I was often frightened myself by this huge rough creature who addressed me in a bantering, condescending way and informed me every day when I went to the house that we were one step nearer to becoming a German colony. 'Hitler's coming! Just you wait, Marraine! He'll get here just as he's got to Belgium and Holland and now France.'

His wife, who was afraid of him, would applaud and encourage him to frighten the other families in the house until they got worked up into a state of real hysteria.

He adored his fragile little girl and so did his wife. She, poor child, seemed terrified of everything and this was not surprising after the appalling journey she had had, seeing her friends machine-gunned and their boats sunk. The Giant's boat had not been sunk – he had brought it safely to Dover and he was proud of it. It was now at Haverfordwest and later on when he had been passed through the screening he would be allowed to join the British fishing fleet, as would all the refugees who had brought their fishing boats to England.

I felt great sympathy for these fishermen who wanted to be with their boats. It was difficult to see why they had been sent to London of all places. As almost all coastal towns were now restricted areas it was understandable that screening was necessary before they were given the freedom of places restricted to us, but it was difficult to explain to them the endless red tape and delays. I would come upon them leaning over the embankment watching the river, their eyes following longingly the movement of every small vessel and craft. When the tide came in they would sniff appreciatively. 'It's a little bit of the sea!' they would say and the hopeless shrug of the shoulders which followed was eloquent of their feeling of frustration.

The middle of the month brought the grim struggle for Paris to a climax. Once again Kathleen, Anne, and I listened to the bulletins of a capital fighting against the invaders – and the fact that this time it was Paris, where I had studied painting, Paris, beloved of all British tourists, made it more heart-breaking. The Germans were attempting to encircle the city and British reinforcements were being rushed to France.

Some of us VADs, on the 13th, were again seeing schoolchildren off, this time from Paddington, They were all going to the West of England. How different was the outlook of those saying good-bye to them to The Giant's. 'See you soon, darling. You'll soon be back, ducks. We'll beat 'em. You'll see. You'll soon be able to come home. Chin up, love. Mother'll come down and see you...' But then they had not seen what The Giant had seen.

On the 15th the newspapers announced that the Germans were in Paris, and at the same time they were publishing pictures of more BEF leaving for France. Masses of laughing young faces going eagerly to fight for Paris, which had now been declared an open city and from which the population were streaming out in one mad panic rush! No one had given them any order to evacuate, they had just packed their possessions into cars, carts, perambulators, bicycles, anything they could find, and in one terrible human stream blocked every road needed urgently by the troops trying in vain to reach the city to defend it. We were throwing in fresh troops, and the Scottish regiments were fighting in epic and heroic fashion. It seemed incredible to read of the two things at the same time our troops being rushed in and the citizens rushing out!

Throughout the next few tense days everyone went about silent and with strained faces. Was it to be another Dunkirk? On the Sunday, the 16th, the French had been ordered to stop fighting, and Marshal Petain asked for terms of peace; but M Baudouin, the French Foreign Minister, with the example of the other conquered countries before him, announced that France would only lay down her arms in an honourable peace. The French army, he said, continued to fight.

The Prime Minister, Mr Churchill, announced that we should defend our island and with the British Commonwealth fight on, unconquerable, to end the curse of Hitler. Then he went on to declare our unification with France.

This speech was perfectly timed. We were all depressed and horrified at the events in France. Was no country going to succeed in checking the terrible and relentless advance of the Nazi troops? They seemed like that horde of Huns under Attila sweeping through Europe and treading down everything which came in their path. The ponderous, deliberate, quiet voice of Winston Churchill was far more effective than the hysterical ravings which one could listen to on the German radio – whether it was Hitler or Goebbels screaming his threats across the waves of the air. Churchill's voice was slow, but its very deliberation had in it the weight and promise that nothing would deflect him from his determination to end the mad lust of the man in the Reichstag. It carried that complete assurance of conviction which we all wanted to hear,

On the Tuesday, the 18th, I had planned a small cocktail party. By the early evening I did not feel like a party – for the placards said *France had fallen*. Mrs Freeth had got everything ready and assured me that people liked a disaster to discuss even more than a mere social occasion! She proved to be only too right. The cocktail party developed into a violent discussion as to the rights or wrongs of the Fall of France. My French friend, Marianne Ducroix, resenting the criticism of her country's defeat, burst into angry tears, shouted that we were all all enemies of France, that we were aiding the Nazis by our gloom and pessimism, that all we were thinking of was our own troops while the fate of the French mattered nothing to us at all.

I tried clumsily to apologize – but I only made matters worse. Marianne left in high dudgeon and I was miserable about it. An uninvited guest revealed himself to be an ardent Fascist and revelled in the disaster. I quarrelled violently with him until I realized that he was drunk. He would not leave the party as Marianne had, but fell asleep on the studio couch cuddling Victoria who, faithless in politics, adored this follower of Mosley. When at last he woke up he was lachrymose and silly, using Vicki's silky head on which to let flow his tears at the stupidity of Britain who, in his view, was marching blindfold to her doom.

Jennie was terribly cast down at the fate of Holland; only Asta was cheerful. Norway was not yet beaten, she asserted gallantly, King Haakon might have arrived as a refugee but the Norwegians would not give in. Her optimism was a tonic to everyone. She raised her cocktail glass high and drank loudly and firmly to her King and to Victory – and we all stood and raised ours too. But none of us had the heart to drink to France – the memory of Marianne's outburst was too painful.

Dr Alice Pennell, in a wonderful sari of red and gold, was looking at my portrait of Kumari, my young friend from Hyderabad, now training as a nurse. Her brother Indi, a most handsome youth, was also present. He had come over for training with the RAF in the Nizam of Hyderabad's special squadron.

It was quite the most unpleasant party I could remember. General de Gaulle, of whom few of us had ever heard, now appeared as the leader of those French who were determined to resist, and made an amazing broadcast that all was not lost – that France would continue to fight. His fine speech that evening did do something to alleviate the wretched events of the day, but nothing could banish for me the picture of Marianne, whose friendship I valued. As soon as I could, I telephoned her flat – but the bell rang into that silence which betokens emptiness.

In the Civil Defence Services we were told of the thousand bombs which had been dropped on Paris during Dunkirk. There had been no panic, and all the ARP Services had worked perfectly. Some of the bombs had fallen on schools, killing and injuring children. The details were released to us for their value in the ARP lectures. Again we had several large-scale practices. By now they were no novelty to most of us – but as a number of personnel were constantly disappearing into the Services, there were always some who had not taken part in a practice.

Our own air-raid sirens were sounding in the Home Counties where the RAF were successfully driving off German planes, attacking during their fresh assault on the Western Front.

The French armies were fighting with epic courage and we listened to the radio bulletins with the same feeling of tragic inevitability which had coloured the broadcasts on the battles for Poland and Finland. In some ways it was terrible to bear these frequent bulletins because the watchful attitude of censorship prevented us from getting the full facts. The ones not disclosed would come later – and were usually not so good. The news of the *Lancastria* had not been announced until the 17th – long after Garth had come home and told us of it.

CHAPTER EIGHT

THE FRIEND most violently affected by the disastrous news was Ruth. She telephoned constantly, and each time the strain in her voice was worse. Her incessant telephoning and letters had become almost a persecution. Her whole problem was one with which I was not able to contend.

Mrs Freeth had become wonderful at soothing Ruth on the telephone, and she had managed to keep her away from the party, but the following morning Ruth arrived quite early. I was shocked at her appearance. Her eyes were enormous in her white haunted face and she talked on one note – her voice having no inflexions whatsoever. She had been very beautiful before she had been so relentlessly treated by her husband. She told her usual story of persecution. She talked always of 'They'. They were persecuting her, listening at her walls, tapping her telephone calls, shadowing her wherever she went. It was useless to argue with her – she was beyond it. Her young daughter, Carla, was at a convent school. It had evacuated, but part of it remained, with a skeleton staff, in Chelsea. Carla was a lovely blonde child who had quite obviously taken after her Aryan father. Ruth was very dark. It was, she told me, quite dangerous to have very dark hair and dark eyes in Germany.

She stood now in the dining-room ignoring the coffee which Mrs Freeth had brought her, twisting her hands and talking, talking on and on in the monotonous level voice which so alarmed me. 'It's no use, no use at all. They'll get me interned. You've heard what Sir John Anderson has said. All Austrians and Germans will be interned. *They* are after me again. I can hear them all the time. I can see them all the time. In every shop, in every bus – even if I take a taxi. I shall lose my job – they won't want a German – let's see your passport they will say – oh, you're *German*. Sorry but it's war-time. You're an enemy alien now...I have to report to the police quite often. *Me!* I've been here since the first horrible purge in Germany. I brought Carla here when she was only six...' She stopped, staring unseeing at me. 'You must help me. You *must*. You're so lucky to be British born. I've tried and tried to get British nationality. It was just about to go through when this war came. Now they won't give it to me. You must make them. You have friends in the Home Office.'

It was useless telling her that no naturalization papers were being considered during the war. Looking at me with those wet mournful eyes she said in a hard tense voice, 'You didn't invite me to your party. It's because I am German. You didn't want to be embarrassed.'

To this I had no answer. I just stared at her; and she burst into a terrible tirade about everyone being against her and that she had believed that I was different.

She got up reluctantly to leave when at half past ten I said I had to go. I knew that I ought to keep her with me, she had a wild distracted look, but I was going out that afternoon: although I had to take a refugee to St Luke's Hospital first I was going to a matinee. The never-ending troubles of the refugees had to be forgotten sometimes and although my instinct was to put off my date and keep Ruth with me for lunch I did not do it. I had consulted Dr Pennell about her, and she, having met Ruth in my studio, had said firmly that she needed medical treatment and that nothing else could help her.

As she went out of the front door Ruth said, 'You're just like the others. You *won't* help me.'

It was half past ten and I was due at the hospital at eleven, so I did not put on my uniform but collected Monsieur F and went with him dressed in civilian clothes.

When we reached the hospital there was a strange doctor on duty who was impatient, and even disagreeable in his manner, and poor Monsieur F crumpled up at his brusqueness. The doctor was one of those Englishmen who seem to think that if shouted at loudly enough everyone should be able to understand English. Monsieur F refused to co-operate and it was a long time before I could persuade him to submit to an examination.

At last it was finished and I was free to go home. There would be exactly fifteen minutes to snatch some food before leaving for the matinee.

But I did not go to see *Dear Octopus* after all. Mrs Freeth greeted me with a worried face as soon as I got in. 'Will you ring Miss Carla at once, please,' she said. 'There's been trouble.'

Carla was fairly calm considering what had happened. She had got home from school and had rung the bell, and when her mother did not answer she had looked under the mat and there, sure enough, was the key of the flat where they always left it. She opened the door. A great rush of gas met her. Choking and gasping, she had the sense to leave the door open while she tried the door of the kitchen. It was locked. She looked in the other rooms. No one. She knew instinctively that her mother was behind the locked door. She tried kicking it but she could not smash it in. Then she rushed down to find the porter. He was at his lunch and she could not find him. She shouted for the neighbours – but no one appeared to be in. It was lunchtime and there was no one about in the streets. She telephoned me but I was out too. At last she found a policeman and he went back with her and broke the door in. Ruth lay on the floor. She had stuffed up every aperture with dusters and cushions and had turned the gas on full. The policeman tried artificial respiration but, finding it useless, telephoned for an ambulance. He waited with Carla until I telephoned, I got into a taxi, and took Victoria, thinking that the dog would help comfort the child. I was horribly shocked.

Carla was waiting for me at the entrance to the flats, calm, pale, and with a stem resigned look on her young face. She didn't want to go into the flat again. 'Is the policeman still up there?' I asked her. She said he was. He was a very understanding policeman, not young, but solid and fatherly. 'Will she recover?' I asked. He looked dubious. 'She was pretty far gone,' he said. 'I couldn't get her round, not even with one of the neighbours, who helped me very efficiently. She must have inhaled a lot of gas and she must have been unconscious for some time when we broke the door down.'

I asked if she had left a letter or anything. Nothing, it seemed. Nothing at all. *She must have gone straight back from me and done this thing.* I thought of our conversation. Had I been impatient, unsympathetic? True, I had been anxious to get away – because of the theatre. Probably I hadn't been sympathetic enough. I often spoke without thinking. What had I said? But Ruth had been in a terrible state when she had arrived because of Sir John Anderson's statement on the refugees and because of the fall of France.

We all went in a taxi to the hospital, where we were told that she had not yet recovered consciousness. We were not allowed to see her.

I collected what Carla needed for a few nights and we went back to Cheyne Place. I had a small spare room, large enough for a child, and Mrs Freeth had already fixed it up and put flowers and some of my porcelain animals in it. 'I knew you'd bring her back,' she said, giving Carla a warm greeting. The child didn't say anything about what had happened until I went to say good-night to her. She was sitting up in bed with her hair hanging over her eyes. 'She shouldn't have done it – it was beastly for me finding her like that. She was bright red as if she'd been boiled. It was *beastly* of her. And if she had died what about *me*? What would happen to *me*?' and she burst into terrible sobs.

I kept her with me for some weeks and the Belgian and French children came to play with her. She was delighted when she found that she could understand Flemish words, which were not unlike German. When I told her that I'd invited the Belgian and French children, she said, flushing bright pink, 'Would you mind telling them that I am Czech? You see lots of Czechs speak German and they'll like me better then.'

Ruth recovered slowly. She was not charged with attempting to commit suicide, but she had to enter a nursing home for treatment for a time. At the convent school which Carla attended the nuns were most kind and helpful. They said that the whole school would shortly be moving to join the section already in the country. The Mother Superior thought that the best possible thing for Carla would be for her to get into the country and forget what had happened. I saw her off with the nuns and their charges, promising to write to her and to visit her very soon. She was excited at going to boarding school for the first time in her life – she had always wanted to be a boarder, she said. I had just sold two paintings unexpectedly in an exhibition and so modest was the sum asked by the convent for Carla that this windfall would keep her there for a year.

Ruth was by no means the only refugee from the Nazis who had tried to commit suicide. The policeman told me that there had been many. Anguish, misery, fear, and bitterness amongst German and Austrian refugees now interned alongside their Nazi oppressors was such that the Archbishop of Canterbury had written to the Home Secretary about their plight, and many MPs were indignant.

After the calamitous events in Belgium, Holland, and France, a statement was put out by the Ministry of Information on June 18th which was headlined in the newspapers. Mrs Freeth brought to me in scorn a paragraph she had cut from a newspaper headed 'What to do if Parachutists should come'.

1. If the Germans come by parachute, aeroplane, or ship you must remain where you are. The order is to stay put. (Germans made use of the population by spreading false rumours.)

2. Do not believe rumours and do not spread them. When you receive an order make quite sure that it is a true order and not a faked one. Most of you know your policeman and ARP wardens by sight and you can trust them. If you keep your heads you can tell whether a military officer is really British or whether only pretending to be so. If in doubt ask the police or the ARP. Use your common sense. Be calm, quick, exact.

3. Keep watch. If you see anything suspicious note it carefully and go at once to the nearest policeman or the nearest military officer. Do not go rushing about spreading a vague rumour. Go quickly to the nearest authority and give him the facts. When parachutists come down near homes they will not be feeling very brave. They will not know where they are or where their companions are. They will have no food and will want you to give them food, means of transport and maps. They will want to know where they have landed, where their comrades are and where our own soldiers are.

4. Do not give any German anything. Do not tell him anything. Hide your food, your bicycles, your maps. See that the enemy get no petrol. If you have a car or a motor cycle put it out of action.

Kathleen produced a photograph from *The Times* of German parachutists. Tough, brutal, and armed. How exactly would housewives prevent them taking any of those things listed by the Ministry? In thousands of homes there were only women now, the men were in the Forces. We were not allowed weapons, what did they expect us to use against these tough shock-troop parachutists? Did they think that if we said sweetly that we were not allowed to give them anything, they would salute, click their heels, and depart?

The wording of the pamphlet which we knew was designed to try and avoid the same panic flight as in Belgium and France caused such hilarity everywhere that every current show included some skit on the arrival of parachutists. In the FAP we went about chivvying one another with the words of the clauses about seeing anything suspicious and *Be calm, be quick, be exact* became a joke in every place of work or exercise which we had to carry out with the Civil Defence.

Perhaps it was that the idea of a Ministry of Information was alien to us after our free Press, but everything done by this new Ministry seemed very comic. We British do not like scraps of advice and information handed out to us as pamphlets. We like to read them in the paper which we *choose* to read. I stuck the pamphlet on the wall and it never failed to amuse me when I was depressed

On the morning of June 25th when hostilities ceased in France we had the first air raid warning since the false alarm of the previous September. Alert and ready in the FAP, we were all sorry when nothing happened at all and presently the All Clear sounded. The sirens were the signal for the preparing of instruments, bandages, splints, stretchers, and all the paraphernalia for sterilizing. Although we had had so little to do that everything was always in apple-pie order, the Alert was an excitement which put everyone on their mettle again.

I think we were all heartened after the brutal air attacks on Jersey and Guernsey by photographs of large numbers of Australians and Canadians arriving in Britain. The Canadian Army had been withdrawn intact and with all its artillery equipment from France. The men had been bitterly disappointed at this withdrawal.

The French disaster hastened the Government's plan to evacuate children to the Dominions and they decided that twenty thousand should leave at once. The first group were to be those between the ages of five and sixteen. Ten thousand were to go to Canada, five thousand to Australia, and the remainder to New Zealand and South Africa. They were to go with escorts, but no parents. Many Chelsea friends who had relatives or friends in America and Canada were trying to make up their minds as to whether or not they should send their children away. The young South Africans whose portraits I had painted had written warmly offering homes to my young niece and my nephews in Bristol. My sisters had decided against it. They thought that families should stay together.

We received more refugees in Chelsea, for refugees were still pouring into Britain. We had Czechs, French, Dutch, and Belgians, now came thousands of Poles, Polish soldiers, aircrews and aircraft in addition to subjects from Jersey and Guernsey. The announcement that we were not going to defend the Channel Islands upset everyone. Those beautiful islands which so many of us knew and loved as holiday resorts were just to be left to their fate. The islands had been demilitarized and already twenty-five thousand of their civilians had arrived in Britain with all troops and their equipment. Everything of value to the enemy had been removed – including most of the potato and tomato crop.

The Ministry of Information's announcement on July 1st that German troops had landed in Jersey and Guernsey and that all telephonic and telegraphic communications had been cut off fanned everyone's fury.

The gloating of The Giant became unbearable when I went to take an English lesson and found the class all assembled in the front room. 'See, Marraine,' he greeted me, 'I told you so. France phui!' he raised his hands in the air. 'And your little Channel Islands. That's the first bit of Britain to be occupied. You see? The water is no barrier to Hitler! Just wait, he'll get here!'

I told him to shut up. The Flemish words for that are very ugly and expressive. He was surprised that I should use such a vulgar expression but I didn't care. It was infuriating to see his great brown grinning face mocking at us while at the same time he was enjoying our hospitality and he and his family were being provided with everything they needed.

One of the young girls in the class went up to him and said furiously, 'If you won't shut up we'll make you...' and with a youth of about sixteen she stood menacingly over him while two older and smaller men rolled up their sleeves. The Giant's wife struck her in the face, telling her to leave her husband alone. The girl responded by pulling the wife's black hair and egged on by the women. A horrible battle started, the men attacking The Giant, and the women, his wife. Instead of ignoring his twitting I had fallen for the bait and lost my temper and this disgusting broil was the result. Through the window of the front room in which this scene was taking place I saw my policeman friend, whom the refugees called Young Bobbie (this to distinguish him from Old Bobbie), walking past. I signalled to him to come in. 'You needn't do anything,' I told him when he obeyed. 'Your appearance will be enough for that great bully.' 'Same one as always gives trouble?' he asked, smiling, and straightening himself up and putting on a very stern face he tramped into the hall and into the room where the fight was in full blood. All the objects I had taken for the lesson had been hurled all over the room, and as they were vegetables and fruit the mess was indescribable, pictures on the walls had been knocked down, noses were bleeding, hair dishevelled, faces red and furious. 'Now then,' said Young Bobbie in stentorian tones, *'and what's all this?'*

At once there was a dead silence and as his stern regard went from one face to another the class sheepishly began brushing themselves down and tidying their hair. 'Tell them all to take themselves off and go back to their own rooms,' he said, 'and say I don't want to hear any more noise from this house.' They went, abashed and shamefaced, and leaving them I walked with Young Bobbie along Tedworth Square. 'You'll see a lot of me if those are any sample,' he said laughing, when I thanked him. The Giant caught us up. He was almost weeping with mortification. All the others were blaming him for the loss of the English lesson. 'Come back, please, Marraine,' he begged. 'I promise you all will be as good as angels!' These last words and *'Please'* were said in his best English, with such a shame-faced engaging smile that it was difficult to resist him. 'They'd whistle for their lesson if it were me,' commented Young Bobbie, and saluting me smartly he walked off while I returned with The Giant.

The room had been tidied, the chairs arranged in rows, but the blackboard had been knocked down and the stand broken in the fight. We propped it up on the mantelpiece and the men promised to mend it if I would lend them a hammer and some nails.

'It is the First of July,' I wrote on the board. 'The Germans have landed in the Channel Islands,' and then I turned to The Giant. 'Translate into Flemish, please,' I said. He repeated the sentence perfectly in Flemish and added, 'Curse them, damn them, *damn* them, I say!'

'Don't swear before ladies,' reproved his wife, whose tear-stained face was scratched right across from the battle. The lesson went on all afternoon and the most zealous pupil was The Giant.

CHAPTER NINE

FRANCE, occupied by the conquerors, was already being used as a base for attacking her former ally, and air raids on the south and east coasts now began to intensify – the German Air Force no longer had to fly such distances with their deadly loads. Air raids and aerial battles over the south coast were increasing not only in intensity but in frequency, and an RAF aerial photograph of Rotterdam after its ruthless bombing by the Germans depressed and frightened people. The headlines in the newspapers always bore the number of enemy planes shot down. Much smaller print was used for what the mothers, wives, and sweethearts all looked for first – the number of British planes *lost*. On the BBC the velvety voice of Bruce Belfrage or Alvar Liddell (who had to announce their identity as a precaution after the seizing of the Dutch radio by the Nazis) would first tell us of some magnificent aerial battle – and in glowing terms state the number of enemy planes shot down. We soon got very accustomed to the quiet, 'One of our aircraft is missing' or 'Eight of our aircraft failed to return...' which ended the announcement.

A storm of public opinion was being aroused at this time over the question of the evacuation of children to the United States and the Dominions. The Government had postponed its scheme because of the need for convoys to escort them. Naturally there were people with relatives or friends there and the money to send their children privately, and the news that several hundred children had reached the United States in the liner *Washington* caused much resentment.

The Overseas League and the English-Speaking Union had offered to raise funds for poorer children to go, but the Government were reluctant to send thousands of children without escorts.

Class feeling was noticeable everywhere now that rationing had begun the levelling of standards for everyone. 'She can't get no more than I can,' was very comforting to some families who had subsisted on bread and margarine for a very long time, and 'Well, the Princesses aren't going so why should *they* go?' was another.

More and more women were finding independence and happiness working in munition factories for the war effort. Thousands of young women were enlisting in the ATS and in the WAAF, as well as working in factories. Domestic servants, already on the decline before the war, were rapidly disappearing, and owners of large houses were closing them and moving to hotels. It was still possible to obtain a good meal in restaurants without surrendering any meat points from the ration books, and the news that Lord Woolton had ordered that after the middle of July only one course, either fish, meat, or game, was to be served at a meal gave great satisfaction to housewives, who had to rely entirely on their ration books. Tea rationing, the news of which followed soon after the Oran incident, caused a tremendous outcry. Two ounces a week per person for the tea-loving nation was not considered enough over which to gossip and discuss their grievances!

We had begun to listen nightly to 'Lord Haw Haw' (William Joyce), whose English broadcasts, far from terrifying his listeners, became a source of vast and unfailing amusement. According to him Britain was disintegrating, collapsing under the weight of the German attacks, and extraordinary accounts of the lengths to which we were driven were given by this ardent follower of Hitler. As it was, the ridiculous affectation and inaccuracy of his broadcasts became the butt of music halls and his latest blunders the joke of the day.

In the German news one could detect the same wishful thinking. Mingled with the stream of threats and abuse from the propaganda chief, Dr Goebbels, was an obvious desire to reassure his own country – and possibly himself – as to the wisdom of what they were doing in the Third Reich. Once when I was listening to this late at night with the window open, a warden knocked at the door. I thought he had come about a light showing – but he had come to see 'why I was listening to the German news'. The campaign against despondency and despair was being encouraged, and several people had been prosecuted for it. Had it been our own warden all would have been well, but this was one unknown to me. He seemed suspicious and asked to see my identity card and so I told him that we had been advised to make sure that a warden was really a warden and not a fake. I showed him the pamphlet about parachutists on the studio wall. He was most indignant and couldn't see that I was pulling his leg. Finally when I told him that I often listened to Germany last thing at night because it never failed to give me a laugh, he seemed reassured and accepted a whisky and soda before he left.

Two days later it was announced that the *Arandora Star* had been torpedoed on her way to Canada whither she was carrying a large number of enemy aliens for internment there. Amongst the

470 Italians on the ship was Joseph Caletta, of the King's Road, Chelsea. I was very upset about this and went at once to see Madame Caletta when I was told that her husband was missing. She was still at her desk in the restaurant, calm and dignified as always. She bore no resentment or bitterness about her loss. 'It was war,' she said, spreading out her hands in a helpless gesture, 'it is no one's fault.'

The *Arandora Star* had been a smallish luxury ship on which I had once enjoyed a cruise round the Greek islands. It seemed extraordinary to think of it as being an internment ship for all those husbands and sons – some of them famous West End restaurateurs known by nicknames to their fashionable clientele. There was much indignation over the whole matter. The Germans had torpedoed not only their own nationals but those of their ally. Madame Caletta's calm acceptance of the ironic situation had something stoic and noble in it. When I expressed my indignation and disgust she said, 'It is far worse for the mothers of all those boys who didn't come back from Dunkirk. They had all their lives before them. My husband had had a good life. We have worked hard and we have been very happy. I have my children.' It was Mrs Freeth who reminded me that German mothers must be suffering too when I was expressing myself violently about the torpedoing atrocities. She was the mother of three sons herself.

When some details of the sinking of the Arandora Star given by the survivors were released everyone was horrified. The ship, before she sank, had been the scene of the most horrible panic, in which Germans had fought and pushed away the gentler Italians, who were no match for them, in a mad scramble for the boats. They were all in their night clothes for the ship was torpedoed at 6am without warning. Almost all the Italians perished. They all cursed the German U-boat but none so heartily as the Germans. Madame Caletta's husband was amongst the Italians lost.

One of the Belgian refugees who had arrived alone without any family was a young girl, Catherine. She was almost nineteen, and very pretty, but looked pinched and worried. Her identity papers stated that she had been employed as a domestic help in Brussels and several of the ladies on the committee were eager to have her in their Chelsea households.

When I questioned Catherine as to whether she would like to do this, she was curiously reluctant to agree. She began to cry and said: 'I am going to have a child – can't you see it?'

Now that she told me it was obvious.

With patience I got her story out of her. An orphan, she had lived since childhood with an old aunt in Brussels, and had worked since she had left school in the household of a well-to-do shop-keeper in Brussels. She seemed to me to have worked long hours for very little money, and to have had little time for pleasure or enjoying herself. When she was eighteen she had met and fallen in love with a young mechanic who worked at a garage near the shop. They planned to marry when she was nineteen, before which age her aunt considered her too young. When the Germans invaded Belgium her fiancé had been called up immediately. He had wanted to marry her before he left for the Front so they went to the Burgomaster but Catherine could not produce her birth certificate and she could not marry without it. She had been born in England during the 1914-18 war when her mother had been a refugee just as Catherine was now. The Burgomaster had written at once to the town of her birth, but before the certificate had arrived her fiancé had been sent to the Front and in the sudden calamitous events she had no idea where he was. When the German troops were advancing on Brussels she had gone one morning to her employer's shop as usual, to find it closed, shuttered, and deserted. A note on the door said, 'Catherine, Gone to the country – advise you do the same.'

She went back to her old aunt. 'Go to the coast,' said the old woman, 'there are thousands tracking for the ports. Make for England. Your parents went there in 1914, and you were born there. If you stay here the Germans will see from your identity papers that you were born in England – and you will suffer for it. *Go quickly* – I shall be quite all right.'

She had helped the old woman to bury everything which she had valued deep in the garden, and to put other things up in the loft before she left.

She soon fell in with a great stream of people fleeing with their carts and bundles for Ostend, and amongst them she found a school friend, Mathilde. The two girls kept together during the whole nightmare journey. They were machine-gunned, dive-bombed, they hid in ditches and hedges when the German planes came remorselessly at them. Many of the families in the great flow had small children and they hampered both the parents and the others. Bombs fell constantly, killing whole families, and machine-gun bullets injured many of them. But the stream of humanity went on like a great caterpillar to the coast. I asked what they had done with the dead and injured. Catherine looked blank. 'What could we do?' she said, in surprise. 'We just left them there.'

She had felt sick and ill from her pregnancy and although she was sturdy she felt again and again that she could go no further, but her friend Mathilde urged and encouraged her on. Just before they reached Ostend and the ships were already in sight a bomb fell right in the ditch into which they had flung themselves when a Heinkel dived low. When the cloud of dust and smoke had cleared she saw that Mathilde was dead. 'She just lay there – without a head,' Catherine finished dispassionately.

There had been British troops embarking at Ostend as well as a great mass of Belgian trawlers and fishing boats. None of the Belgian boats would take her – they had all their own friends and families. A British boat on which troops were embarking took her and several women with her, after warning them that they stood a greater chance of being torpedoed, bombed, or machine-gunned because of the troops on board. They did not care – they were past caring now and accepted gratefully. Just as they were leaving harbour a Heinkel dived and released two bombs and one of them hit their ship. Catherine found herself in the water and clung to a piece of wreckage until she was rescued by a small fishing boat. Several British soldiers were picked up by the same little craft, the owner of which did a splendid job hauling survivors of the British ship on board in spite of the constant bombing going on all around. They got away safely although pursued for some way by German planes. 'Then,' finished Catherine, 'the RAF chased them back and lots of them fell blazing into the sea, and it was getting dark and we made for Dover and the WVS gave us cups of tea.'

She said wryly that she had hoped that the explosion which hurled her into the water would have lost her the baby – but no, it was still very much there and would be born *illegitimate*. She was extraordinarily sensitive about this. As several girls I knew were in the same condition and seemed to accept it as part of the war effort this was surprising. 'In Belgium,' she said, crying again, 'they write *bastarde* on the birth certificate.' I couldn't believe this, and assured her that in Britain we did no such thing and that in any case her baby would be British as she was. I said I would write at once for her birth certificate and this I did.

Next day I took her to a pre-natal clinic where they said that apart from anaemia she was in good health which, after all she had been through, was encouraging. The baby would be born early in October. Catherine was somewhat reassured by my promising to look after her and I got her transferred from the house where The Giant and his wife were, to one of the other houses for which I was responsible. Here there was a very kind woman, with her husband and two children, who would, I knew, be good to Catherine because I had told her the girl's story, Madame R being one of the very nicest of the refugees.

I felt sorry for all these Belgian children with no schools to attend. All London schools were now closed, and except for the English lessons which I was giving them, they were learning nothing. Later they would have to have some kind of schooling. The Lycée Français was willing to take some of them, but it had evacuated to the north.

King Leopold had not followed his Government to London but was said to be living in complete seclusion at his palace at Laeken with his mother, Queen Elizabeth, while his three children were in France. The refugees still discussed him violently and some of them seemed unable to believe anything good of him, or to give him the benefit of the doubt as to whether or not his intentions were honourable.

The Giant, having got it into his head that he would have a better chance of being allowed to fish with the British Fishing Fleet if he could speak English, set his whole heart on learning it, and his unfortunate wife had to listen to his homework all day and hear him repeat it. Their little daughter corrected them constantly. When I asked The Giant why he was so violently anti-Leopold he seemed nonplussed. 'Are you a Communist?' I asked him. His great swarthy face went dark red. '*Me?*' he shouted, beating his great chest in the blue jersey in which he had arrived and which he always wore. 'Me? A Communist? That's funny, that is! I may grumble at Leopold because he killed his wife by driving too fast – a lovely woman and a good one – but just let anyone attack him and I'd fight for him.' I forbore to point out that his King had been attacked and that far from fighting for him The Giant had fled.

He had, however, become one of the most diligent in the English class. I had managed to get his wife some wool to knit him another jersey. We had nothing large enough for him amongst the clothing at Crosby Hall and his blue fisherman's one needed a wash. She could be seen now with her knitting needles under her arm in the continental fashion and a piece of The Giant's enormous jersey in the making. He was inordinately vain about his size and despised the smaller men, amongst whom he stood out like Gulliver amongst the Lilliputs.

CHAPTER TEN

My SISTER in Weymouth was the first member of my family to experience an air raid and her account of the heavy attacks on Portland and Weymouth on August 11th was vivid and frightening. She was working in a munition factory there and described the raid as a terrifying experience. Sixty German planes had been shot down and twenty-six of our fighter planes were missing. My sister, however, seemed stimulated rather than frightened herself. Small and frail, she had always been fearless and nothing ever daunted her, two qualities which I envied her.

She described the work of the Civil Defence and Fire Services as magnificent. There had been a lot of casualties, she said, but no one knew how many. This was a subject on which we were to be kept in ignorance all through the war. For reasons of censorship the names of places bombed were never disclosed nor were the number of casualties until some time after the event.

Refugees had been arriving from Malta, and we VADs were now sent in pairs on duty to some of the hostels where they were living in communities. Far less stolid and sensible than the Belgians, they were rather temperamental, although charming. They were not easy to help or advise, but I found them fascinating as types and some of the children would have made lovely models. All were indignant at having been evacuated from their homes and sent to London, and it was useless trying to explain that it was unavoidable as Malta had to be defended at all costs.

By the middle of August I was very tired. London was hot, dirty, and airless. The sand blew about from bursting sandbags, and the streets did not get the same cleaning as they once had. The deserted houses with dirty windows or shuttered ones were depressing. I suddenly felt that I couldn't face one more refugee or listen to one more complaint, and I was depressed as three leading hospitals had rejected me for general training on medical grounds.

I went to Plymouth to visit my mother for a long weekend. The journey down was appalling. The train was absolutely packed with troops and naval ratings and so crowded that the corridors were impassable. There were a great many parents going to visit children evacuated to the west.

War-time Plymouth was very different from the town as I had last seen it. The Hoe, from which one looks out at that lovely bay with its landmarks of Mount Edgcumbe and the Breakwater, was full of barbed wire entanglements and whole areas of it were forbidden to the public. Sand-bags were everywhere, and at night it was strangely alien without any lights. The town was full of troops and naval ratings, WRNS and ATS. My mother's friends were all in the WVS or in the Red Cross. She was annoyed that she was too lame to do much herself except knit for a number of organizations and attend weekly sewing parties. I spent most of my time on Dartmoor where we had lived before my father had died. The moors looked the same – ageless and unchanging, with the bare bones of the earth showing through those parts where the heather and undergrowth was sparse. There appeared to be a good deal of building being done – they were making an aerodrome and various army dumps, but these could not make any appreciable difference to that vast expanse of landscape. I did some long walks, enjoying the grandeur and silence of Dartmoor. Usually, unless you get off the moor itself and descend into the small villages and hollows where the farms huddle in surprising lushness after the bleakness of the moor above them, you can walk all day and never meet a soul except the herds of Dartmoor ponies. But now, in August, I met members of the Mounted Home Guard, former followers of the Mid-Devon Hunt patrolling the moors. They looked splendid on their mounts silhouetted against the sky-line as they scanned the horizon for parachutists and anything of a suspicious nature.

From one of the farms, as I passed, I heard shrill Cockney voices and the soft Devonshire-cream voice of a woman remonstrating with them, and saw a group of London children who had been received as evacuees by the farmer and his wife. It was extraordinary to hear that familiar Cockney slang out there in the wilds of Dartmoor. I asked the woman how it was working out for we had been hearing of the troubles of those evacuated and those who had to receive them, often against their will. The farmer's wife, a plump, pink-cheeked woman, said bluntly that 'they be terrible ignorant – don't know a pig from a sheep', but that they were settling down and learning and the boys were helping her husband. She loved them in spite of the extra work they caused her. I asked the three boys how they liked Dartmoor after London. Without exception they replied that they liked it fine. The two little girls were silent. They missed the shops, said the boys scornfully. They actually came from Chelsea! I promised to visit their parents when I returned there and tell them that their children were well and happy. The journey back to London was far less irksome than the one down – people were not travelling into London, they were travelling out of it.

On my return I found that there was a lot of trouble again with the refugees over the food in the canteen, Seraphine having failed to satisfy them. A new rota was made out and was to be strictly adhered to with two women cooking each week, and in this way every man would get some of his own wife's cooking as well as that of others. Suzanne sorted this all out as she overcame many other difficulties, for the French-speaking refugees were just as full of complaints if less pugnacious than Flemish ones, and some of their problems were more complicated, and consisted of quite delicate points of propriety which Suzanne received with commendable solemnity.

Catherine, who had been spending most of her time with Mrs Freeth, was relieved to see me back again.

When I got back she was in the kitchen helping Mrs Freeth to cut up a rabbit. She had put it on a board and was attacking it with a chopper. The expression on her face was so vicious that I asked her why she did it. 'She asked to do it – she likes it,' explained Mrs Freeth. 'I pretend that this rabbit is Hitler – and this is what I'd like to do to him!' said Catherine, bringing the chopper down on the revolting mess on the board. For a prospective mother this was pretty horrible – but remembering what she had been through owing to Hitler's march on Belgium I didn't say anything but just went away and was violently sick. I have always jibbed at eating rabbit – partly because they are so charming and partly because my father considered them vermin. After that exhibition by Catherine I could not swallow a morsel of rabbit even when food became terribly scarce later in the war. It was already becoming more so daily.

And now we had Canadians in Chelsea, and the billeting officer came to every house and flat to ask householders to billet one or two. It was difficult to find billets for them because so many people had gone away. I agreed to put one up in the small spare room or on the divan in the studio, but explained that I was getting married soon and would not have much room then. It was settled that one should come temporarily in the small room. Kathleen had also taken one in Penty's room as Penty was still in the country. Kathleen, worried about her own future with work falling off in the Disabled Men's Workshops, had rented the ground floor of the house opposite where Elliot Hodgkin had his studio, and was turning it into a small shop – a sort of boutique. She had a flair for dress – and knew how to put on her clothes and how others should put on theirs. She had found a very clever cutter and was starting up on her own. She began to get orders quite quickly for she had a wide circle of friends and there was a real need for such an establishment in the neighbourhood.

I was doing four-hours shifts at the FAP now that many VADs were away on holiday, and frequently Kathleen and I would lunch together. The Canadians ate at midday in their mess but we provided their breakfast and evening meals. The young man allotted to me was really an American who had volunteered with the Royal Canadian Army Service Corps. He was a delightful person, enormous in stature but rather shy, gentle, and detached. His home was in St Louis and he was lonely, as they all were in a strange land without friends or relatives. We all wanted to show them that we were grateful for their having volunteered to come to our aid, and Mrs Freeth and I adopted Larry immediately as one of the family.

He was soon accompanying me on my rounds to the refugees, and in a very short time produced chocolates and sweets for the children. He spoiled them thoroughly, and was delightful with them. We went on some exciting shopping expeditions taking all the children with us in turn, so that they could choose their own toys. He loved children and was at his best with them.

Kathleen's billetee, also in the Royal Canadian Army Service Corps, was even larger in build. He was about six foot five. My young American liked to be called Larry, simply that. His surname was Lawrence and he did not care for his Christian name. Kathleen's billetee, Cecil Stainton, was also rather shy. He walked with the easy lope of the hunter, and before he joined up had been a trapper in Hudson Bay. There was something very refreshing about both these men, and I liked them.

Margerie Scott's broadcasts and letters to friends in Canada had brought a batch of parcels for the refugees. Lovely parcels, thoughtfully and beautifully chosen. Blankets, soft and fluffy, not old and threadbare as were those given by householders when they were turning out. There were jerseys, coats, socks, and shoes, all of the very best quality, every kind of garment, and in the pockets were bars of chocolate and sweets, and every small toilet article which a refugee could need. Naturally they caused trouble as well as delight. Those with old coats resented others having new ones, and arrived at the Town Hall asking permission for the old things to be changed for new. *New lamps for old*, we called this transaction! But parcel followed parcel, and packing cases followed them, a continuous stream from the generous Canadian people to the refugees of Chelsea so that soon everyone had something new.

The long pause was over. There had been enemy air activity in the country for some months, especially on coastal towns, and at the end of July the enemy made a large-scale attack on Dover, sending waves of fighters into the terrific aerial battle which developed. Seventeen German planes were destroyed in thirty minutes, so fierce was the fight. It was said that the Germans had used Red Cross planes for reconnaissance before this attack. All we could be thankful for was that for some reason known only to themselves the Germans had not made their attack during those glorious days in June when the ships had been as thick as shrimps in Dover Bay. I remembered the faces of the French troops looking apprehensively at the sky, and the children who had arrived from Belgium and Holland cowering down under anything which appeared to give them shelter.

PART II

PERFORMANCE

CHAPTER ELEVEN

Towards the end of August Richard had a week's leave from his Ministry and we decided to get out of London and do some long walks, and with this purpose in view we went to Newlands Corner, which is a splendid centre for walking all over the Downs. There was a hotel there which had been a private house and it had a good library, which was essential as we both loved books, and it had delightful gardens. There had been constant short Alerts in London the preceding week when I had been doing several shifts as relief at the Control Centre while some of the telephonists were on holiday.

The warning system was given by the use of colours. Purple was the colour used for the first warning, denoting that enemy planes were sighted approaching from the coast. Then followed the yellow, which was a general signal for readiness by all ARP Services, and then the final red, which was the signal for the sounding of the Alert for the general public. The wardens' posts all had telephonic connexion with their various points and huts, and from these the reports of incidents and requests for Services were telephoned to Control. It was very exciting and also alarming to know that these signals were actually real ones – and no longer practice ones. I think we all had butterflies in our stomachs as we waited after the red signal for the incidents to come through. We were all keyed up to efficiency after the long wait for action and the innumerable practices and rehearsals, and everyone was determined to come up to scratch so as not to let down our indefatigable chief, Mr Cane. But after the Alerts came through nothing further happened, and the white signal – which meant the sounding of the All Clear for the public – would come, finding us all relieved and yet rather disappointed that we could not prove our worth and justify our long training.

We left for Newlands Corner on the 24th. Mrs Freeth, who refused to have a holiday, saying that she would look after my billetee, Larry, to whom Kathleen had offered to give meals with Cecil. The country round the Hog's Back was looking glorious and the weather was wonderful – hot and sunny, absolutely perfect for a holiday and for leisurely, if not arduous walks. Richard's friend, Delves Molesworth, whom we called Moley, and who was also in the Ministry, came down with his wife, Eve, to visit us there. The first few days were glorious and we walked miles across the Hog's Back and followed the old bridle paths on the top of the Downs. It was clear and we could see the landscape spread out as a map below. Then we began hearing distant sirens frequently – but as the country was so open it was difficult to know from which direction they were coming. When we asked at the hotel no one seemed to know – and the few walkers on the Downs were not interested.

There had been continual aerial activity in the area round the Hog's Back ever since we arrived, but the hotel manager told us that it had been so ever since Dunkirk. Now, at the end of August, we began seeing dog-fights overhead and watched our Spitfires chasing Messerschmitts and engaging in exciting battles, and in the still summer air we could hear the gunfire from the combatants and could see parachutists descending and the planes crashing down with a spurt of fire from their tails. It seemed impossible at first to believe that these were actual deadly battles and not mock ones as we had watched at aerial displays at Hendon. It gave one a strange, shaking, sick feeling of excitement to watch their every movement as though we were following with rapt attention a mock battle at Hendon, but never before had we seen such a thrilling exhibition of aeronautics! Twisting, turning, their guns blazing, the sunlight picking them out in the clear sky, they would dive under, over, round, and then straight at their opponents until one would fall in a trail of smoke and flame, often with a gleaming parachute like a toy umbrella preceding the final crash to earth.

It was horrible – but it had a macabre fascination impossible to resist. And after gazing spellbound I had to shake myself and face up to the realization that this was war – not mock war. This was the real thing and the queer excited sensation of suspense and apprehension which was causing the butterflies in my inside was one which thousands of us were to have with us very frequently, and I was glad that Richard was with me. He had been through unspeakable horrors in the 1914-18 war in France and was not under any illusion about what we might face in this one. And I thought then – nothing matters if you are with the person you want to be with – the importance of an event must always be relative, and because of this we would be able to endure what Churchill had told us to expect.

One German plane came extremely low, dropping papers all over the Downs and I collected a great bundle of them. They were two different pamphlets, both extracts from Hitler's Reichstag speech; one was headed, 'A last Appeal to Reason' and the other 'From the Führer's Speech'. I already had one which my sister had sent me entitled, 'The Battle of the Atlantic is being lost', but these were the first I had had literally thrown at my feet.

Richard said that we were dropping pamphlets all over Holland, France, Belgium, and Norway and Denmark as well as over Germany. Paper warfare seemed extraordinary to me, but propaganda had proved its danger and value already.

The battles in the air continued all day and during a very fierce fight a German plane flew even lower than the one which had dropped pamphlets, machine-gunning right across the Hog's Back. It seemed to be coming right at us as we stood there gazing at the battles in the sky, and Richard dragged me suddenly into the shelter of some bushes as bullets spattered in our direction and all round. Vicki was down a rabbit hole and I thought she might get a bullet in her stern so I insisted on hauling her out. Richard was angry with me and dragged us both under cover again. He knew more about machine-gun bullets than I did, having been severely wounded by them in the 1914-18 war. When the plane had gone we hunted all round for a parachutist or a body fallen from a plane – but we could not find anyone. Distance is very difficult to judge from a great open space like the Hog's Back, but the German pilot had certainly machine-gunned the actual spot where we were standing watching the fights so it seemed logical to conclude that there was some target in our locality. It was an alarming experience, but it aroused in me nothing but furious anger. It was late afternoon, almost dusk, when another wave of German planes came over and flew in the direction of Croydon, which we could see from where we stood.

That night the sirens sounded much nearer, and everyone was awakened in the small hotel and guests were asked to go to a somewhat inadequate air-raid shelter which had been erected in the garden. The planes were dropping flares and small incendiary bombs. Richard organized the men into parties to put out these incendiaries. There was a naval officer on leave staying in the hotel and Richard asked him to head one party. To everyone's astonishment he refused – and would not leave the shelter at all. The hotel manager himself was splendid, as were the young waitresses who, frequently absent when needed because of the presence of Canadian troops in the neighbourhood, had returned from what the manager called 'rolling for victory', and joined the fire-fighting parties with enthusiasm. It was exciting stumbling about and extinguishing the firebombs with sand and stirrup pumps. We had all been instructed in the use of stirrup pumps but actually to use them for bombs was quite exhilarating. The bombs were small and easy to extinguish. I could not bear to be in the shelter and felt far safer in the open. We could see a great blaze which seemed to be in the direction of Croydon – certainly near London or on the outskirts. The thought that the raiders had actually got so far through the terrific defence being put up by our Spitfires gave us a terrible feeling of fury and resentment. The grass and heath were very dry from the last week's hot weather and caught fire quickly as the small incendiaries fell, and we beat them out with branches, in organized lines, just as we had been taught would be necessary if undergrowth were alight, and although everyone was upset at the sight of the flames in the distance it was fun beating out the burning heather and it brought its own exhilaration.

When at last the All Clear went the manager gave us all drinks and we sat in the lounge and read the pamphlets which I had picked up that afternoon. They caused much amusement because they revealed such a mistaken assessment of the British character. We telephoned Kathleen in the morning. Chelsea had had Alerts ever since we left – and last night a long Alert and they had heard the planes and bombs – everyone was upset and alarmed. She herself sounded quite unperturbed, however. She had the keys of our flat in case of fire and said that they were sleeping in the shelter but it was too small and very draughty – she hated it.

By the next night most of the guests in the hotel had left. After all, like us, they had come on holiday and wanted a peaceful place such as one expected Newlands Corner to be. There were several Alerts during the day, which was still and sunny, and again we watched aerial battles – although not so many. Soon after dark, however, the sirens sounded again and there was immediately a great rush of wings like a drove of hornets, a sound which was to become all too familiar, and another terrifying battle took place in the sky. Watching the doomed planes diving to earth with a plume of fire showing up in the dark sky was fearful. Again we could see a great light as of a huge fire in the direction of London. We spent most of the night out fire-watching. In the morning we again telephoned Kathleen. She did not sound so placid; there had been more Alerts, both day and night, the night raid had been horrible, with planes circling and the sound of bombs not so far away – she had not slept at all but Cecil and Anne had slept through most of it, she said. The milkman had told her that the bombs had dropped on Hammersmith and that there was a lot of damage. She was rather nervous and said that there was now general alarm. She mentioned something about an unexploded bomb but was very vague.

We decided to return at once, and left Newlands Corner to do some last-minute shopping for food in Guildford. Mrs Freeth did not expect us back until the following week and there would be no food for the week-end. In Guildford I found a duck. This was a treasure as poultry was unrationed and, planning to have a feast, I found late green peas and apples. The food in the hotel, as everywhere now, had been quite inadequate and we were both hungry.

On the journey to Waterloo we heard people talking about the bombing of Croydon and Hammersmith as if they could not really believe it. At Waterloo we met Moley. We did not ask him where he had been. We had already got into the war-time habit of not asking anyone anything – a curtain of hush-hush was rapidly descending on us all. He did, however, tell us that things were rapidly warming up in London and the last few nights had been very broken, with constant sirens shattering the peace of the capital, and that people were tired and depressed from lack of rest. The bombing of Hammersmith had been quite heavy, but the ARP Services had worked splendidly and that was what concerned his Ministry most.

We invited him to return with us and share the duck which I was going to cook that night for dinner – Blitz or no Blitz. As Eve was away he readily agreed. When we reached the Royal Hospital Road, however, it looked as though we would not get the duck, for to our astonishment Cheyne Place was roped off from exactly where No. 33 started, and a policeman was guarding it. When I lifted the ropes of the barrier to go into the house he came over and told us that there was an unexploded bomb in the neighbourhood and that we must evacuate the house.

At the beginning of the war we had all been told to have a packed suitcase always ready for emergencies. I had had one but as time went on and nothing happened I had removed one thing after another from it until it was empty.

I asked if I could go in to collect some clothes. The policeman was dubious –but when we pressed him to tell us where the bomb was he did not seem to know – his orders were to guard that piece of road and warn the occupants of a certain number of houses which might be affected. It seemed to me that the person most affected if it went off would be him – for he was standing in the middle of the street! A warden came along and said he didn't know exactly where the bomb was but we'd better do as the policeman said. Then Major Harding Newman came along – he was our Deputy Chief of ARP and he knew me well. I asked him where the bomb was supposed to be. 'Over there,' he said, pointing in the direction of Burton Court, 'somewhere in the grounds. As a matter of fact I don't think there is any danger here, it's just that this is in a direct line and there is an open space between it and these buildings. It's a precaution.'

The policeman said that we entered at our own risk, which we did cheerfully enough, stepping over the barricade. Inside everything was in perfect order. Kathleen came down with Anne, excited and full of the previous night's events. Both our billetees had been sent away by the authorities until the bomb was removed – the Army were taking no risks. When Anne had gone upstairs I asked how she and Cecil were getting on together. Anne seemed to like him, said Kathleen. They were going out together, and Anne was teaching him to dance. She said this as if she were not too happy about it. I knew that she found the Canadian rather a rough diamond. Kathleen minded such things as table manners and the more superficial niceties which from much travel I had found were of no real importance at all. She had been brought up in a world which placed value on them. I liked Cecil, and was glad that Anne was liking him too. She had been unhappy long enough; if Cecil could help her to get over her former disappointment then I welcomed it. Kathleen said that they had slept in the shelter at the back of the house for the last few nights, but that if I were willing to sleep in my own home – then she was.

We had the duck – but long before I had begun cooking it the sirens had sounded. They went at about six o'clock and there was a rush of planes just as we had heard at Newlands Corner. Nothing seemed to be happening around us – Richard and Moley kept a sharp look-out for incendiaries, and later we went up on the flat roof to watch the raid.

We never tasted anything better than that duck – and bombs or no bombs we were determined to enjoy it. Richard had been living at the Guards' Club for some time and it had been so crowded that food had been very short. We fell upon the roast duck and there was absolutely nothing left of it but the bones when we had finished with it. We all slept in my hall and dining-room that night. It seemed to us to be the safest place with its one wall of ferro-concrete and its others protected by the archway. It was quite noisy, and for the first part of it we went out in turns to watch and deal with the small incendiaries which were falling just as they had done on Newlands Corner. It was fun and Anne enjoyed it too. She told us that neither Cecil nor Larry were allowed by their Army Regulations to help in fire-fighting. None of the troops in the Duke of York Barracks were permitted by their Regulations to do so either, and the wardens found it as infuriating to see all those khaki-clad males and be unable to enlist them in the fire-parties, as the men themselves found it galling to have to stand about and do nothing. Larry and Cecil, Anne said, had hit upon the ingenious device of borrowing civilian jackets and coats that they were not conspicuous and passed with the other civilian fire-fighters. As Richard was as tall as both of them I foresaw his being asked to lend some of his clothes.

In the morning Mrs Freeth arrived punctually as usual. I was astonished to see her and asked her if the policeman had let her through the barrier. 'Lor,' she said, 'that thing's been there for days – that didn't stop me. The policeman doesn't come on until eight o'clock – I come at half past seven!' She told us that it had been quite exciting up her way, which was Westminster, and she seemed exhilarated, not frightened, by the raids. Chris, from the Control Centre, knowing that the doubtful bomb was in our area, had kindly gone down to see that she was all right. She came down when I telephoned that I was back and gave me all the news of the raids.

The refugees were excited and hysterical when they told me about all the Alerts they had had. The actual wailing of the sirens had an appalling effect on some of them – on others, like Catherine, it had none. To those who had already suffered from the Luftwaffe on their long trek out of Belgium and France it was what they had always expected and they bore it stoically. The ones who were hysterical and implored me to get them moved out of London before worse happened were, I found, those who had actually endured far less than the stoics. The Giant was one of the worst complainants – he burst out with imprecations against everything and everyone. It was useless to point out that he could have stayed in his own country as millions of others had done, he merely said that Britain had always set herself up as impregnable and they had expected safety. I got so angry arguing with him that I gave it up and left him to it. His wife was sullen and the child even whiter and more pinched. I saw that they all knew their shelters and had everything ready to take as soon as the sirens should sound. It was quite a task, for they all wanted to take the small bundles they had brought from their own countries with them – and some of them were heavy and the shelters none too large. They had already a great respect for Miss Reid, their warden.

At the FAP everything was calm and placid; those who had been away were back from holidays and I told them about the exciting aerial fights on the Hog's Back and showed them all the pamphlets before giving them to the Town Hall. Betty Compton's two small daughters were in the country, as were most children now, and I was wondering if some of the small Belgians should not be evacuated. This seemed difficult because the authorities were not willing that alien adults should leave London until all their screening was over, and the parents, quite naturally, were not willing to be separated from their children who had already suffered so much. I talked to Margerie Scott about it and she agreed with me that it was a pity that the children, including the Maltese, must stay in London. But it was difficult to find accommodation now outside London – the raids had sent thousands more Londoners fleeing out to any place which could take them. It was rumoured that we might get some of the East Enders in Cheyne Hospital.

Catherine did not look well. That she was unhappy I knew. She was not afraid of the air raids, she told me, it wasn't that at all. She didn't care if she died – and that would be as good a way as any other. I could see that normally she was a gay light-hearted girl when she forgot her unhappiness and was interested in something she was telling me, or joking with Mrs Freeth her eyes would twinkle and she had dimples in her cheeks. There were little crinkles at the corners of her eyes and mouth which proclaimed her as the type who normally laughed easily. But now, as the time for her confinement drew nearer, she was becoming more and more depressed and silent. I tried to reassure her about everything, telling her again and again that her baby would be exactly the same as any other baby, but she had got the idea that her child would be a 'bastarde' implanted firmly in her mind, and she was convinced that her fiancé would be killed – or was already dead.

I had told Richard about her and the coming baby and of how I felt responsible for Catherine. Why I felt so, I couldn't explain, but I did. There was Carla, too, happy for the moment at school near Ascot, where I visited her whenever I could. One of her school-friends had invited her there for the August holidays and Carla was enjoying a stay in a very jolly family. Ruth was still in a hospital having treatment for a severe mental breakdown, and I felt as responsible for Carla as l did for Catherine. The child already looked to me for all that she needed and wrote affectionate letters telling me everything that happened at school.

The bomb was removed next day without mishap – and we were told that it was a dud one. I exchanged news with all our little colony, as we called that small piece of the Royal Hospital Road where we lived, the Ferebees in the grocer's shop opposite, Miss Chandler in the chemist's, Sally at the newspaper and cigarette shop and the girls in the Post Office in Oakshott's on the corner of Tite Street. They all had something exciting to tell of the last few nights. Chelsea had had its first bomb and everyone was excited, if not apprehensive. In the King's Road, where I went shopping, the feeling had changed too. In that short time since I had been away the whole feeling of London had changed. Now that Hammersmith and Croydon had been heavily bombed the Londoners were not taking the Alerts so lightly; more and more were going to shelters and in the streets people were beginning to look apprehensively at the sky as those French troops had done at Dover.

Our billetees returned with the removal of the bomb, indig-nant that they had been sent away while women had stayed. I felt for them – Army Regulations did seem difficult to understand and Richard said that they appeared to be purposely obtuse. As I had thought, the first thing they asked him was if he had any old mackintoshes or jackets!

In the late afternoon of September 7th the sirens had sounded and we heard many planes about – they did not seem to be dropping anything in the Chelsea vicinity, but we heard a lot of gunfire far down the river. Presently the All Clear sounded. Soon afterwards, about six o'clock, they sounded again and fires started almost immediately. We could see a red-orange glow in the sky. Wardens out in the streets marshalling their shelterers said that the docks had been attacked very heavily and every Fire Service had been called there. Presently, instead of darkness following the sunset it remained light – a curious yellow-orange light almost like sunrise. We went up on the roof and saw a terrifying sight far off down the river. A monstrous fire was obviously blazing and its gloriously reflected flames in the river cast the glare upwards and right over London. It was absolutely terrifying! As it got later the bombs began whistling down everywhere – and more and more planes came droning over dropping them.

It was a terrible night, there were continuous loud whistling whooshing sounds followed by dull, ominous, heavy thuds which shook the houses and then came several loud, reverberating explosions which shook the very ground of the streets. More and more German planes zoomed overhead as they had done on the Hog's Back, and they seemed to be circling over London, Again and again they returned to drop more and more bombs into the inferno which we knew – and could see – was devouring our docks. There was not a single gun to chase them off – and it was so light from the great fires that we could almost see to read on the roof and it was unnecessary to make use of our torches. Again and again we went down below as planes came right overhead, and we heard the whoosh of a bomb, only to return in a lull to watch the progress of the fire. By now the area of glowing red-orange light was vast – it gave us a horrible feeling of complete impotence in the face of its magnitude – so great was this bonfire display reflected in the heavens that we felt like Lilliputians watching monstrous aerial Gullivers at work.

Kathleen had tears running down her face – she could not bear to see it. As for me I felt fury – a wild anger of which I did not know I was capable. I found I was shivering with some kind of emotion hitherto unknown to me – it was similar to the one I had felt when Catherine was describing the bombing and machine-gunning of the trail of refugees. From the roof we watched fire-engines racing and wardens cycling on their urgent errands. I had telephoned the FAP although I was officially still away, and was told to remain on call. They were fully staffed at the Control also.

The All Clear did not come until five o'clock next morning and we heard then that there had been terrific battles all round London and that eighty-eight German planes had been destroyed. When I went out people were stunned by the magnitude of the raid and the endless succession of German planes which had circled London. Like me, they were under no illusions, they knew that the long-promised Blitz – threats of which I had listened to again and again on the German radio – was here.

Early next morning, a Sunday, we heard something of the appalling destruction which the vast and savage attack of the previous afternoon and night had caused to the docks. The firemen had, some of them, fought the fires for more than twenty-four hours and were still fighting them, for as they had put out a blaze fresh waves of the Luftwaffe rekindled it. Woolwich Arsenal seemed to have been the foremost target for the first waves, and they then bombed Tower Bridge, Poplar, Bermondsey, and West Ham, where their targets were the East India Docks and the great Surrey Commercial Docks. All the small residential houses round them were wiped out – and before the fires could be extinguished darkness fell, and more and more waves of German bombers hurled more and more bombs into the fires the blaze of which provided them with a perfect guide and target. The whole East End had been ablaze and was still smouldering – and this was the awesome and terrible glare which we had watched from our roof in Chelsea.

Later some of the firemen who had been rushed to the area from every borough told us something of the horrors of the burning docks – how the tea and sugar and flour which burned as fiercely as any fuel, the petrol and oil, the wood and paper, all went up in one vast inferno.

I went round to the refugees to see how they had stood the night. They were quieter than I had expected – and all had been in shelters, marshalled there by Hilda Reid. Some of them were bitter that they had been put in London after their experiences in escaping to England. On the whole I found the women more resigned in their acceptance of the air raids than the men. The men told me that they felt doubly bad because they had taken the responsibility of bringing their families to Britain, and had apparently brought them out of the frying-pan into the fire.

Chelsea had had several bombs during the night and they had felt the reverberation of them in their shelters, as we had in the house.

The Giant was rather quiet – he seemed very shaken, not by the bombs and the raid, but by the behaviour of the shelter occupants. Some of them, he complained, had been very rude to the Belgians, saying that they were *Germans*. At this, The Giant, who understood quite a bit of English now, had doubled up his fists and shouted that if anyone called him a German he would knock him down. There had been an uproar and the shelter warden had quelled it and restored order. Catherine told me that many of the people had complained at having foreigners in the shelter to which she went. It had not been too pleasant – quite apart from the crowding and the smell and the lack of sanitation. One family told me that they only felt safe in the Knightsbridge Underground and that they intended to ask for a place regularly there. When I said that it was a very long way to go they said they didn't mind that – if they could sleep in safety when they had arrived there, and that they intended going as soon as dusk fell – they would not wait for the sirens. The Royal Hospital, which was to prove a constant target, had had a bomb drop in Ranelagh Gardens. It was unexploded and the whole area was roped off and closed to the public until the Bomb Disposal Squad came to remove it. We were soon to become familiar with these wonderful REs who, oblivious to danger, would remove the fuses in these unexploded bombs, or UXBs as we called them in Civil Defence and in the Control Centre. If the bomb could not be put out of action it would be conveyed through the cleared streets escorted by police on a conveyance which was painted bright red and marked BDS.

In the studio, except for some flakes of plaster on the carpet, everything looked the same. The heavy bomb which had fallen in Ranelagh Gardens and those in the river near Swan Walk had not even shaken the Green Cat from his lacquer pedestal. Serene and aloof he sat in the window in the sunlight, surveying with contempt the activities in the street. Everyone begged me to put him down in the cellar with some of the paintings which I had stored there now. But I would not move him. Was he not the Guardian of the Home? He must be treated with respect. His place was in it – not below it. But I looked at him as he sat there and I wondered if he were going to prove the truth of what Ah Ling had said. *'As long as he is intact he will guard your home and all that is in it.'*

CHAPTER TWELVE

AFTER THE FIRST few days of the Blitz on London we realized with indignation and resignation that this was a horror which had come to stay – for there were no guns to drive off the raiders circling round with their monstrous loads like a swarm of death-dealing hornets. The noise enraged us – it seemed an outrage that this should be happening over our capital. My anger amused Richard, who said that I was merely wasting valuable energy in reviling and cursing the Nazis. Finally, after several outbursts, I saw the wisdom of his argument. What was the use of cursing? The Luftwaffe was here – over London now whenever it felt like coming – its pilots knew it only too well from their days on the civil aviation lines. But the question on everyone's lips was, Where are our anti-aircraft guns?

Those first days of the Luftwaffe's Blitz on Chelsea were dramatic and tragic, and in them the much-resented and ridiculed air-raid wardens came into their own and showed us the stuff of which they were made. Our Chelsea ones were magnificent! The first to rouse people after the sirens sounded, they hurried to the shelters, ticking off the names of the residents in their areas as they arrived, then back they went to hustle and chivvy the laggards and see that those who chose to stay in their homes were all right. The first to locate and report the bombs to Control, they were the ones to guide and direct the Services sent by Control to the 'incident (a word to which we were to become all too accustomed). It was the wardens who soothed and calmed the terrified and comforted the injured and the dying. They carried children, old people, bundles of blankets, and the odd personal possessions which some eccentrics insisted on taking with them to the shelters. They woke the heavy sleepers, laughed at the grumblers, praised the helpful and cheerful, and performed miracles in keeping law and order during those first dramatic weeks when the Battle of London was being fought in our skies. At the height of the bombing in the raids I would meet Nonie and Tishie Iredale-Smith, wardens of our own area, immaculately uniformed and groomed amongst the half-dressed and dishevelled shelterers, running to waken and hurry their 'flock', lists in their hands, ticking them off as they were located; George Evans, our post warden, calm and imperturbable; Major Christie; Connie Oades on her bicycle: small, pretty, and efficient, she was capable of dealing with numbers of disgruntled shelterers and even drunks in the shelters.

One of the first horrors was a direct hit on Cadogan Shelter, a public shelter under a block of flats in Beaufort Street. The blast killed a large number of people as it blew in the sides of the shelter, amongst them Jean Darling, the shelter warden. Our first casualties at FAP5 were quiet and shocked. None of them wanted to say much – I think the dirt and mess with which they were all covered and their anxiety for missing relatives or friends was uppermost. The casualties' indifference to injuries, cuts, and abrasions astonished us just as the dirt upset all our arrangements. The effects of shock when they first arrived, although we had been trained to recognize them, varied very much in individual cases. What did emerge from this first unfortunate tragedy was a feeling that shelters were not safe – that had the victims stayed at home they would still be alive. To this there was no answer – it was the duty of all Civil Defence personnel to encourage the public to use the shelters.

Digging on this terrible holocaust was still in process on the afternoon of the next day, September 9th, when the sirens sounded again in broad day-light. I was walking with Vicki to the Town Hall to report to Control and see when I was needed most as a stand-in, when the sirens went. Almost at once there were terrific noises of planes overhead, explosions, and activity in the sky. The first great thud came as I reached the turning of Flood Street, by which time wardens were out and shouting to people to take shelter. Everyone was going about his or her usual jobs and did not seem inclined to obey. I continued on my way but walked a little faster. 'Take cover,' called a warden on a bicycle sternly. 'Going on duty,' I retorted. 'Hurry then – and get under cover,' he insisted. Just then there was a terrific explosion and I threw myself down as instructed with Vicki under me. When I got up there was a great cloud of dust and glass was flying about. I felt distinctly sick, but Vicki took not the slightest notice of the appalling noise – had I not known that she had excellent hearing I would have concluded that she was deaf. Up in the sky, very low indeed, a raider was being chased by a Spitfire and as it was chased it was unloading its bombs at regular intervals above the King's Road. I ran on to the Town Hall, shouted at by indignant wardens all the time. One caught hold of me as I reached the King's Road. 'Why aren't you taking cover?' he demanded. I pointed to Vicki. 'Dogs aren't allowed in shelters,' I said. 'The sirens sounded after I left home with her.' 'Well get under cover *at once*!' he ordered. 'I'm going on duty,' I said. 'I don't care where you're going. *Get under cover*...Look out!!!' I threw myself down again as another deafening explosion rocked the King's Road, and another, then another.

I was now very frightened and went into the Town Hall and took shelter in the labyrinth of its bowels where Control was. Vicki showed not the slightest sign of perturbation at all the noise and I was thankful as many people had had their dogs destroyed, fearing that they would not be able to stand the noise. Mr Broad, the veterinary surgeon, told me that he had done nothing since the Blitz began but destroy people's pets – cats, dogs, and birds. It was a lamentable task for, as with doctors, his job was to save life not destroy it, and he said that some of the animals he had been obliged to put down were beautiful healthy creatures.

I reported to Control, who were excited and busy. They were fully manned and did not need me for the time being but asked me to stay in case I was wanted later on. Here I learned where the bombs had been unloaded. The first one I had heard as I went along the Embankment had been on Cheyne Walk, very close to Whistler's lovely house in which we held our meetings. The second had been on Bramerton Street, then King's Court North (a block of flats just west of the Town Hall), then on Swan Court (this was the cloud of dust), Smith Street, and the last one before the Spitfire caught up with the raider had been on St Leonard's Terrace.

The All Clear went quite quickly. The raid had been short and sharp, the raider having obviously been chased in from the outskirts where, as we had seen from Newlands Corner, the RAF were intercepting the Germans in their constant attempts to get through to the capital.

I noticed that the Town Hall clock had stopped precisely at ten to six. Outside it was still sunny and lovely. The mess was awful. All the Services were out – fire, heavy rescue, ambulances, and all the wardens – a most impressive sight. It was difficult to get back to the Royal Hospital Road. Flood Street, Manor Street, and Smith Street were all blocked, as was Bramerton Street. The streets were full of plate glass, whole shop windows were out, the special wire-supports and the much vaunted sticky paper and cellophane advocated by the Government had not been of any use at all. There was scarcely a window left anywhere. Worried about the refugees, I managed to get through Manor Street because I was in uniform. The whole of one side of Swan Court had blown out, leaving the flats exposed like a doll's house which opens on hinges, and there were all the rooms on display to the public eye like the Ideal Homes' Exhibition shows them! The glass was so thick that I had to carry Vicki, otherwise she would have been cut. I went quickly back to Cheyne Place and put her safely inside.

Kathleen was all right but was worried about Anne, who would be on her way home. I was equally anxious about Mrs Freeth, who always went home all the afternoon and usually returned about six. She would have been on her way when the raid started. The dogs, Spider and Susan, said Kathleen, were terrified. She had decided to send them to the country. Mrs Freeth arrived as unperturbed as Vicki, and informed me that Victoria Station had been hit. I reported quickly to the FAP to see if I was needed. They had casualties, mostly from flying glass, but not many, and were also fully staffed, so I was sent to see how the refugees had fared. I knew from Control that a bomb had fallen on St Leonard's Terrace. The Belgian women would have been in the canteen preparing a meal at the time it had fallen. They were all right, they had been in the shelter – but eloquent indeed – far more so than the casualties. The other refugees had been marshalled to shelter by Hilda Reid and were all loud in their anger and criticism. Raids ought to be at night – why in the day? Why indeed, except that the Luftwaffe chose to come! That there would have been far more had the RAF not intercepted them we already knew.

At the FAP I had been told that Dr Richard Castillo was out with the Mobile Squad from St Stephen's Hospital. A bomb had fallen on Bramerton Street and I feared it was on his house. One of the most agonizing strains suffered by the staffs in the Control was having to record and deal with the reports of bombs which had fallen on homes – sometimes those of their own families, relatives, and friends. Their job was to take the reports of incidents and carefully note the time and place. Dr Richard Castillo had been out working for hours on the Cadogan Shelter tragedy and had just gone out again with the Mobile Squad when his own house was demolished in the day-light raid. He had been working during the morning with two wardens, Bert Thorpe and Mathews, who were preparing bodies for removal. Both his house and Thorpe's, which was in Smith Street, had been demolished by this day-light raid while they were again on duty. Digging on Dr Castillo's house was going on – but his wife and daughter and his little son, known to have been in the house at the time, had not been found and were presumed to be dead.

This was the first tragedy of someone known to us all in Civil Defence. Dr Castillo was well known not only because of his work in the Service, but also as an excellent doctor to the patients of his large practice in Chelsea, of whom I was one. Dr Alice Pennell lived in Bramerton Street, but at the far end, not the King's Road end, and although her home was damaged by glass being broken and she herself badly shaken, they were both all right.

The digging on the site of what had been Dr Castillo's house in Bramerton Street was to become a classic in the story of Chelsea's Blitz. The first to reach the heap of ruins was Jo Oakman, a doctor's daughter and a clever painter, with another warden. They and the Reverend Arrowsmith and his curate began working frantically with bare hands at the debris. They had not been scrabbling long when they heard a voice calling and it proved to belong to one of Post Don's messengers, a seventeen-year-old boy called Fox. After some hard work and help from other wardens he was released almost unhurt, with only superficial cuts and bruises. It was a miraculous escape – for the whole house had fallen into the basement and he had apparently been at the back of it when the bomb fell.

Heavy rescue arrived with all the paraphernalia for rescue work but there was no further sound from the site, no answer to their calls and signals, and it seemed that young Fox was the only survivor. What had been a happy family home was now reduced to ground level, with the basement, where the wife and children of Dr Castillo were known to have been, filled in with huge blocks of masonry and heaps of debris. Desolate and grim, it was a reminder that the raider had passed that way.

Four days later, when the heavy rescue were continuing to dig in the debris, they heard a faint cry of *Mama* which came from what had been the basement. Using blocks of wood to shore up the walls they made a tunnel some twenty or thirty feet long through which, with infinite patience and determination, they managed to squeeze. Seven and a half hours after they had first heard the cry they reached Dr Castillo's twelve-year-old daughter, Mildred, who was buried up to her neck in debris. This little girl, whose heroism became a by-word in Chelsea, had been buried for four days and four nights and had been conscious most of the time. She was given tea through a rubber tube and biscuits, and she asked for her rosary before undergoing the terrible ordeal of being pulled inch by inch through the long tunnel by her rescuers. This was a tortuous, agonizingly perilous task which took hours, and all the grim persistence and humour of the rescuers was needed, as they wriggled backwards inch by inch pulling their little charge to safety. At last it was achieved – she was out – and all three rescuers safe too. Her mother and little brother, Richard, were found dead in the ruins – Mildred was the sole survivor.

During the long period while the tunnel was being made the whole of Chelsea had held its breath for Dr Castillo in his anguish and suspense. No one who has not watched a perilous task such as the rescuers, George Woodward, Wally Capon, and George Pitman, performed to save Mildred Castillo can have any idea of the superb courage needed for such a feat. The slightest misjudgment, the smallest false movement, the most infinitesimal slip – and the whole structure could crash down and bury the tunnellers. Theirs was a double peril – for they had not only to reach their goal but to return from the gates of death with the child. They were not young men – few of the heavy rescue were young. The young were disappearing all too fast into the Services, leaving older men, and the women, to deal with the Blitz.

This epic of that day-light raid made a tremendous impression on us all. Here was a child – and not such a robust one either – who had survived a terrible ordeal with a courage and fortitude equalled only by that of her father's devotion to duty even in his terrible loss. The names of the rescuers were on everyone's lips during the next weeks. When I spoke to Wally Capon later when he was working on a site clearing debris he said, "S all in the day's work – I'll get you out if you're ever stuck in yourself!'

The bomb which had hit a house in St Leonard's Terrace was an oil bomb – a nasty messy affair. Fortunately it was not one of the most beautiful of the old houses in that terrace and it was not the home of our Medical Officer for Civil Defence, Dr Symes, in charge of our light rescue and stretcher parties, as we had feared when it was first reported to Control. There were not many casualties from the raider's flight from the Spitfire but he had left a trail of damage everywhere.

The bombs had shattered some gas and water mains and our gas and water seemed to be mixed up with air in the most extraordinary way! To get enough gas to boil a kettle was difficult. I went at once and bought two electric kettles – it seemed to me that this would probably be a frequent occurrence now. My mother had told me that in the 1914-18 war they had all made hay-boxes to save fuel. These, she said, were excellent for keeping food hot, once it was cooked. Mrs Freeth and I constructed one from a box given us by Mr Ferebee, whose wife was most interested in the idea. That we should have to get accustomed to going without baths was also evident if there was to be no gas. One of the things which often gave me the jitters was the idea of the contents of the open grate at one end of the huge studio being distributed over the room by one of the terrific explosions which frequent bombs in the river caused. We were very near the river and it was obvious that the Luftwaffe were trying to get the power stations and the bridges over the Thames. Bomb after bomb would go in the water, making loud long explosions without damaging any of the bridges. That they would do this had been foreseen and small makeshift bridges had been constructed near the permanent ones from Battersea Park to the Embankment.

On the night of the 11th the full barrage of our anti-aircraft heavy guns opened up. The noise was appalling – but the effect on the morale of us Londoners was miraculous! 'Now they're getting it! They'll shoot 'em down now! They'll soon put an end to their nightly circling...' Joy greeted the angry bark of the guns, which now mingled with the whooshes of bombs and the wail of sirens taking up the cry in one area after another, and pieces of shell and shell-caps were to be added to the objects arriving from the sky. It was a magnificent barrage on that first night – and it increased nightly. Day-light warnings were constant now as well, and we could get caught anywhere at any time. I met Suzanne out shopping in the most elegant tin hat I'd seen. She looked as if she had had it especially designed for her – but it proved to be French and to have belonged to her brother in the 1914-18 war. If we went out with our tin hats hanging over our shoulders in a raid we could be ordered to put them on our heads by the wardens. I had a horrible one which was both heavy and far too big. Richard was working a great deal at the Ministry now with Mr Rock Carling the surgeon, who had become special adviser to the Home Office and with whom we had become very friendly. He thought that as I was out so much at night I should have a tin hat which I could wear, and he produced one for me which was much better, and on which I not only painted my name and identity number as directed, but also several adornments from my paintbrush. Even so it was nothing like as elegant as Suzanne's – the French, it appeared, showed their graceful flair for hats, even tin ones!

When the sirens wailed in day-light the shops closed – and we could get shut out without having bought anything. The same thing happened at railway stations. Dr Graham Kerr was finding this – and that any taxi driver willing to bring her to the FAP needed a large bribe. After all, the public had been enjoined again and again to take shelter – even ordered to. The authorities could not foresee that the raids would become such a daily and nightly occurrence that all these injunctions would break down of themselves. People had to be fed – the housewives had to shop – people had to get somehow to their jobs – life had to go on, bombs or no bombs.

Dr Graham Kerr was finding a lot of patients complaining of general malaise and their complaints ranged from headaches to 'just can't take any food'. She put this down in many cases as the result of sleepless nights in shelters, and much of it to fear. She said that they made such a faint-hearted attempt to adjust themselves to the new sleeping conditions. Many people complained to me that they resented the lack of privacy– they hated having to be seen in undignified stages of undress but admitted that they felt 'safer' when together with others. They could not stay alone – they felt too nervous.

The Blitz was providing something besides bombs. It was making people talk to one another. People in shops, in the buses, in the streets often talked to me now. They opened up amazingly about how they thought and what they thought – how they felt and what they felt. They all liked to see the nurses' uniforms – and were loud in their praise of the nurses, the firemen, and the wardens. But they did not like the indignity of sleeping publicly in a bunk in a shelter with hundreds of others. The Blitz was doing something else – it was continuing the slow difficult process already begun before the war of breaking down class barriers.

Another shelter received a direct hit in our area on the 13th and very early in the morning we had many casualties at the FAP which Dr Graham Kerr dealt with. This was the large shelter of Manor Buildings, an LCC block of flats in Flood Street. The water main had been severed and the poor sufferers were soaking wet. We put them all with their feet in hot water and wrapped in blankets until they could be got dry things. They were all filthy and had a lot of cuts and bruises and were all suffering from shock. Shelters were rapidly getting a bad name and some of the casualties said that it was obvious that they could be seen from the air! Residents in Paultons Square had no gas at all as a bomb had severed the gas main. It had also killed one of the wardens in the hut there.

The bomb and everyone's special bomb was still a subject of endless interest and possibilities – but they were coming so thick and fast that everyone had a better story than his neighbour. All over London people were full of stories of the Blitz, but life was going on as usual – in spite of it. September 14th was a date which few of the personnel at Post Don will forget. In a further daylight raid another shelter was hit – this time under a church. The Church of the Holy Redeemer is a massive building and I had been there several times to see the shelter in the crypt because some of our refugees liked the idea of this shelter so much that they wanted to change to it. It was very close to Cheyne Hospital and when, at first, two of them did go there, I had gone to see that they were all right; but we persuaded them that it was too far and that their own was just as safe. It was a very popular shelter – perhaps because, like the refugees, others felt that nowhere would they be safer than under the protection of the Church – and at the time the bomb fell it was crowded.

The bomb was recorded by one of us telephonists in the Control Centre at 18.35. The message said that there was fire and casualties trapped in Holy Redeemer Church in Upper Cheyne Row. Requests followed in rapid succession for ambulances, blankets to cover the dead, fire services, and reports came in that there were many casualties.

The bomb had struck the church at an angle through a window in a most extraordinary way and had penetrated the floor and burst among the shelterers, mostly women and small children. Here George Thorpe, who we knew as 'Bert', lost his life with those women and children he had visited to reassure them – as he always did, although he was not the shelter warden. He knew that they were apt to become nervous and needed moral support in the heavy raids and he used to drop in there to boost up their courage and cheer them up. He had just despatched Jo Oakman on duty and gone there when the bomb fell. The bomb exploded right amongst the shelterers, A woman who was in the shelter told me about it when I visited her afterwards in St Luke's Hospital. She was badly injured and said that the scene resembled a massacre – in fact, she compared it to an engraving she had seen of the massacre of the women and children of Cawnpore in the Indian Mutiny, with bodies, limbs, blood, and flesh mingled with little hats, coats, and shoes and all the small necessities which people took to the shelters with them. She said that people were literally blown to pieces and the mess was appalling. She herself was behind a pillar or buttress which protected her somewhat; and there was a pile of bodies between her and the explosion for it was still day-light – no one had gone to their bunks.

Jo and Len Lansdell were quickly at the scene, followed by all the ARP Services. They could not get into the crypt at first because the body of a very heavy woman barred the only entrance. The explosion had set fire to the great heaps of coke stored there for heating the church and the smoke from it made it difficult to see. Jo and Len Lansdell immediately set to work with stirrup pumps to try to extinguish it before the whole place became a crematorium. The body of Bert lay there face downwards. Jo, who had spoken to him only a few minutes before the bomb fell, turned him over. She said afterwards that she wished so much that she hadn't, so that she could have remembered him as he had been when he had sent her on duty. His equipment, which was taken back to his post, was described to me as being bright red with blood – as was everything which had been in that crypt.

The work of the ARP Services that night was magnificent – by nine o'clock in the evening the casualties were all extricated and were laid in the grounds of the church with the Home Guard in charge, and wonderful work was done by Dr Castillo and Fr Fali, of Tarapore. In our FAP we had numbers of casualties again, including some rare and interesting fractures which Dr Graham Kerr commented on for the instruction of us VADs. To watch her at work, deft, neat, cheerful, and competent, was a lesson in itself.

After a heavy raid with many casualties such as this one there was a task for which we were sometimes detailed from our FAP and to which both our Commandants disliked having to send us. This was to help piece the bodies together in preparation for burial. The bodies – or rather the pieces – were in temporary mortuaries. It was a grim task and Betty Compton felt that we were too young and inexperienced for such a terrible undertaking – but someone had to do it and we were sent in pairs when it became absolutely necessary. Betty asked me if I would go as I had studied anatomy at the Slade. The first time I went my partner was a girl I did not know very well called Sheila. It *was* pretty grim, although it was all made as business-like and rapid as possible. We had somehow to form a body for burial so that the relatives (without seeing it) could imagine that their loved one was more or less intact for that purpose. But it was a very difficult task – there were so many pieces missing and, as one of the mortuary attendants said, 'Proper jig-saw puzzle, ain't it, Miss?' The stench was the worst thing about it – that, and having to realize that these frightful pieces of flesh had once been living, breathing people. We went out to smoke a cigarette when we simply could not go on – and some busybody saw Sheila smoking and reported her for smoking when in uniform and on duty. Betty Compton, who invariably supported her VADs, was most indignant about this, as indeed she was about us having to perform such a task at all. I thought myself that butchers should have done it.

After the first violent revulsion I set my mind on it as a detached systematic task. It became a grim and ghastly satisfaction when a body was fairly constructed – but if one was too lavish in making one body almost whole then another one would have sad gaps. There were always odd members which did not seem to fit and there were too many legs. Unless we kept a very firm grip on ourselves nausea was inevitable. The only way for me to stand it was to imagine that I was back in the anatomy class again – but there the legs and arms on which we studied muscles had been carefully preserved in spirit and were difficult to associate with the human body at all. I think that this task dispelled for me the idea that human life is valuable – it could be blown to pieces by blast – just as dust was blown by wind. The wardens had to gather up pieces after a bad raid – they had no choice – and someone had to assemble them into shrouds for Christian burial, but it seemed monstrous that these human beings had been reduced to this revolting indignity by other so-called Christians, and that we were doing the same in Germany and other countries. The feeling uppermost in my mind after every big raid was *anger*, anger at the lengths to which humans could go to inflict injury on one another.

That first visit to work in the mortuary made a deep impression on me, and on the following Sunday when 'Rockie', as we called Mr Rock Carling, came to lunch I went for a walk with him in Battersea Park and he talked most understandingly to me about such things, so that I felt better about it all. He told me that he and Richard had visited mortuaries in all parts of the country because one of his jobs was to ascertain what form of death resulted from the blast or actual bursting of the bombs. He told me that once when they were in Gillingham mortuary and a terrible raid was on, Richard had remarked coolly that at least they were in the right place if they were killed.

On September 15th Buckingham Palace was bombed, and mingled with the people's anger at this outrage was a kind of warm gratitude at the personal sharing by the monarch himself in his country's ordeal. Two bombs fell on the Palace but neither of them exploded. Unexploded bombs were a nightmare – sometimes we would awake to find ourselves surrounded by barred-off streets because of these UXBs. There had been one recently in Cheyne Court, a few doors down from No. 33, and we had been obliged to evacuate while it was removed. The young, eager-looking officer of the REs who came to take it away was blithely contemptuous of the danger to himself while insisting that we all go away while under his directions the bomb was removed. Bombs were his life, he told me – he knew them as a mother knows her children. I wondered if his mother knew of the appalling risks which he was running continuously – he looked so young and so full of life.

I had gone to Suzanne while the bomb was being removed, as we were not allowed in the neighbourhood. She had a deputation of Belgians full of complaints. I was surprised at the way in which they were standing up to the nightly shelter life. I thought they were splendid. Madame C. said to me when I commented on this, 'Well, we *are* frightened, you know – and if we were alone we would make a noise – but you British are so quiet that we dare not make one wail!'

Just occasionally a list of places which had been bombed was released on the news. The withholding of the whereabouts of the incidents seemed ridiculous to those Londoners who passed the gaping holes and melancholy mounds of debris on their daily journeys to and from work, but we were told that it was important that the Germans should not get to know exactly what they had bombed. That they had a pretty good idea was apparent from their own news, which included details of many buildings destroyed by them.

Richard and I were married during one of London's heaviest day-light raids. Because of this none of our guests turned up for the ceremony – and, what was more important, neither of the witnesses did. We went out into the deserted street and found two taxi-drivers, who were philosophic about bombs – saying that bombs or no bombs they had to eat and what was the use of staying alive if one's stomach was empty? They acted willingly and charmingly as witnesses, and afterwards tossed up as to which of them should drive us to the Guards' Club where we had invited our friends to lunch. The All Clear sounded before we reached there and most of the guests turned up, although some were late because they had been on duty during the raid. Anne had got leave from her office and came with Kathleen. When we got back to Cheyne Place Mrs Freeth had tied a white ribbon round Vicki's neck and had put flowers everywhere and Mr Ferebee had sent over some champagne.

In the evening some friends came in to drink our health, but the sirens went very early and most of them had to rush away on duty. We spent the first night of our marriage putting out incendiaries with Anne and Cecil and Larry, who had now moved out as a billetee but was welcome to come in whenever he liked. It was exhilarating, especially as we drank champagne in between the bouts of fire-fighting. When there appeared to be a lull in the dropping of these small fire bombs we decided to go to bed. There were now high explosive bombs being dropped and the barrage was very noisy. One bottle of champagne had been opened but not drunk, and as we appreciated the fact that French wines were already scarce we put it in a pail of ice, intending to drink it last thing before going to bed – but we forgot it.

In the early hours of the morning we were both awoken by a loud explosion in the room. 'It's a fire-bomb come through the window,' I said, for the plop was exactly like the plopping explosions of the small incendiaries which we had now become accustomed to extinguishing. But there was no sign of a fire-bomb – the champagne cork lay on the bed and the ceiling was splashed all over with champagne! I was astonished that it could explode to such a height and make such a mess as we surveyed the diminished remains of our wedding toast.

On September 19th the King and Queen came to Chelsea. Their visit was unofficial and quiet, but news of it leaked out and a large crowd lined the King's Road when they were driven to Bramerton Street, and cheered them loudly. They were taken to Dr Castillo's demolished house and shown how Mildred Castillo had been rescued from it. All the Rescue Squad were presented to their Majesties and shook hands with them. George Pitman told the Queen how they had got her out safely, and the King commented, 'You have done absolutely grand work.' Pitman answered, 'It's all in the day's work, sir, we all get the same pay.'

Wally Capon was fifty-four at the time of the rescue and amused the Queen by saying, 'People in these days think the old 'uns are no good and only the young 'uns matter. Now the old 'uns are showing what they can do.' Their Majesties walked through a number of side streets to Cheyne Row and the Church of the Holy Redeemer and were given an account of the terrible holocaust there on the night of the 14th when Bert had been killed with the shelterers. I had only just learned that Bert had been in the RAMC at St Mark's Hospital during the 1914-18 war.

There were many of the Borough's officials and dignitaries lined up to receive the King and Queen although their visit was supposed to be informal. I had been visiting Dr Pennell and so got a first-class view. When the crowd was approaching the damaged Holy Redeemer Church the Queen walked away from the group of officials surrounding her and going up to a group of wardens, mostly women, asked to be introduced to them. Amongst them was Jo, and Len Lansdell, the Deputy Post Warden, both of whom had done such magnificent work in the Holy Redeemer incident, and the Queen spoke to them all. Len Lansdell is a shoemaker with a wonderful personality and as many wisecracks as an American movie, and I had heard everywhere of his bravery and devotion to duty. I liked this incident very much. It seemed to me that

Queen Elizabeth, with her usual thoughtfulness and perception, had understood and appreciated the merits of those who, though not perhaps the star performers, nevertheless formed the vitally necessary core of the whole structure without which such deeds as those of the three heroes of the Castillo incident could never have been achieved.

Hundreds of us had a close-up view of the King and Queen that day, and the knowledge that their London home had just been bombed made a link between them and the victims of the tragedies about which they had just been told. They left a warm glow of pride and affection wherever they went. Queen Elizabeth, exquisitely dainty and so much prettier than any of her photographs, gave us all her lovely heart-warming smile, and King George, looking careworn and strained, had a sincerity which was unmistakable as he talked with the ARP personnel, giving everyone the feeling that he shared our sufferings to the full.

On the following Sunday, when he broadcast from Buckingham Palace, King George spoke of the wonderful work of the ARP Services and of the creation of the George Medal which was to rank next to the Victoria Cross in honour. His praise must have cheered thousands of ARP workers who had begun to lose heart at the prospect of a whole winter of experiences such as September had brought them. He spoke of the loss of the evacuee ship *City of Benares*, which was torpedoed on September 17th without any warning 600 miles from land. It carried ninety children and nine escorts. Eighty-three of the children were killed or lost, and seven out of the nine escorts also. Most of the crew and the ship's Captain went down with the ship and Colonel Baldwin Webb, MP, who was accompanying the children to Canada, also lost his life.

This had cast gloom over the hearts of many parents who were contemplating sending their children across the Atlantic under the Government scheme. When the few survivors were able to tell their stories of the last moments of the *City of Benares* the nation's fury broke out. What must have been the feelings of the parents who had sent their children away as they thought to safety? Their little friends sent into country districts in England, Wales, and Scotland were still safe and happy. *'Sink their ships, sink their ships,'* was the cry everywhere, just as those who had been bombed begged, *'Give it them back, give it them back.'* We were apparently doing both those things, judging from the reports of neutral countries such as Sweden. Fury, resentment, and detestation of the crime of the *City of Benares* was expressed all over the world. Two of my small cousins lost their lives in this disaster. Their mother, who had worried herself sick as to whether or not they should go to Canada, had given in finally to her husband's wishes and parted with them.

CHAPTER THIRTEEN

CHEYNE HOSPITAL, now that most of the refugees had been found homes, had been receiving bombed-out people from the City and East End. After the docks fire at the beginning of the Blitz there had been a number, and more came as the East End, and especially Bermondsey, suffered heavy attacks which rendered thousands homeless. Some of these people were very dirty – so dirty that the others, put with them into the former wards of the hospital now used as dormitories, refused to sleep there with them. They 'stank', they said, so much that it was beyond bearing. Some of these offenders were ordered to take a bath by the Medical Officer, but they were people who had never seen a bath, let alone taken one. Most of them were very old and to us VADs there fell the task of bathing them against their wish. To see the bodies of some of those to be bathed was a revelation in the way others in our capital lived. Peggy Rowles [now Mrs James Dowdall] and I, who were often paired together, had to bath an old woman whose body literally resembled the bark of a tree – so thick and ingrained were the layers of dirt. She was resentful and indignant at this outrage performed on her by 'young chits', as she called us. I explained to her that she was going to have a special medical bath which would do her rheumatics good – and she was somewhat mollified. We had trouble in coaxing her into the bath and it took loofahs, flannels, and scrubbing brushes to get the dirt off her. We were sweating and soaking when this revolting task was finished and the poor old soul dried and dressed in some of the clothes from Crosby Hall. After this there came the loathsome task of delousing their heads – and then treating the hair for nits. For hours some of us would sit in a small room overlooking the Thames dealing with lousy heads. One woman whose long and beautiful hair was literally alive asked me if I did it because I liked it. I said no one could like such a job. 'How much do they pay you for it?' she then inquired. When I said that I was a volunteer and was paid nothing she said tartly, 'Why don't you leave the bloody things in peace then – if I don't mind 'em why should you?' Why indeed?

When I got home Mrs Freeth would insist on my washing everything in carbolic and said she couldn't see why such filthy people couldn't be 'just fumigated and done with'.

Many of our East Enders never took their clothes off at night in peace time, and since the Blitz thousands had never taken them off at all. But others, who, in spite of all they had gone through, were clean and respectable, resented the dirty ones being near them. Another revelation was the sanitary or rather insanitary habits of the bombed-outs. They seemed to have got used to using buckets or the floor in the shelters where they had been sleeping, and rather than find their way in the dark passages to the lavatories they used the fire buckets. As *these* were filled with sand and constantly needed when we had incendiaries, the horrible surprise of those dealing with the bombs can be imagined. When we remonstrated with them they demanded chamber-pots, and it seemed to me that the easiest way to get rid of their revolting habits would be to obtain some of these articles.

As usual, I went to Margerie Scott. She said she had a case of them – but no transport to get them to the hospital. So urgent did the problem seem to me for hygienic reasons that I said I would take some down myself for the forthcoming night. I left the Town Hall with half a dozen of these articles piled high in my arms. Paper was a commodity impossible to obtain and except for a newspaper which we wrapped round the unwieldy pile they were bare, shining, and vulnerable. I staggered down Shawfield Street with them. There was unfortunately a wind and the newspaper was blown away after a few preliminary flaps. Now I thought, it only needs the sirens to go for the whole lot to tumble down when the bombs drop. I could only just see over the top of the things, which were growing heavier and heavier as I walked. It became increasingly evident that sooner or later I would either have to put the pyramid down and rest or it would fall! The moment came when I could go no further. I heard steps hurrying behind me but I could not turn round, and, pausing by the steps of a sand-bagged house, I was endeavouring to lower the things without cracking them when a familiar voice said, 'Sit down on the steps and I'll take them from you.' I slithered onto the steps, almost causing a tragedy by not judging the distance, but a firm hand steadied me and the pile of china was removed deftly from my aching arms and set down on the steps. I looked up. My saviour was a slim khaki-clad figure with a lock of fair hair falling over his eye in a way it always had. Rex Whistler [he painted the frescoes in the dining-room of the Tate Gallery], in the uniform of the Welsh Guards, consumed with mirth, was counting the pots as he laid the pile down. 'What in God's name are you doing with these lewd articles?' he said. 'Oh, oh! If I only had a pencil and paper! You can't imagine how you looked staggering along with these.' I could imagine only too well. The wind had blown my hair about as it had his. I was surprised that his was still quite long – Richard had told me that the Guards were strict about close-cuts. My face must have been red with anxiety and exhaustion and the squat round cap of the Red Cross uniform did not suit me. I said I knew I looked awful. 'Awful? You looked enchanting – who would expect to find a girl staggering about in broad day-light with these!' and he went off into hoots of infectious laughter. Rex could always make me laugh. He had a quality of never having grown-up yet being completely mature.

We sat there on the stone steps surrounded by white china chamber-pots and smoked a cigarette and exchanged news. I had no idea that he was in the army and he did not know that I was in the Red Cross. He was curious as to the destination of the china articles and in spite of his elegant uniform he insisted on accompanying me to Cheyne Hospital and carrying half of them. We giggled all the way and tried some juggling with several very near accidents to our precious burdens. 'Do you often walk about with such interesting things?' he inquired as we approached our destination. I told him about the East Enders, of our having to bath and de-louse them, and I told him about the old woman whose body was like the bark of a tree. Rex always liked unusual and fantastic models and he was absolutely fascinated, and when we had deposited our burdens and he had seen with what joy they were received, I introduced him to some of our 'patients'. He came back with me to Cheyne Place and enjoyed one of Mrs Freeth's famous cheese omelettes with me while I told him more about what I was doing.

He was stationed 'somewhere on the coast', he told me, and it was all quite fun. Yes, he was painting and drawing there. My aunt had known Rex's mother when she had lived in Abbot's Langley and he and his brother Lawrence were children. We had both been taught drawing by Professor Henry Tonks whom we had both loved.

Rex was very encouraging about my work and implored me not to give it up but to try and do some drawing every day – even if it were only a sketch or a scribble. He said that I could get a permit to draw bombed buildings from the Ministry of Works and that they were excellent practice.

To see and talk to this original and delightful person was indeed a breath of fresh air. Just as he was leaving, after parting reluctantly from 'Miss Hitler', as Vicki was now called, he held out a sixpence. 'I owe you sixpence – don't you remember?' he asked. I didn't. But apparently several years previously I had once lent him sixpence at a party at which he had arrived without any money. He had refused to take more than his exact fare back, which was typical of him.

A few days later I received a post-card from him and on it was the most delightful drawing of myself with the pile of articles which had so amused him. Richard and I loved this drawing – as did all our friends. The card bore no postmark – war-time censorship on coastal towns forbade it – but from something he had said I concluded that he was stationed somewhere in the Brighton area.

We VADs had to do day and night duty in pairs at Cheyne Hospital now that the bombed-outs were there. These poor souls – especially those from Bermondsey, Poplar, and West Ham – had already been through terrifying and appalling horrors about which they loved to talk, each vying with the next in gruesome details of the heavy attacks on their boroughs in which they had lost their homes. They were panic-stricken when the raids became localized and noisy, as they frequently did. Cheyne Hospital, being on the river, got the full impact of the bombs, intended for the power station and the bridges, which missed and fell in the Thames. We all hated being sent there on night duty because the old people panicked easily.

One night Peggy and a VAD named Elizabeth Mason were on duty there and there was no Sister-in-charge. The Blitz was bad, and the old people became hysterical and Peggy, not knowing how to calm them, gave them all sleeping tablets. Later in the night when she went the rounds they were all sound asleep. The guns barked, the bombs whooshed down unnoticed by the sleepers. When she was ready to go off duty early in the morning some of them were still asleep. Peggy had a sudden horrible fear that they had died of an overdose of sleeping draught. Supposing they had? What would happen to *her*? She had acted on her own initiative. She waited about and then as time went on she began trying to rouse them, and then crept from one to another, her heart beating with apprehension. But they were all awaking quite happily, and one old woman said to her, 'Oh, nurse, I haven't had such a lovely night since the Blitz started.'

Asta Lange had a friend who simply drank herself stupid every night with brandy, of which she had got in a wonderful stock. One night she fell down the whole flight of stairs when a heavy bomb fell, but she simply lay at the bottom dead to the world and quite unharmed. Asta was worried as to whether the brandy would last out the Blitz and whether her friend would have developed such a taste for oblivion in it that she would not be able to live without it.

There were other kinds of escape. Music was one for me. After I had first had to fit together the pieces of flesh which had been my Chelsea fellow citizens I had put on a record of Tchaikovsky's *Pathetique* and revelled in its self-pity and yearning. Perhaps it was its unanswered question of *Why? Why? Why?* which seemed to fit in with the inevitable query which must have troubled all those who did these tasks. For the violence and its grim aftermath, like the symphony, urged one terrible question only...*Why?*

Mr Churchill had said that he promised us nothing but 'blood, tears, toil, and sweat'. The Blitz was certainly bringing the blood, tears, and the toil, and it seemed to be bringing a great deal of dirt to some of us. When I stopped to think of the disgusting and revolting chores which the war was meaning for me I often rebelled violently, and wondered if a Florence Nightingale role really appealed to me – I loved fun and was considered frivolous by my family. There were days when I felt I didn't want to do one more thing for one more refugee or one more bombed-out person, although they compelled my compassion. I didn't want to enter one more hospital or smell the stench of one more shelter. And there were times when Richard was away – and they were all too frequent – when I was afraid. When I had to go out sometimes during a heavy raid in answer to a call from a family or from the FAP or the Control Centre, I felt that I just couldn't go. And I would look out of the window and see the wardens and the AFS men and women cycling or running to their posts and I would think of Dr Castillo or Dr Phillips out with the Mobile Unit and I would put on my tin hat and scrub my hands in anticipation of more dirt and go – with a sigh for the rapidly fading memories of the lovely travels which I enjoyed before Hitler had upset the world.

I wondered if the wardens felt as I did, and I asked some of them. 'Lord, yes,' replied one whose courage had been proved a dozen times already, 'some nights I'm so bloody scared that I have to make myself go on the bloody beat,' and another one, a woman whose coolness in danger I envied and admired, said, 'There have been times when literally I've had to drag myself from railing to railing to reach the end of my beat.' No one would have dreamed that she felt like that and I admired her even more for her candour. I could never detect the slightest sign of fear in Richard. He was always completely cool and whimsical about the incidents in which he and Mr Rock Carling were frequently involved on their dangerous tours of the bombed provincial cities and the coastal towns. On the nights we were not on duty he would count bombs dropping and he would sleep absolutely soundly.

We had never yet slept in a shelter – I had had to do short spells of duty in several to relieve shelter nurses, but never for the whole night. We felt much safer in our own home. There were often unpleasant incidents in the shelters and men who were drunk would interfere with the habitual shelterers who wanted to sleep. Fights would break out sometimes. Diminutive Connie Oades, when shelter warden, was quite capable of dealing with huge tough drunks but sometimes other wardens were not so successful and the police had to be called. The drunks liked to sing – and so did the majority of the shelterers – but not all night. One shelter warden in the Knightsbridge Underground told me that he felt for all the world like the housemaster at a large mixed school for adults when he was obliged to try and keep order, mollify those insulted, pacify those who were frightened, and settle quarrels over the allotment of places. 'The only thing I lack – and could use,' he finished wryly, 'is the traditional cane.'

There had been several odd nights without raids now but it still seemed too dangerous for Carla to come to us for Christmas. She kept on writing. Would she have to stay at school – all alone with the nuns? Surely she could come just for a few days? Besides, she wanted some new clothes – she had grown! Her skirts could not be let down any more. I was worried about Carla. In every letter she assumed that I was going to adopt her. She never mentioned her mother, never asked me how Ruth was. It was no use telling her that the war might go on for years and that even then if her mother was still mentally ill there would be her father to consider. She had replied to this without any preamble. 'I hope he is dead by now – killed by a bomb or in a battle – he helped to kill all Mother's relatives. As to my brothers I do not acknowledge them as brothers. They are all Hitler Youth fanatics and they call Mother dirty names.' After this it seemed wiser to let her think that we would adopt her if it were ever possible, and to reassure her that at any rate I would always look after her. She was a brilliantly clever child, the nuns told me, and had a straight, realistic approach to everything. She appeared to have no relatives in Europe except the father and brothers in Germany, but occasionally mentioned an aunt of whom she had been fond who was now in Brazil. After much trouble I found an address which might possibly find this woman, and I wrote her about Ruth's breakdown and Carla's plight.

Early in October Chelsea mothers and young children under school age were evacuated to the West of England. This involved a fresh spate of work for the WVS, the Red Cross, and St. John's Ambulance. I was glad to see them go. Several times during the Blitz I had seen perambulators with a toddler leaning out, left outside houses, or a child playing unconcerned in a sand-pit during an Alert. They were a headache to the overworked wardens. Not all of them went, many women would not leave their husbands, although the Government had stated their intention of providing mobile communal centres to feed the grass widowers.

October proved a bad month for bombs in Chelsea – almost as bad as September had been. On the night of the 14th we had one of the worst fire attacks we had as yet had. Thousands of incendiaries rained down – and were put out by the householders, fire parties, and Fire Services. The following night St. Stephen's Hospital was badly damaged and some of the nurses and Sister Skinner were killed, and there was a spectacular crater in the Fulham Road which we all went to see. All the mains were severed, gas, electricity, and water. The raid, in brilliant moonlight, lasted six hours and was very noisy. The severing of gas and water mains was one of the worst results of heavy explosives – and one which did not appear to have been foreseen. The speed with which temporary repairs were effected with the help of the Royal Engineers was amazing.

The Royal Hospital seemed singled out for attention by the Luftwaffe, just as it had been in the 1914-18 war. Bomb after bomb – some unexploded, some delayed action – were dropped on the buildings and grounds. The Pensioners insisted that Hitler knew that the place was under the administration of the War Office, and that it was bombed with intention. Its position on the Thames between two bridges was the obvious reason for its constant bombardment, but the old men preferred theirs. They were soldiers still, as they proudly pointed out – and it was right that they should be considered a target. What they did not accept was the fact that the three bombs that had been dropped on their infirmary had injured their nurses. After these bombings the place would be set to rights and put into some sort of order in an amazingly short time. All around Chelsea the piles of debris and rubble were growing as houses in succeeding streets and squares were destroyed, but in the Royal Hospital all rubble was cleared away at once, gaps in roofs tarpaulined by the War Office, and every brick and tile of the historic and much-loved place was preserved for use in the eventual repairs.

I would go to Suzanne after a bad night and find all the family down in the huge basement kitchen which was always warmed by a wonderful old kitchen range. After the sleepless nights we always felt cold the next day, and they would offer me some hot porridge, coffee, or tea – whatever was going – and we would sit there talking of the night's events. Maurice, whose work at this time seemed as endless as was his responsibility for the welfare of the old men, would be grey-faced but cheerful, his delicious wit unimpaired by the horrors of the nights. He and Captain Townsend seemed absolutely indefatigable!

During a heavy raid on the Fulham area the big cemetery in the Old Brompton Road received an HE bomb, and we were telephoned by friends to come and see the Resurrection there! I did not find it resembled Stanley Spencer's idea of this event at all. It was very horrible indeed. The historic little churchyard in the Royal Hospital also had its ancient tombstones heaved up unceremoniously by the blast of a bomb. More gruesome still was the incident in Lower Sloane Street. A house there was badly damaged and the wardens found a number of corpses in the basement. They reported their presence and asked for the usual vans to remove them. They stated, however, that the corpses appeared to have no injuries, and to look extraordinarily peaceful; in fact they did not present the appearance associated with bomb or blast casualties. After medical inspection and inquiries, the bodies were found to be embalmed subjects of an undertaker, whose business premises having been destroyed, was using the basement of his private residence to store those waiting to be taken long distances for burial – a long wait now that transport by sea and air was almost impossible.

The October days were bright and sunny and the parks and the grounds of the Royal Hospital were unusually lovely in their autumn colours, but the nights were violent and not made for sleep. All kinds of horrors could occur while people were in shelters – as on the 16th when seven bombs fell on Chelsea, severing a water main and flooding all the basements between Milmans Street and Seaton Street, so that when the poor shelterers emerged in the early hours of the morning they were met by wardens and police whose job it was to evacuate them all from their flooded homes to Rest Centres. It was now a common sight to encounter a little procession in the early mornings – the sleepy, bewildered family, preceded and followed by laden wardens carrying bundles, suitcases, babies, pets, pots and pans, and all the paraphernalia which the displaced would not or could not do without. Grumbled at and cursed at for so long in the phoney war, the wardens, men and women, were now welcomed when a bomb had fallen or gunfire at night was at its height and most frightening. The noise of the heavy guns was shattering, having a reverberation which was in itself a threat, and many people were more disturbed by them than by the planes and falling bombs. Riley Street was completely demolished at this time, but as everyone had been evacuated from it the bomb was really a blessing, for this street had long been an eyesore and a terrible slum. I had once lived in a small cottage in Apollo Place, into which Riley Street runs, and had been astounded at the cleanliness of the children after having been shown the homes from which they came.

In Seaton Street there were many casualties and eleven dead, while the damage was widespread and grim. One casualty was never found and the place where she was known to have been was hallowed in a small religious ceremony. Fred Purver, a warden from Post Don, had been killed in the wardens' hut in the Paultons Square incident, and Robert John Hanson, warden from Post F, was killed at Pelham Court on the 13th. Civil Defence was a dangerous job for those out on duty in the raids, and the Government's statement a few weeks after this, that injured Civil Defence workers would receive thirteen weeks' full pay instead of the two weeks' hitherto granted, and that a grant of £7 10s would be made towards the funeral expenses of volunteers killed on duty, was poor comfort. When the raids were at their height, and we had to be out, we would console one another with the Government's promise of a £7 10s funeral! None of us thought that flowers would be included!

Bernard Newman came to Chelsea and gave us a very exciting lecture in the middle of October. He spoke about Hitler's secret weapon, about which we were all talking and wondering. In the broadcasts from Germany there had been much talk of this secret weapon which was to destroy us all! Bernard Newman told us that Hitler could have no worse weapon than panic. He had seen its effects in Poland and Belgium and France. 'Those battles were not lost by the soldiers but by the civilians. *Panic comes from rumour!*' He went on to say that the French ran away from rumour, their morale was undermined months before the German advance, and the same thing had no chance of succeeding in Britain. Morale was so magnificent in Britain that he was confident of the outcome.

There was no need to emphasize the danger of panic to us in Chelsea, where we had its evidence before us every day in our many refugees. I thought of Catherine's story of the long trail of people hampering the troops, and being bombed and machine-gunned but forming up again on their trek to the coast. The lecture was thrilling, and was called 'Spies, in Fact and Fiction'. We enjoyed it immensely, and afterwards went about in the FAP feigning suspicion of one another as a guard against such possibilities as those of which he had spoken. There was no need of warnings about morale in London. In the heaviest Blitz I had seen people strolling about as if nothing was happening and when chivvied by a warden they did not run. *It was not done to run!* Nor to show any sign of fear! The Civil Defence – especially the AFS personnel themselves – behaved with the greatest nonchalance in the most appalling danger, and showed no signs of what they were feeling. Two of our stretcher-bearers at FAP5, Desmond and Michael, would stroll about waiting for the ambulances as if they were merely waiting for a bus or train while bombs were whistling down near them. When the ambulance arrived they would load the injured as stolidly and deliberately as if it were a taxi into which they were handing their guests after an evening out! I don't know if they or the wardens felt as cool as they looked, but the thing was to affect a joking 'don't care' nonchalance everywhere. A sort of Kismet theory was the fashion. 'If your number's on a bomb it'll get you,' was Mrs Freeth's way of putting it. 'Can't do nothing about it, if it's going to get you it'll get you,' was old Granny's.

October had been a bad month for raids in other places besides London. At the end of the month the Ministry of Home Security announced that during October there were 6,334 killed and 8,695 injured and detained in hospital from the air raids.

I think it was about this time that I had the absolute conviction that my number would be on one of the bombs. Richard's assurance that the chances were one in a million made no difference. I just knew it. On the 9th Mr Churchill asked in his review of the war, what had happened to the promised German invasion? There had been rumours of an invasion at the time of Dunkirk, and several times since. But we had not been told of this and were being constantly reminded to mistrust rumours and not to spread them, so if we got letters from friends near the coast who had seen or heard anything suspicious we took no notice and told no one – except our best friends or colleagues at work!

Now the Prime Minister had openly mentioned the word *invasion*, and what is more had asked what had happened to it, where was it?

Mr Churchill's reviews of the war, just as his naval reviews had been when he was First Lord of the Admiralty, were a delight and inspiration to all except a few of his most bitter critics. He told us now how he had himself visited every possible scene of bomb damage and his comment was: 'In all my life I have never been treated with so much kindness as by the people who have suffered the most. One would think one had brought some great benefit to them instead of the blood and tears, the toil and sweat which is all I have ever promised. On every side there is the cry "We can take it," but with it there is also the cry, "Give it them back!" He went on to assure the nation that we were battering them continuously with all our forces.

Coming so soon after the King's broadcast praising the ARP, this speech by Mr Churchill was a tonic to the fainthearted, the weary, and the pessimistic, as were all his speeches. They did something for me which is indescribable. The reports from neutral papers at this time that the evacuation of school-children from Berlin had already begun did much to strengthen the statement that we were battering the Germans. The children were being sent to Austria and East Prussia.

Reports about the Blitz by Lord Haw Haw were extraordinarily revealing in their mistaken assessment of the British mentality. For some reason or other this misguided man frequently chose to address himself to the people of Leeds. He would announce that they were going to be bombed that night – that their town-hall clock hands stood at some certain time, making it appear as if the Germans had some spies amongst Leeds' citizens and some way of communicating with them. Manchester was another town to which he addressed his tirades. He sounded to me extremely like some of the followers of Mosley – only they were neither so comic nor so imaginative.

The German News Agency reported at this time that Hamburg had suffered terribly from the RAF raids, a whole working-class district having been wiped out, and told of the continuous bombing of Hamm, Cologne, Hamburg, Dortmund, and Berlin. It helped to bolster up people in their nightly endurance of the Luftwaffe, but there must have been many aged, sick, and frail people in Germany enduring the nightly bombing as there were children. From some of the casualties we attended I found that they thought of this too – not all of them gloated over our reprisals. 'The wrong people suffer,' said one old woman to me when we had finished bandaging her after she had been dug out of the ruins of her home. 'That Hitler now, why isn't he at the Front with his men? He made the war. My sons have both had to go – they're in safe billets in the country far from bombs – *it's old Mother who has had it.*'

A cousin of mine who was a Brigadier-General had been sent to Northern Ireland. His wife was in Richmond and taking very little notice of the nightly raids. When he came home on leave he was horrified when the sirens went and the bombs began to fall. The indifference of his wife to the Blitz amazed him. He had never heard a siren or a bomb until he came home on leave.

One lovely sunny morning Mrs Freeth was hanging out of the studio window cleaning the glass and shaking her duster. The sirens had sounded some time before but nothing much had happened except some gun-fire. Suddenly the noise of planes burst on us and a plane came so low that its shadow could be seen on the sunny studio wall. 'It's a German! It's a German!' she shouted excitedly. 'Look at the black crosses on it –' But now the sound of machine-gun fire and the clatter of bullets was shattering the stillness. 'Come in! Come in!' I screamed. But she was as delighted as if she had seen a rainbow and leaned far out gazing up at the sky. I could not resist joining her. A car came swerving and skidding down the Royal Hospital Road and, pulling up with screeching brakes, came into the archway under the house.

'There's bullet marks all over his roof!' cried Mrs Freeth. We heard the bell and went down. It was an army car driven by a corporal and its passenger was a very young captain. Richard told him to come inside and Mrs Freeth, without a word, fetched the brandy and gave him a glass. He was shaking and could not speak. Presently he asked us if it was often as noisy and dangerous in London. 'Lord yes,' replied Mrs Freeth, 'we have it like this nearly every day!' He was reassured when we said that it was the first time a plane had come so low over Chelsea. We told him about the raider being chased by a Spitfire over the King's Road on September 14th, but this was the first time we had known the Royal Hospital Road to be machine-gunned. We heard afterwards that the plane had been brought down near Victoria and that the pilot, who had landed by parachute, had had a very rough time from the public. The army car had the marks of several bullets on it and the windscreen was shattered. The young captain was, he told us, stationed in a very quiet part of the country and had just been detailed on regular missions to London. No wonder he wanted to know if this was the usual state of affairs in the capital!

CHAPTER FOURTEEN

It was at the height of one of these bad nights in October that Catherine telephoned that her baby was on the way, and that she wanted me to go to the hospital with her. The sirens had started wailing almost as soon as it was dark and there had been several appalling thuds and explosions. She said that an ambulance would be coming soon – could I hurry? I did hurry – all along Cheyne Walk there was activity – and it was only too obvious bombs had found Chelsea again. There were wardens blocking off streets, ambulances and fire engines were dashing round corners, and things kept falling with a clatter as I put my tin hat on while I ran.

Catherine was calm but her set face and compressed lips were enough. She was quite oblivious of the Blitz, as she always was – it might not have existed. All that agitated her was that she should reach the hospital in time. There were few hospitals in London now which could take maternity cases and Catherine was going to St Mary Abbot's. I saw her into the ward and into bed – Sister didn't think that she was yet ready for the Labour Room. While I was there several of the patients were asking to be put *under* the beds. The Sister allowed me to stay although I was not wearing uniform. She told me that I could come in and out as I liked in future provided that I wore Red Cross uniform. She was very kind and efficient and I felt that Catherine would be all right except for the growing intensity of the Blitz. I asked how the patients stood it. 'They're not too bad,' Sister said, 'sometimes we get one who panics – that's dangerous – they all panic then. We have to be severe.' Before I left she had put a card over Catherine's bed. When she had gone Catherine looked at it and burst into tears. 'Isn't she sweet?' she said, pointing to the name on the card. At first I couldn't see what she meant. Her name was on it – that was all – then I saw that the prefix 'Mrs' had been inserted and it was this which had caused the tears. 'The others won't know,' she said, crying again.

She was abnormally sensitive about being unmarried. I left when two nurses came to take her to the Labour Ward – her pains had started. She clung to me and cried – but silently and stoically. I knew that she would bite her lips until they bled but that no sound would come from her during her labour. Catherine was one of the bravest girls I had ever met. She had always been obliged to fend for herself and neither bombs nor guns had any fears for her. What she shrank from was the condemnation of her fellow-refugees, their smug references to marriage lines. Her British birth certificate had arrived and she was delighted with it. Her one thought was to join up with one of the Services – she was British and she wanted to fight for Britain. It was very late when I left St Mary Abbot's. The Sister had promised that they would telephone me when the baby was born. Richard was away on a tour for the Ministry – Mrs Freeth was sleeping in the hall on a camp bed. She awoke to inquire anxiously after Catherine.

I was so tired that I fell asleep after counting twenty-three bombs. It was extraordinary how soundly I slept now that the Blitz was on. Before it had started I often found difficulty in getting to sleep – but now I was no sooner in bed than sleep came. I sometimes thought that should a bomb hit the house while I slept thus, I would know nothing and never wake up – and this was how many people died. I had seen them dug from the ruins, their faces peaceful as they lay in their night clothes. It was only horrible when they were laid on the pavement or in the street uncovered, with their faces turned up for all the world to gaze at while blankets were awaited to shield them from the curious.

We could always judge the intensity of the previous night's raid by the time at which the milkman and the newspaper boy arrived. The post was surprisingly punctual no matter what had happened. The bread van which came from the King's Road was also a comment on the previous night. The milkman as usual knew all about last night's bombs. I knew that the Royal Hospital had had three UXBs because Suzanne had telephoned me. She also told me that St Mary's Church in Cadogan Street, where the refugees mostly worshipped, had been hit. The milkman was rattling off a string of streets, Lower Sloane Street, Lacland Place, Riley Street, and St Stephen's Hospital had all been hit. There were UXBs all over the place – Sydney Street, Tetcott Road, and Shadburn Street – and it was a job to find a way anywhere, so many streets were barricaded off. He had just started telling us about the pub, the Six Bells in the King's Road, being hit when the baker, who had arrived and was listening, cut in with, 'That was the night before last.' 'Excuse me,' said the milkman politely, 'but it went last night – it was all right yesterday when I went by on me rounds.' 'It was the night before last,' insisted the baker. 'Our bakery is only a few houses down – don't you think we heard the bloody bomb in the bakery?'

They would not leave it alone and became very heated. I knew that the baker was right from the Control Room – the Six Bells had been hit by an HE two nights ago, but it was impossible to get a word in, they were shouting so angrily at one another – *all about a bomb*. It was extraordinary how heated people became about times and dates of bombs. It had been another bad night – that was certain. In the middle of this violent argument the telephone rang. It was the hospital. Catherine had a daughter. She was fairly well – they were not too satisfied. I could come and see her if I wished. I was thankful for the news that she was safe – I had heard from Control that Kensington had had a very bad night and the milkman said that the hospital had been hit. Mrs Freeth was terribly upset until the baker assured her that the milkman was a ghoul who liked to exaggerate every incident and add on a few of his own. But he had been right about the hospital.

When I got there I found Catherine in a different ward. The one she had been in had been damaged. She had only just been brought back from the Labour Ward after the baby was born when the bomb had fallen. She had been placed under the bed as so much glass and plaster was flying about. She was quite conscious for they had not given her an anaesthetic – but she was terribly exhausted. She had not cared when she heard the bomb fall and the explosion which followed. There had been a lot of mess and dirt; the nurses were tired and the patients seemed tense and strained. I did not like the look of Catherine – or her apathetic attitude towards the baby. 'She doesn't want to look at it – she isn't interested,' said the Sister. I thought she was too ill to care – and I told Sister a little of what she had been through. 'She had a pretty awful time last night,' she said. 'The bomb fell just as she was being brought back after the birth.'

I was shown the baby – she was exquisitely pretty. Most new-born infants are only beautiful to the mother, but Catherine's baby was lovely – like a curled-up rose. 'She is lovely,' I said enthusiastically as I held her close to Catherine. 'I should love one like her – she's adorable.'

'You can have her,' said Catherine tersely, turning her face away from the child.

In the evening when I returned again she was feverish, with brilliant eyes and flushed cheeks. She was still refusing to nurse or even touch the child. I thought she was ill. She had some fever, they admitted. Her hands were dry and burning hot as she clutched mine and she seemed slightly delirious in her talk. I could not stay longer as I was on duty and had a number of refugees to attend to. I promised to return the following evening and bring her several things which she wanted.

Next evening she had puerperal fever and was being moved to an isolation hospital.

I do not enjoy riding in ambulances. They have a curiously shut-in air as if they are a cage. I cannot imagine why they have to be so completely devoid of windows. It was unpleasant to feel that I could not see what was going on – to ride in darkness through the noisy violent night was quite terrifying because it was obvious that Catherine was alarmingly ill. She was wildly delirious, calling for her fiancé – not lovingly as if she needed him, but reviling him for what she had suffered. It was horrible, because in consciousness not one word of complaint had passed her lips. She had accepted her lot and indeed said bluntly that she had played her part in it – that she had not been seduced but had been as willing as her fiancé. It was this engaging frankness which I liked so much in her. It would have been easy for her to have played the part of the innocent maiden seduced against her will, for she had been only eighteen when it had happened, but no, she insisted, she knew quite well what she was doing – what she did not know was that there would be any difficulty in getting married, that the Germans were going to invade Belgium.

I thought about this now as I drove with her, wrapped in blankets in the ambulance through the black noisy night, right across London, with her baby in my arms. When we drew up at the fever hospital and were directed through a garden to an annexe I saw with dismay that it was only a one-story building like an army hut – and offered little protection from the bombing. But we were there – and Catherine was unloaded and the stretcher taken in. She would not let go of my hands and I had to unclasp her fingers when the nurses came to take her. And now she cried out in despair – she was quite oblivious to what was going on. She was living in some terrible world in which she felt only the need to cling hard to someone she knew. I had been nursing the baby all the way and it was with reluctance that I handed over the tiny bundle of life to the nurses, who exclaimed with delight at it.

For the next two weeks Catherine was desperately ill and I spent my time between the FAP and her bedside, neglecting the other refugees except for their English lesson. They resented it, and remarks about the wages of sin being death were frequent – as were comments on the doubtful moral attitude of the British. Suzanne was amused by this and told me about Snow White and the Seven Dwarfs. Snow White was a French woman who had taken into her home seven ARP wardens whom she called *Les Arpes*– hence her nickname. She had justified their being there by saying that she helped their morale by her comforts – whether or not she helped their *morals*, as Suzanne laughingly said, was another matter. Another pretty French refugee had such an admiration for the RAF who looked after Blossom, the balloon in Burton Court, that nothing seemed able to prevent her climbing through the barbed wire to offer her comforts, as she called her personal charms, to the heroes. Complaints were made to Suzanne about this. It was difficult to deal with, but her delightful sense of humour combined with her own Gallic common sense made Suzanne's approach to such a problem a marvel of diplomacy. Whenever I had any such worries I invariably confided them to her.

One evening, at the end of a week, I thought that Catherine recognized me again. She was paler and quieter. 'Am I dying?' she asked me. 'Of course not, you're getting better,' I said. 'I don't care one way or the other,' she said. 'If I die will you take the baby – she is to be named after you anyway. The priest was here last night – but I was too tired to talk to him – he said the baby must be baptized and that I should make my confession – but I didn't want to – and Sister sent him away.'

'Don't think about anything but getting better,' I told her.

But the Blitz was so bad that evening that I began to wonder if any of us would be alive in the morning. The patients were terrified, and Sister, fearing a panic, was entertaining them. She and two nurses, with bed-pans on their heads and gas-masks on their faces, marched up and down the ward pretending to be air raid wardens. Sister was a little shrimp of a woman but she had the courage of a lioness and in a few minutes she had the panic averted and the patients all laughing. 'Come and do a turn while we take a breather,' she begged me. A huge bomb shook the building and some glass clattered down. 'Come on,' called Sister entreatingly. 'All I can do are cartwheels – and Russian dancing,' I said, and tucking up my Red Cross dress into my belt I took the floor and did cart-wheels round the ward while Sister and the two nurses provided the music by singing and banging on the bed-pans. Hearing the patients laughing heartily was lovely, and when doing cartwheels it is quite impossible to think of anything else. When the applause had died down the planes had passed over and were giving some other part of London their attention. 'You'd better go while it's quieter,' whispered Sister. I looked at Catherine – she was asleep. She looked like a small tired girl with her hair in two pigtails. The baby was asleep in a cot at the foot of the bed.

I went back by the Underground. At each station the plat-forms were massed with sleepers – just like the men at Dover after Dunkirk. I had to change at Piccadilly – there was a narrow piece of platform for the passengers marked with white lines. The stench was frightful, urine and excrement mixed with strong carbolic, sweat, and dirty, unwashed humanity. I spoke to the nurses on duty there and admired their stamina. I don't think I could have stuck out even one long night in that atmosphere. But they, fresh and trim, alert and calm, were there attending to the many aches and pains of that mass of humanity. We hated being sent as shelter nurses from the FAP and the smaller shelters in our district were not to be compared in stench and discomfort with the Underground ones. These girls did it regularly; they were heroines indeed.

Returning one night from one of these visits to Catherine, when she was still desperately ill, I took a short cut through a side street from the hospital. There was no transport and walking was the only way of getting back to Chelsea. There was the usual raid on, and it had been very noisy, but now it was quieter and only occasional bursts of gun-fire shook the silence of the streets. Passing a gap in a terrace I saw a little group of people bending over what seemed to be a hole in what had been the basement of a house but which now appeared to be filled in with debris. A car stood in the road with the notice 'doctor' on it. It was dark, but I could see that there were three men bending over the hole and one woman. The woman wore nurse's uniform.

As I hurried by she turned, said something to the others, then called to me, 'Nurse!' I went over. The man bending over the hole straightened up, but I could not look at him because of the appalling sound coming from the hole. Someone was in mortal anguish down there. The woman in nurse's uniform, who was tall and very largely built, said sharply to me, 'What are your hip measurements?' I said, above the horrible moaning from the hole, 'Thirty-four inches.' One of the men took a piece of stick and measured it across my shoulders, then across my hips, and then put it across the hole. 'Easy – an inch to spare each side,' he said.

'Will you let us lower you down there to help that man trapped and in great pain?' he asked. 'We're all too large for the hole – and we daren't widen it until the Heavy Rescue Squad come to shore it all up.'

'What must I do?' I asked fearfully, for I was tired already, and the black hole was not inviting.

'Just do as you're told, that's all,' said the large nurse. 'All right,' I agreed.

'Take off your coat,' said the doctor. I took it off. 'And your dress,' he said. 'It's too dangerous – the folds may catch in the debris and bring the whole thing down – better without it.' I took off the dress. 'Fine,' he said shortly when I stood in the 'black-outs', as we called the closed black panties which most of us wore with uniform. 'It'll have to be head first. We'll hold your thighs. Go down first with this torch and see if it's possible to give a morphia injection or not – I doubt it. Ready?' 'Yes,' I said faintly for I was terrified. 'Better hold the torch in your mouth, and keep your arms tight to your sides,' he said. 'Can you grip the torch with your teeth?' I nodded – it was as if I was having a nightmare from which I would soon waken. 'Ready?' Two wardens gripped me by the thighs, swung me up and lowered me down over the hole. 'Keep your body absolutely rigid,' said the doctor. 'Don't be afraid – we'll hold you safe,' said the large woman. 'I ought to be doing this – but I'm too big.'

The sound coming from the hole was unnerving me – it was like an animal in a trap. I had once heard a long screaming like rabbits in traps from children with meningitis in India, but this was worse – almost inhuman in its agony. The torch showed me that the debris lay over both arms and that the chest of the man trapped there was crushed into a bloody mess – great beams lay across the lower part of his body – and his face was so injured that it was difficult to distinguish the mouth from the rest of it – it all seemed one great gaping red mess.

The blood had rushed to my head from being upside down. Fortunately I had done some acrobatic dancing and had been held in this manner previous to being whirled round in the dance, so that keeping my body stiff was not too much of a strain, but the stench of blood and mess down there caught the pit of my stomach and I was afraid of vomiting and dropping the precious torch. There was plenty of room for my arms at the bottom of the hole so I took the torch cautiously from my teeth and began trying to soothe the remains of what had once been a man. He could still hear, for after I had repeated several times the formula we had been told to use to reassure trapped casualties, 'Try to keep calm – we're working to get you out. You'll soon be all right... Very soon now', the horrible screaming stopped, but the gap which had once been a mouth was trying to say something...it was impossible to catch what it was... so unintelligible were the sounds. 'Pull me up,' I called, and put the torch back in my mouth and kept my arms rigidly to my sides as they hauled me up. On my feet I felt violent nausea and vomited again and again. They stood back, and the doctor handed me a huge handkerchief. 'All right?' he asked when it was over. I was deeply ashamed, apologized, and told him what I had seen. 'Have to be chloroform,' he said shortly. 'Have you seen it given on a pad?' I nodded. He took the bottle with a dropper from his case and a cotton mask. 'I'll hold it in my mouth,' I said. 'When I'm down, if someone shines the torch down I'll be able to see.' The terrible screaming had started again down there. All I felt now was the urgency to stop it. 'How many drops?' I asked. 'All of this,' he said grimly, 'and hold it over the face as near to the nostrils as you can judge. Try and keep yourself from inhaling it – be as quick as you can.'

I took the pad and the small bottle in my mouth. The big nurse lay down on her stomach by the hole – I thought it was asking for trouble for the whole structure was perilous and one false move could bring the whole pile down on to the trapped man and extinguish what small flicker of life remained there. But she did it very cautiously and carefully, so that she could shine a torch down for me. 'Ready?' asked the two tough-looking men in overalls. I nodded. They gripped my thighs and swung me upside down and lowered me again into blackness.

'I'm back again, you see,' I said to the terrible anguished thing down there. 'The doctor has given me something to help the pain – they'll soon be here now to get you out.' I was dropping the chloroform on to the pad now. 'Breathe deeply – can you?' A sound as from an animal – a grunt – came from the thing which had been

a face. I held the pad firmly over him. 'Breathe deeply...deeply...
deeply...' There was a small convulsive movement of revulsion...
another fainter one – and then the sounds stopped. All was quiet.
The chloroform was affecting me, and it was all I could do to call
'Ready!' and they hauled me up. I disgraced myself by violently
vomiting again and again – this time intensified by the chloroform
and the stench of blood, for there were other bodies down there
– I had seen the pieces. The big nurse held my head, and hastily
pulled my dress back on me and then buttoned me into my coat. 'All
right?' asked the doctor, taking my wrist professionally. 'Breathe
deeply yourself now – go on, several big deep breaths.' I recovered
quickly, and said I'd be getting along – it was very late.

'I'd drive you home,' he said, 'but we're wanted elsewhere. That'll
keep that poor fellow quiet until the rescue squad arrive to take over
so that I can get down myself. Thank you, nurse. You did very well.'
All I wanted was to get away – I was going to be sick again. 'Run
along while it's quiet,' advised one of the wardens. I went – but I
did not run – all the way back to Chelsea I vomited at intervals. Mrs
Freeth, bless her, had waited up for me. She took one look at my face
and fetched the brandy. 'No,' I said when the smell of it reached me.
'No. A cup of tea.' 'I've got that – I was going to give you the brandy
first. How's Catherine?' she asked anxiously. 'Not bad news, is it?'
'*Catherine?* She's the same – no change,' I said. An awful shivering
had taken hold of me – and nothing could stop it. I had never seen
anything like that horror in the hole. Mrs Freeth's comment on this
episode was short and terse and was confined to my having removed
my dress. She thought the man could have waited a bit longer – but
she had not heard his screaming as we had.

I lay in bed and I thought of all those times we VADs had been
dropped into holes for the rescue men to practise on us – and I
thought of the times my sister and I had had a craze for acrobatic
dancing and learned to be held upside down by the thighs or ankles.
Who would have thought that such things would ever have been so
useful? Any more than that my knowledge of Dutch and Flemish
would have stood me in such good stead.

The guns were suddenly barking in short sharp bursts again.
Something crashed down very near. 'They're chasing them off
now – they always make that noise when it's nearly over,' called
the calm, comfortable voice of Mrs Freeth, who was sleeping in the
kitchen across the hall. 'You know what?' I called back. 'You would

have done for that job – you're even smaller than I am – you're tiny.' 'Not with my dress off – and all,' said Mrs Freeth firmly. We said good-night. I clutched Vicki's warm body to me and slept.

On the day Catherine was to come out of hospital Mrs Freeth and Madame R scrubbed, swept, and polished her room, we put flowers in it, they lit the fire in the open grate, and we unpacked the great parcel of clothes which had come for her baby from Canada; for Margerie Scott had written about Catherine and those generous people had sent everything she could possibly need for the baby. One of the local residents had given a lovely cradle and this was waiting ready in the room.

It was difficult to get transport of any kind – the petrol restrictions were so stringent that taxis were few and ambulances could only be used for the really sick and injured. Catherine was convalescent – but the hospital was a long way from Chelsea and she was very weak after the fever. I was hoping to get a taxi because there was the baby as well, but I could not find one anywhere near the hospital. Sister telephoned several places for me but it was useless.

While we were waiting in the hospital one of the doctors came in. 'Would you mind riding with a mental case?' he asked me. 'She'll be quite quiet – and there'll be room for you if you wouldn't mind taking her first. The ambulance can go on with your patient.'

I asked where she was to be taken. It was to a small nursing home quite near us. She was to stay there until her family decided where she was to be sent. Sister saw that I was rather dubious. 'She's all right – you needn't be alarmed,' she said. 'She's quite quiet, but we can't keep her here because she's a mental case. We need her bed.'

And so Catherine, the baby, and I rode with the mental case. She was a young woman – and must have been pretty when in normal health. Now she was not only pale and emaciated but she had a tic on her face even when apparently unconscious. She was on a stretcher and tied down. I viewed this with some apprehension but was assured that it was only so that she should not fall – she was not violent. Nevertheless it was an uncomfortable journey for it was late afternoon and there was a day-light raid. The sirens howling had a startling effect on the mental patient. She began howling too – in a low long drawn-out wail which was horrible. Catherine's baby began to cry too and the noise of all these wailings was so extraordinary that Catherine and I burst into helpless giggling. The ambulance stopped and the driver came round and opened the door. 'What d'yer like to do?' he inquired, looking anxiously up at the sky. 'Them b—s are at their bloody game again. Shall I drop yer and the baby by a shelter?'

'And *her*?' I indicated the mental case. Surely we could not take her into a shelter on a stretcher. He shook his head. 'She can stay in th'ambulance. She don't know the difference.' 'She does,' I said. 'She's been wailing ever since the sirens started.' 'Oh well,' he said indifferently. 'Make yer mind up – I can't stay here. There's a shelter over there...' Catherine had clutched her baby tighter when the sirens started and to my question as to whether or not we should get out and take shelter she said firmly, 'No. Please let's go on.' A warden came up and put his head in. 'Better get below,' he said. 'It's quite lively.'

I indicated the patient on the stretcher. 'We can't take her in a shelter,' I said.

'Why not, what's she got – plague?'

The driver tapped his head significantly. '*Loopy* – ought never to have got sent to us.' The warden looked puzzled, but only for a moment. 'You can draw the ambulance under those trees there,' he suggested, 'or under that bridge a few hundred feet on.' 'And have the bloody bridge on top of us? No, thanks – if the passengers agree we'll get moving. Okeydoke, Nurse?' 'Okeydoke, Mama?' Catherine blushed a bright pink at being addressed as Mama. Then she began laughing again as both the baby and the patient started howling. 'You do so at your own risk,' said the warden disapprovingly.

'What the hell am I to do then? With a loony and a new-born baby no shelter'll welcome us.' 'Oh, let's go!' I said impatiently. At the beginning of the Blitz all traffic had ceased when the sirens sounded – and passengers and driver went to shelter. Now that there were sirens all the time the traffic took little notice unless the police or wardens stopped them and ordered them off the road. 'Suits me,' said the driver. 'Don't make no difference to me. Drive this bleeding hearse whether it's raining cats and dogs or bombs – it's all the same ter me.' He slammed the door and the engine started up.

'I went to hospital in a raid – and I had the baby in a raid – now I come out in a raid –' said Catherine, beginning to giggle again. 'She ought to be named Raida.' She cuddled the child to her while I tried to soothe the young woman, who lay moaning as if she were suffering horribly.

When we reached the nursing home, which was quite near the King's Road, the patient did not appear to be expected. I wanted to get Catherine back as she was looking alarmingly white. At last a male attendant came out and he and the driver grumblingly carried the moaning one inside. 'Thank heavens she's gone,' he said, as he came out mopping his brow. 'Gave me the willies, that moaning did – worse than the sirens – they do 'ave a fixed time limit for 'owling.'

Mrs Freeth and Madame R were waiting for us in Catherine's room and made a great fuss of the baby. 'What about the night?' asked Madame R anxiously. We all go to the shelter – we can't leave her alone in the house.' It was quite obvious that Catherine couldn't sleep in a shelter, and it was already dusk. Madame R was perfectly willing to stay in the house with her but she knew that her husband would not allow it. I foresaw that for a few nights at least, until other arrangements could be made, I would have to sleep there with Catherine. Richard did not like this although he was awfully patient and understanding about our home being invaded at all hours of the day and night by refugees, wardens, and friends on shifts from the Control or the FAP. I had lived alone there until we married and it had been open house – it still was.

Now that it was bitterly cold at night Mrs Freeth and I always kept a great pot of soup on the stove. Tea was rationed – and not everyone drank coffee – but soup was popular. Anyone who dropped in – wardens, AFS, VADs, or refugees and friends – could always have soup, and Mrs Freeth's soup was extremely good. She shopped on her way to Cheyne Place very often and was a very clever manager.

Old Granny, who lived in Paradise Walk, got into the habit of dropping in every morning for her soup. Her husband went to Covent Garden and fetched vegetables in the early mornings in an old cart with the horse Beauty. We all called the old woman 'Granny', and she was a grandmother many times over. She did not know her age and had no idea where she had been born, and now that they were getting old and times becoming hard she was anxious to get an old-age pension; but for this a birth certificate had to be produced – and Granny had not got hers or her husband's.

She had a face which I can only describe as luminous – the pale skin had a transparency which was extraordinary, as had the eyes, which were as clear and had the blue-tinted whites of a young child. I liked old Granny. She had had a hard life – and if she was so set on a purpose as to appear perverse, almost arrogant, on the subject, it was understandable when one realized the odds against which she had battled all her life to bring up a large family. They had a man lodger – I think he was some kind of relative – and they lived over a kind of stable or garage in which the cart and Beauty were housed; but now that the Blitz was so bad the two old people slept with Beauty down in the stable. The horse was terrified of the Blitz and they slept one each side of her, holding her and patting her all night.

Granny had an ulcer on her leg and asked me if I could dress it for her. She would come to the kitchen every morning and I would bandage the leg, and then she would drink her soup or have a cup of tea and tell us all the news and all her troubles. The horse was very cold, she told me, and she had no coat for her. She felt that if Beauty had a covering she would feel less frightened of the bombs. When I gave her a thick double-breasted blue overcoat of Richard's which he seldom wore, for Beauty, she was delighted. That night when I went to visit her because her leg was particularly painful, I saw the two old people fast asleep, one each side of the horse, holding her legs, and draped over her was Richard's overcoat. There was something quite lovely in the scene. They used to leave the doors unlocked, as we were all supposed to do in the Blitz; and sometimes they left it slightly ajar. I had not the heart to wake Granny up to dress her leg and I stood there looking at this trio – and I went home and sketched what I had seen – I thought it so moving.

Richard was not very pleased about the coat. He did not wear it much but he had liked it. I could not ask for it back – so agreed to buy him a new one. This I did – but he is a very big man and the blue one had been specially made for him. He liked it better than the new one. Apparently Beauty only needed it at night for, when returning from night shifts, Richard had the tantalizing spectacle of seeing Grandpa huddled in the coat, in which, being a small man, he was almost lost, driving the naked Beauty to Covent Garden. He teased me about this for a long time – as he did about my passion for all animals. Mrs Freeth urged me to get it back and give them a blanket for Beauty – but Richard said he did not fancy it after Beauty had worn it as a nightshirt!

We had moved a divan bed from upstairs to the dining-room on the ground floor now that the Blitz had become a nightly occurrence, and had put two camp beds in the kitchen, which was a large room across the small hall. A mattress was on the floor in the hall for guests, who often had to stay the night when the Blitz was too noisy for them to find transport. The dining-room had a large and very charming bay window looking on to the pavement of the Royal Hospital Road and we used to eat at a small table in this window when we were alone, but when we had guests we had to eat in the huge studio upstairs. There was only a short, easy flight of stairs to the studio. Mrs Freeth would serve dinner up there absolutely unperturbed by any amount of plaster which fell whenever there was a bomb nearby. Not all our guests enjoyed this, and on several occasions their appetites were not very large, but the sight of tiny Mrs Freeth, absolutely immaculately turned out in a diminutive lace apron serving them as calmly and efficiently as if there was nothing happening at all, forced them to hide their fears and conform to her rigid idea of what was what. I admired her enormously. Once when one of her twin sons was sleeping in the kitchen with her and the bombs were appallingly loud and frequent the boy complained a little. I heard his mother say, 'What's the matter with you? Nothing's hit you – time enough to holler when it does!' Her husband had been in the Grenadier Guards and was a night-watchman – he was a fine man of whom Richard thought a great deal and was now doing a dangerous, lonely task guarding a large city building all through the bombing, with no word of complaint or sign of fear. The twins were fifteen at this time, sturdy boys and splendidly brought up. I don't think I could have got through those winter months of the Blitz without Mrs Freeth. I was alone so much – as she was – and together we could face far more than we could separately.

CHAPTER FIFTEEN

OUR NEIGHBOUR at No. 1, Swan Walk, the oldest house in Chelsea, was David Fyffe, whom Richard had known in India. He was in the Ministry of Information and had not been long home from Bombay. We were fascinated by the house which he had been lent; it was said to have a strange history and had an underground passage leading to the Royal Hospital. David told us that there was supposed to be another underground passage from it to a subterranean tunnel under the Thames and that long ago the house had been used for escapes. It had an ageless, matured, much lived-in feeling and could have been a house of ghosts – although David had never seen any he was always hoping. Its beautiful panelling was of an earlier date than that in the Royal Hospital and the house stood back from Swan Walk in a paved garden. It could have had no prouder occupant than David, who loved showing its beauties and extolling them. The staircases were the original ones – twisted and tortuous, even dangerous – but one could imagine no others in such a house, and we descended one to the room in the basement where he slept in the Blitz.

Since he and Richard had met again after returning from India, David had been dropping in to us for meals sometimes. He seemed lonely.

On the morning of November 1st he telephoned and asked us to come in that evening for a drink with him as he had something special to tell us. Over sherry in the gracious, elegant little dining-room he told us how, the previous day, he had been examined by two well-known specialists and passed as a first-class life for an insurance policy. He had, we knew, returned from India worried about his health. He suffered from terrible headaches and frequently felt giddy, and he had an obsession that he was suffering from a tumour of the brain. He was a bachelor of thirty-seven, a very sensitive, charming person. We liked him immensely and were delighted when he confided to us that there was a girl of whom he was very fond and whom he had for some time wanted to marry. He had hesitated because of this fear of his about the tumour, but now that the two entirely independent specialists had convinced him that his fears were groundless he was going to propose to her. Her name was Rosemary, he told us, and in a few days or so he hoped to introduce her to us as his fiancée.

We drank to his future happiness and hoped that she would accept him. He seemed fairly sure about this, but he was a modest man, in spite of his excellent brain, and he said that Rosemary – Rosie, as he called her – was a very pretty, charming, and capable girl, and he was aware that a great many men must feel the same way as he did about her. We asked him back to dinner with us – but he said he was feeling very tired as he hadn't been sleeping well, so we left him at about 7.40 p.m.

I was due at the FAP on night-shift, and Mrs Freeth had gone home. When her husband had a night off from his night-watchman duties she usually went home. I changed into uniform quickly. The sirens had gone early and the usual noise had started. One tremendous thud shook the whole house – so that even Vicki pricked up her ears and looked startled. Plaster fell from the ceiling and several things fell down in the studio above. I ran up and saw that two decorative plates had fallen and a picture had come down from the wall but the Green Cat was still erect and aloof in the window. Plaster was thick all over the studio floor like snowflakes. The bomb must have been very near. I listened, but could hear none of the activity which usually followed such a thud. The guns were barking noisily against the usual droning of the planes, but I could detect no ambulance bells, none of the excited shouts of wardens who often hailed and guided the fire and ambulance and rescue Services with 'Here ... over here...right...left,' as the case might be.

I went out and looked down the Royal Hospital Road but beyond the fact that the sky behind Cheyne Place seemed full of a haze which I took to be the first November fog, I could see nothing unusual and not a soul was about. We had scarcely begun our meal when the telephone rang loudly. I picked up the receiver. It was the young valet who looked after David and who had let us both out of the house not more than forty minutes previously. His voice was frantic. 'Will you please come at once – I think my master's dead,' he said. I asked him to repeat it, and handed the receiver to Richard. I heard Richard ask him what had happened and he repeated, 'My master is dead...*please* come over, *please*.'

We went without further questioning. I only stopped to throw my nurse's cloak over my dress and apron. The valet – he was only a youth awaiting his call-up – met us at the door. 'Downstairs,' he said. He could scarcely speak, and was terribly pale, but his control was remarkable. He took us into the room which David had shown us less than an hour previously as the place where he now slept during the Blitz.

David lay on the bed in his pyjamas. He was a curious livid colour and his eyeballs were turned up. 'He *is* dead,' said the boy, breaking down now. By the bedside was a glass and a bottle containing some tablets and my first thought was that he had taken some drug and was in a coma. I felt for a pulse but could find none in the wrist. His body was rather cold, especially his feet, but there seemed to me to be a faint pulse in the neck.

I said to the valet, 'What happened after we left, tell us quickly.' 'My master said he felt sleepy,' he said. 'He said he didn't want any food and that he would go and lie down for a bit. He undressed and got into bed. He asked me to bring a glass of water. While I was getting it that great bomb fell and the house shook. As I came from the kitchen with the water I heard a funny noise – a sort of gurgling groan – and I came in and found my master like this.'

'Who is his doctor?' I asked quickly. He told me and went up at our request to telephone him. He came down almost at once to say that the doctor declined to come as the Blitz was so bad. We telephoned two more doctors – neither could come. I was frantic – I felt that David might be saved by an injection or some urgent treatment. I could still discern a faint pulse and was trying to keep him warm. Richard shook his head. 'I don't think it's any good,' he said. I telephoned Dr Thompson at St Luke's. 'Get an ambulance and bring him here,' he said. *An ambulance – in this Blitz.* How was I to get one when we could not even get a doctor? I telephoned the FAP and explained what had happened. The FAP said that it was difficult but they would send a stretcher-party as soon as they could.

They came after what seemed an age. Getting the stretcher down the twisting narrow stairs was bad enough, and it was a grim party of men who stood by the bed. The leader was a man I didn't know, although I knew two of the other men. He looked at David and said, 'This man looks dead – we don't take corpses – we've got our work cut out to take the injured.' He looked at me challengingly. I said, 'I think he's alive – I'm not a doctor, how can I know? – but there *is* a pulse...' But he did not want to take him, and said, 'Will you state, *as a nurse*, that he is not dead?'

Except for the woman at the Samaritan with whom I had stayed until her death I had only seen violent deaths and I hesitated. Richard was about to intervene but the stretcher-party leader said, 'No, it's a nurse's opinion we want. Do you say that this man is alive?' and he stared challengingly at me. 'Yes,' I said stoutly. 'He *is* alive – but if you don't hurry he will die before we can reach the hospital.' 'Very well then,' said the leader. 'On *your* responsibility.' Then began an agonizing journey up the twisting stairs, which were never made for a coffin or a stretcher carried by stalwart men. It took an endless time to get the stretcher-party up. Richard and I were guiding them – and seeing David's body at all angles as they turned, raised and lowered, was macabre, but at last we were outside where the ambulance waited. It was a terrible night, with sudden violent rain and wind. The noise from the barrage and the bombs seemed intensified as the wind hurled the sounds at us as it rushed up Swan Walk from the Thames. The stretcher-party leader was morose – he was angry about the whole thing, and was muttering about *stiffs* and wasting his time. The young valet undertook to go in the ambulance with his master to the hospital. I said I would report to the FAP and follow on to see the doctor.

Richard had to go on fire-watching duty. I telephoned the FAP that I might be late because of David and ran off. It was dark and wet and I thought I would take a quick cut through Shawfield Street to the King's Road. As I hurried through the rain with my tin hat on, it seemed to me that the curious cloud of mist or fog which I had noticed behind the Royal Hospital Road was as thick as a blanket – so thick and dark that it was difficult to see. But how could it be fog with all this wind and rain? I was carrying a masked torch such as we all carried in the black-out. It was so small a light that it revealed little, but I saw what the cloud was – it was dust, a great cloud of dust which was still rising in spite of the rain – rising from what appeared to be a great gap in Shawfield Street where a row of tall houses had stood. It was too dark to see properly, but I had seen enough to be too shocked to move, and I collided violently with someone whom I found was a half-dressed terrified woman. For a moment I was speechless, all thought of David driven out of my head. By the light of my torch I saw that the woman and I were standing on the edge of a vast crater – it loomed on every side seemingly never-ending – and the houses which had stood on that piece of ground had simply vanished! 'There are people buried there,' the woman cried, clutching at my arm. 'Come and help me get them out. The bomb fell some time ago – and no one's come yet!' She was pointing to some mounds beyond the crater. I stumbled over to the heap with the horrible fear that there might be another such crater – it was too dark to see properly. Just then a woman warden appeared before us. 'It's no use,' she said. 'You can't do anything – better to wait for the experts, they're on their way.' 'Taking their time,' said the woman violently. *'Listen to them.'*

And I could hear voices now – it was horrible... voices coming from the mounds of the ruined houses, from people entombed like the dead but fighting to get out. 'They're in the basement,' went on the half-dressed woman. 'They mostly sleep in the basement but I don't – I was just undressing in my own room when it come – and I found myself in the street.' With her as guide I went over to the mound from which the voices were coming...'Help...help...' they were crying, a thin distraught frantic wail. 'It's all right...they're coming...it's all right...they'll get you out. Keep calm...' I cried again and again, as close to where the wails were coming from as I could judge. It was horrible standing there listening to them and not being able to help and suddenly I felt frantic and started grabbling and scratching at the debris. 'Don't do that,' called the woman warden. 'It's dangerous...wait...they're coming now.' And almost at once there was sudden violent activity in the dead, ravaged street; the wails were drowned in the jarring of brakes, the screeching of engines, and sudden short sharp commands. In the thick evil-smelling blackness it was an eerie and ghastly sight to see all the preparations being made, the paraphernalia unloaded. Did any of us realize how terribly dangerous and treacherous it was to have to excavate, shore up, and tunnel in such complete blackness for buried bodies – living or dead? Did we appreciate it until we saw it? I know that I had not until I watched the tunnelling for Mildred Castillo and that had been mostly in day-light.

It was almost impossible to recognize the individual ARP personnel and for them to recognize one another in the oblique pin-pointed rays of light from masked torches – only triangles and sharp cubist squares were illuminated – and by the angle of a nose, the quirk of an eyebrow, the set of a mouth the owners of the faces were identified. Overhead the searchlights made beautiful, intricate patterns as they tracked the raiders and pinned them in their beams, and all the time the nauseous drone of the raiding planes and the sharp bark of the ack-ack guns made a background against which the sharp terse orders of George Evans, the Incident Officer, were shouted. It was a terrifying spectacle and none of the violent sound-accompaniment drowned for me those voices still wailing from the ruins, and I called again, 'It's all right – they're here. They're here. They'll get you out.' The woman warden was now trying to soothe them. But their cries were beyond soothing. They could hear the guns and the bombs coming down – one could hear it in their frantic voices.

I started digging again with the half-dressed woman but the warden stopped us. 'I've tried that – it's hopeless. Better to wait for the experts.' *Better to wait!…better to wait!* The half-dressed woman burst into loud hysterical weeping. I pulled her nearer to me. 'Where's your home?' I asked. She pointed to a heap next to the one with the voices in it. 'Have you anyone in there?' I asked her. She shook her head. 'My mother is away – went yesterday,' she said, 'but all those in there…' and she began crying again. I saw that she was bleeding from her arms. I felt frantic…they were being as quick as they could under appalling difficulties but to be buried in that heap of bricks and debris with the rain now pouring down making it heavier and heavier. Oh God, I thought, let them be quick and get them out or let them die quickly.

The Incident Officer was taking charge now, and there were more and more men appearing on the scene. He shone a torch on me. 'Get under cover. You shouldn't be here,' he said, and he told the weeping woman with me to report to a warden so that she could be taken to the FAP. One of the heavy rescue men was a friend of mine – the one I called Tapper because he was an expert on tunnelling and shoring up and had told me a lot about it. 'Tap it gently first before you start anything,' he had said. 'Tap it – like this. Listen to the sound – if it's holler you can tell – and you'll know if it's holler or solid muck you've got to get through,' and he had tapped in various places in the ruins on which he was working and asked me to tell him which it was – solid or hollow. But I had not his skilled, highly developed technical sense of sound – it all sounded the same to me. 'Never do anything without testing first. Don't go scrabbling at it like your sausage-dog digging for a bone,' was another of his maxims. 'Make up yer mind where ye're going to tunnel and test it all the way – *like this…*'

I saw Tapper now, grim and business-like, getting ready to work. 'Are you on duty? If not get under cover,' shouted a warden to me as a bomb whistled down near us. I looked round for the woman who had been with me. She had vanished. The voices were still calling from the mounds – and there were others now from other places impossible to locate in the darkness and noise. *And suddenly I remembered David.* What was I doing standing fascinated by the grim scene and distracted by the sounds? *David – he might be dead by now.* I turned sharply. 'Take care – there are holes and it's dangerous everywhere,' shouted a warden. But I had started picking my way across the heaps and pits, stumbling all the way. My stomach felt full of butterflies again – my breath was short, and it hurt as I stumbled and panted up what had once been Shawfield Street to the King's Road. I could see that there were many fires – the glare in the sky showed that – and things were rattling down, crashing masonry, bits of shell-caps, tiles dislodged, and chimney stacks. In the King's Road a warden stopped me. 'Are you on duty?' I nodded and ran on to the hospital.

I was not long after the ambulance – it had had to make several detours. There were other casualties arriving as I hurried in, bomb casualties. I lent a hand to the nurses while Dr Thompson made a preliminary examination of David, who had died soon after arrival at the hospital. He said it appeared as if he had a tumour of the brain. This was startling after David's fears and the happenings of the day. There would have to be a post-mortem, he said. I told him all I could, the valet had already told all he knew. I asked if it would have made any difference if we could have got help immediately and he said that no opinion could be given until the cause of death was known.

I went back by Smith Street as Shawfield Street was now barricaded off and I felt too exhausted to argue with wardens and police. They would let me through because of my uniform but I would not be allowed to help. I was supposed to be at the FAP. It seemed incredible that David was dead – when only a short while ago we had been drinking to his future marriage.

At the FAP they were busy – there were several casualties, including the woman with bleeding arms. I was very dirty from scrabbling in the debris and when I took off my cloak my apron was stained from helping at St Luke's. I hoped Sister-in-charge wouldn't notice it as I scrubbed my hands and took my place with the others who were attending to casualties. As Richard was on fire-watching neither of us would have been at home had the valet accepted our offer of a bed for the night. Kathleen was sleeping in the basement of her little shop – she had made a very comfortable shelter there, and sometimes all three of them slept there when the Blitz was very bad. It *was* a bad night – the All Clear did not go until five o'clock. Nine houses had been totally demolished in Shawfield Street and about twenty others were so badly damaged that they would have to be pulled down – they did not know the number of casualties.

After coming off duty from the FAP and having a cold bath (there being no gas again) and some coffee I went to see how the refugees had stood the night. The big bomb which had devastated Shawfield Street was very close to their shelter in Tedworth Square. They were subdued and silent. They had heard – but they had not seen. Shawfield Street was barricaded off and guarded still. But news travels – they all knew far more about the casualties, the deaths, those still buried, than any of the wardens did. 'Are they still digging?' they asked. They were still digging – and they continued all that day and on into the night. It rained most of the day and the mess was awful. When the sirens wailed again at 6.20 p.m. they were still digging and the trapped inhabitants were able to hear not only their rescuers still working but also the warning of the commencement of another night of bombs. It made them frantic so that no amount of assurance that they would soon be out could calm them.

A policeman called during the morning to ask me for an account of what had happened at David's the previous evening. He explained that this cursory police investigation was now used when possible in place of an inquest. I told him all I could and he said he would come back in the evening and see Richard, who was at the Ministry. David had died from a coronary thrombosis – there was no tumour of the brain. The doctor thought it possible that the tremendous thud of the Shawfield Street bomb which had shaken the house caused the heart attack which had killed him. Yet some condition must have been present when he had seen those two specialists the previous day? The doctor said, no, not necessarily, it could have been caused solely by the shock. But it was difficult to understand this – David was a young man and it seemed monstrous to think that he was dead. Dr Thompson assured me again and again that

I had done all I could – that nothing would have helped. It was a strange and in many ways unsatisfactory business and, combined with the horror of Shawfield Street, was a nightmare which was so engraved on my memory that I can relive every minute of it now.

George Evans and the whole of Post Don did magnificent work that night. The bomb was Chelsea's biggest yet and it had been difficult to locate quickly. The night had been so black, as impenetrable as thick velvet. The crater made by the bomb was so enormous that several buses could have parked in it. The wonderful accuracy of the records of residents and their whereabouts every night, checked and kept up to date every day by the wardens, was never better demonstrated than in the Shawfield Street tragedy. When all the bodies had been retrieved, and all the injured dealt with, there was a Mrs Lanham still missing. According to the wardens' records she should have been there, and so they dug until they found her. Some of the diggers were those who used to visit Mrs Freeth and me on their way home and so we were kept up to date with the search for Mrs Lanham.

The bomb had fallen on a Tuesday, November 1st, and it was not until a Saturday, December 7th, that Mrs Lanham's body was found. When it became certain that it was not in the debris they began digging in the crater, and they found that she had been sucked by the terrific blast right into – almost under – the crater. There was relief as well as satisfaction when her body was found. As with every Chelsea incident, every person had been accounted for – and the incident could be closed. In spite of the size of the bomb and the appalling damage to buildings, only twelve people were killed and six seriously injured and only six treated for light injuries at the FAP, and it was very reassuring to the apprehensive to think that all those tons of TNT had only killed twelve people.

November 3rd was our first bomb-free night since the Blitz had started. Shawfield Street was now open again but it was a terribly depressing spectacle. They were still digging there. There were very few residents now, almost all of them had evacuated. Nevertheless there was a wonderful spirit apparent in those few who remained. More than half its houses had now gone, for the HE bomb which had fallen on it was the heaviest we had experienced so far. We were getting a great many incendiary bombs and Hilda Reid told me how, when a fire-fighting party had to be formed for what remained of Shawfield Street, it consisted of a widow with two young boys of sixteen and seven, an elderly couple with a boy of sixteen, and an elderly invalid chef with an invalid daughter. These were the remaining residents.

When, one night, incendiaries fell, this fire party, helped by an unknown lady from Radnor Walk, found a fire bomb blazing in the annexe of an unoccupied house. They climbed over the garden wall with buckets and equipment and attacked the bomb, which had fallen on a dining-room table with the remains of the family's breakfast still on it. They put it out most effectively and turned to attack a second bomb which they had located in the ruins and found it had been extinguished. They were so indignant that they sent a deputation of formal complaint to Post K that the Town Hall be asked to do something 'about people from another street without even badges, and without invitation, coming and extinguishing bomb No 2 which they themselves had been perfectly capable of dealing with.'

A lady living in the same street whose family was connected with the War Office lamented bitterly that she had missed the Fire Blitz. She had heard the people laughing and talking in the street and thought it was those girls with the Canadians; and subsequently discovered that it was the people with their bombs!

On this night Richard and I had a wonderful time. He belonged to a fire-fighting party for our part of the street and incendiaries were falling everywhere. They were small and pretty, like fireflies coming down, and the sky looked fantastically beautiful. They were easy to extinguish with sand or a stirrup pump provided they were tackled immediately. We put out quite a number and were joined by Anne and Cecil, who enjoyed it as thoroughly as we did. In Tite Street a fire had started in an unoccupied house. We could see through the windows that the front room was blazing and the furniture and carpet alight. There was no time to find the warden who might have the keys to the house, so Richard picked up a brick from the gutter and hurled it through a window of the room. I followed suit with another, smashing the glass, so that it was possible to climb in from the area steps. It was such a relief to hurl those bricks, it released some of the anger which we all felt against the murderous raids. We were climbing in when Major Harding Newman came along and proceeded to smash his way into a house farther up the street.

The incendiaries fell in a peculiar way – it was impossible to see whence they had come! Suddenly they were all there. They were quite small – about eighteen inches long – and were made of thermite, Richard told me. They were in magnesium alloy containers, and weighed very little, but the height from which they were dropped gave them sufficient momentum to penetrate roofs and slates and they ignited on impact. They fell with little plops, rather as insects fell in India when coming in contact with the lamps – they reminded me of that. They were quite easy to extinguish with sand or smother with anything as one did an ordinary fire. Mrs Freeth picked them up with a pair of coal tongs and dropped them triumphantly into the coal bucket where they burned themselves out. In the road and on the pavements they burned harmlessly. A plane could carry thousands of them – and apparently did.

A letter from my mother in Plymouth described one of the terrible fire raids there. From her windows she had a very good view of the distant town and docks. 'It was the most beautiful sight I have seen for a very long time; the sky was alight with dancing lights and they had a blueish green shimmer like a firefly – then a wonderful bright crimson. They came down in thousands – truly like "fire from Heaven" – and everywhere I could hear laughter and shouting as people put them out. While I was watching one came right through the roof of the kitchen and started to blaze on the floor. I picked it up with the tongs and hurled it into the garden where it burned harmlessly on the grass. Another landed on the tiles of the front porch and I reached it with a broom handle and managed to push it over the porch on to the gravel path where it could harm nothing. It was so exciting! and the rain of fireworks was kept up for hours. I stayed up all night in case any more came but they seemed to be dropping them in the direction of the town.'

I thought this was not bad for my lame mother who was past sixty.

The nightly ordeal went on, but the day raids were beginning to be less frequent now. Also, we began noticing that the Luftwaffe did not care for the very dark nights but began making their greatest attacks at the time of the full moon. Thus, each month, the whole ARP, as well as the public, consulted their diaries. When would the full moon fall? The wonderful intricate pattern of searchlights focusing on the raiders for the anti-aircraft guns was beginning to be feared as much as the formidable Spitfires who intercepted the raiders with increasing accuracy. Nevertheless, the strain was beginning to tell on a great many people. The wardens and fire-men slept in their posts, either by day or night according to their shifts. They slept in damp, often soaking wet dug-outs, on camp beds or hard cots – ready to jump up at a minute's notice. They battled with mud, blackness, wind and rain, and every form of discomfort, as did thousands of people in their Anderson shelters, often at the bottom of their gardens. In spite of this their posts were places of fun, warmth, and the intimacy which shared danger was bringing to everyone. There were many painters amongst them, and they used their brushes and skill to adorn the bleak ARP posts – Adrian Daintrey, Theyre Lee Elliott, Hans Tisdall, Norma Bull, Elliot Hodgkin, and Jo Oakman were only a few of them. Post K was already famous for its decorations by Adrian Daintrey. They all boasted artistic adornments and many of them gardens, cultivated by their inmates, which were not only useful but attractive. It seemed a pity that in the FAP wall decorations and the like were forbidden as being unhygienic. We had camp beds provided with rugs. Our quarters were always immaculately scrubbed and polished – no matter how many casualties we had had in – and we had to be impeccably turned out. Our aprons were snow-white and starched stiffly, as were the muslin squares tied behind our heads in the butterfly bow. Sometimes a very important visitor would come to inspect the FAP and Sister-in-charge would inspect us all first! Quite often visitors came to the Control Centre while we were on duty there to watch us take and relay the messages. Now that the Blitz was an accepted fact we were always on our mettle and no relaxation was possible. The heaviest burden fell on those wardens who did a full-time job all day and then turned out for their warden's duties at night. I don't think anyone had foreseen that this would involve every night. Mr Graham Kerr was one of those who did long and dangerous beats, as was Nonie Iredale-Smith, whose job it was to keep the Embankment clear so that the ARP Services could travel in and out of Chelsea.

Mrs Freeth and I frequently gave tea or soup to heavy rescue and demolition workers who were still busy digging in Shawfield Street, Manor Street, and Flood Street. They caught the bus almost outside No 33 and had taken to dropping in. It was they who had named Vicki Miss Hitler – because of the captions and cartoons frequently appearing now in which Hitler was depicted as a dachshund. Mrs Freeth was indignant about this and would turn on the men, threatening them with no more soup or tea. They all had nicknames – Smasher, Crasher, Tapper, Dibs, and similar ones. They would call out whenever Vicki and I passed them at work on the sites, 'Hello, Miss Hitler, how's Adolf?' and they would chaff me and say that if I got buried they would dig me out and *perhaps* Miss Hitler too because at least she was not afraid of the bombs.

The custom of addressing everyone by nicknames or Christian ones was prevalent everywhere. Richard said it was so in the Ministries too, and that he considered it a bad practice there, because in times to come when the personnel were changed who would know what official was meant by minutes signed 'George' or 'Dick'? We were all known by our Christian names at the FAP, as were the wardens at their posts. It gave some sort of equality to the heterogeneous mixture of people all working together in the common cause. There was a general apologetic feeling lest any member should think that another considered himself better than his colleague. Christian and nicknames not only dispensed with any kind of formality but evoked a feeling that every man was as good as another.

CHAPTER SIXTEEN

CATHERINE'S TROUBLES were not over. She had only been back from hospital a week when she began running a temperature again. For a few days I nursed her in her room, staying with her all night, but when the fever rose alarmingly there was no alternative but to send her back to the hospital. They were fortunately able to find her a bed but they could not make arrangements for Francesca, as the baby was to be named. There was nothing to do but to take her home with me. When Richard arrived home that night he was somewhat surprised to find a baby in a washing-basket in our downstairs room. He was most amiable about the visitor, merely remarking that she seemed a bit premature and that all the neighbours would think the worst!

Francesca was a very good baby and slept all night until Mrs Freeth or I made her morning feed. It was I who lay awake fearing that every bomb whistling down might be fatal for her. I understood a little of what some mothers must have felt with that small basket close to my bedside. Everyone agreed that Francesca was unusually lovely and unusually well-behaved; Kathleen and Anne adored her and Mrs Freeth was wonderful with her. Miss Hitler was not so sure about the newcomer. She sat by the washing-basket in a protective way but when I picked its occupant up in my arms she showed her jealousy very plainly.

It was difficult to understand Catherine's attitude to Francesca, but she was still ill – and she had suffered so terribly. She was an excellent mother in some ways – but she did not love her baby, she said. When she came out of hospital again she seemed more like her former self. She kept Francesca immaculately dressed, and attended to her needs punctiliously – but something was lacking in the relationship. And now the trouble of the shelter began again. Catherine was perfectly willing to stay alone in the house with Francesca but all the other occupants went to the shelter and persuaded Catherine to go too. Francesca was carried there in the washing-basket every night, one of the young refugee children willingly helping by taking one handle.

Hilda Reid told me that there were complaints: the habitual shelterers did not want a new-born baby, it might cry and their sleep was already disturbed enough. They were quite unpleasant.

Hilda Reid, a splendid warden, was adamant – the baby stayed in the shelter until other arrangements could be made. The Belgian Government were opening a nursery in the country for expectant mothers, babies, and toddlers. Catherine was willing that Francesca should go to this nursery but she did not want to go there herself. Many people made a fuss about the baby being taken to the shelter every night and representations were made to me that it was scandalous that the child should be exposed to such a thing as a damp shelter in winter. Francesca was extremely healthy in spite of all that Catherine had been through, but obviously a public shelter was no place for her, any more than it was for the thousands of children sleeping in them every night as naturally and soundly as they did at home. I had watched mothers give their children a toothbrush and a mug of water in their bunks, wipe their hands on a towel, brush their hair, and tuck them up with some pet toy animal just as if they were in their own beds at home. The sight was infinitely moving. The small Belgian and French children had become absolutely accustomed to shelter life, but all their mothers said it was a scandal that Francesca slept there.

Catherine came to me in tears. She knew the real reason, she said. It was because Francesca was *illegitimate* and they didn't think that she should be with their children. Such ideas seemed ridiculous to me but they were very real to Catherine, and I realized that she was desperately unhappy. I wondered if she were missing her fiancé and worrying about his fate. She said she did not care for him any more. All she wanted was to get into one of the British Services. There were several Belgian and French girls who had been born in Britain during the 1914-18 war when their mothers had been here as refugees. Three of the ones we knew had joined the ATS. Catherine wanted to do the same. She had a flame of patriotism for Britain which had sheltered her mother and now had given her and her child refuge. She wanted to learn to parachute, to use a gun, to do all the dangerous things which soldiers do. Part of this came from her intense hatred of the Germans and the atrocities they had committed on her fellow-refugees. There was her friend, Mathilde – whom she could not forget lying in the ditch without her head.

One of the officials from the Belgian Government, now established and working in London, was making the necessary arrangements for Catherine and her baby to go to the nursery home in the country. There the mothers, if they accompanied their babies, were required to help with the work of the nursery, we were told. Catherine was not very taken with the idea. She did not want to leave London – she liked it, she said.

Suzanne thought that it was high time Francesca was baptized. Owing to Catherine's illness the ceremony had been delayed. Suzanne made all the arrangements and a famous Monsignor, who was a friend of hers, baptized Francesca in the Catholic church which most of the refugees attended. It had already been bombed and the roof was patched up with tarpaulin. We had tried to make a christening robe but it was difficult to obtain any net or muslin. Mrs Freeth washed one of the mosquito nets which I had brought back from India and Kathleen and her cutter made the most exquisite robe from it. The church was cold and the day was bitter, so Francesca went to her christening in my white fur evening cloak. She looked adorable. One of the young refugee boys was to stand as godfather, and I as godmother. We stood there making our promises for Francesca with Suzanne and Madame R and her children round the font. Afterwards we had a small party in the studio. Mrs Freeth had made and iced a cake and put white flowers everywhere. Miss Hitler had a white ribbon and came in for almost as much attention as Francesca, who behaved perfectly and allowed everyone to nurse and pet her. Shortly after this the day came when Francesca had to go to the nursery home, which was in Worcestershire. Catherine was to go with her, as everyone had persuaded her that it was most unnatural to want to be separated from her baby. I saw her off with a Belgian nurse and several expectant mothers. Catherine cried bitterly when I said good-bye and I felt a traitor – having bowed to the weight of public opinion and persuaded her to go.

Three days later she was standing on my doorstep! She hated the nursery although it was well run and everyone was kind to her – she had had to run the gauntlet of all the expectant mothers' questioning and she did not like it or them. She had left Francesca there and come back – she wanted to go into one of the Services. Her room was still as she had left it, the cot standing stripped and empty. I telephoned the Town Hall – she could have her room back, they said, but she would have to work if she had not her child to look after.

She was not at all strong after her terrible illness and Dr Pennell said firmly that she was not fit for any work and would have done well to stay in the country where the food and air would have benefited her. I did not add my appeal to those made to her to go back. I saw that it was useless. There are women who are not especially maternal – why it should be considered unnatural I don't know. Catherine might have been by instinct maternal, but events had changed her. She had this burning desire to do something active for Britain just as Marianne had to do something for Occupied France. Marianne was training somewhere in the country for work which I understood was very secret. She had written to me several times and had once come to London wearing the uniform of the Free French which General de Gaulle's followers were wearing. Catherine's envy at the sight of Marianne in uniform was so great that the flame of patriotism in her was fanned afresh. She was not yet strong enough and Dr Pennell said she would only spoil her chances by failing the very strict medical examination, but that in six months' time she might pass her as fit enough.

The first evening that Catherine was back in her room I went round there. The sirens were late in wailing. We sometimes hoped now that they would not wail at all. There had been several bomb-free nights, of which November 3rd had been the first since the beginning of the Blitz. She was sitting with her hands folded in her lap by the fire. In the corner was the cot, on the floor the bath in which she had washed Francesca. There was something so utterly forlorn and desolate in her whole bearing that I went and put my arms round her. She covered her face with her hands and burst into a storm of weeping. I said, 'You miss Francesca?' She nodded, weeping more heart-rendingly, but when I suggested that she go back to Worcestershire and join her, she shook her head violently. 'No,' she said, 'that's not my job. I have other work to do. I *must*.'

One evening when we had guests several Belgian women came round in a state of great distress. They had all come out in great red spots, they said, all over their arms, legs, and bodies. I looked at the arms presented for my inspection. I had never seen spots – or rather eruptions – which looked like these. Apparently all the inmates of one of the Tedworth Square houses for which I was responsible had come out in these strange and revolting lumps. It was, needless to say, the house in which The Giant was, and he was one of the worst sufferers.

They regarded me with a strange expectant interest when I went back there with the women. Two of these were sisters whose husbands had both been left behind. Both had a small daughter.

Although sisters, or perhaps because, they quarrelled terribly. One child had red lumps all over her, the other had none, and this was the cause of a further outbreak of bickering between the sisters. The mother of the child afflicted with the lumps looked at me with arms akimbo and a challenging smile. 'What do you think that *these* are, Marraine?' she demanded. I said I didn't know. But I had a horrible lurking fear of what they were. I asked the two sisters to accompany me to Dr Alice Pennell. I can see her now, in a splendid royal blue sari edged with gold, examining the plump freckled arms held out for inspection – then asking the two women to show her their chests. Then she told them to dress and said to me laughingly, 'Don't you know what these are?'

'Insect bites?' I hazarded.

'Bugs,' she whispered. 'Yes. *Bugs!*'

I told her that all the inmates of a particular house had been attacked. 'You'll have to report this to the Sanitary Inspector,' she said laughing. 'The house will have to be fumigated and possibly things in it burned.' Now the Flemish word for bugs is *wandluis*, and they are by no means strangers to Belgium, yet when I had to tell the sufferers from what they were suffering their fury and indignation knew no bounds.'*Bugs!*' They were not accustomed to such disgusting things! Horrible! What a dirty country England must be! It was nothing to do with them – didn't I inspect their rooms every week? Didn't I examine their sanitary arrangements? It was nothing to do with *them*! 'I knew it! I knew it!' cried one of the sisters excitedly. 'But I wasn't going to say anything until Marraine said something. *She* didn't know what these lumps are – and she's a *nurse!*'

Dr Pennell was laughing at my discomfiture but she told the women to calm down and produced some lotion for the affected parts. She said that she had better give me a large bottle for the other bitten ones. We went back quickly as the Blitz had started but these two sisters were not in the least interested in bombs – no, *bugs* was the agitated topic. They were far more frightened of them. 'Do you think we got them in the shelter, Marraine?' they asked. But not all of the bitten ones went to the same shelter – no, it seemed to me that it was the house.

The next morning I went to the Town Hall and talked to a charming officer of the Health Department. He came with me to the house in question and we began a long, exhaustive search. He told me a great deal about the life history and habits of the bug – none of which I knew, and which I found fascinating. He told me how bugs hibernate and can lie in the ground in the foundations of old buildings and then, when a new and modern building is erected on the site, they can come to life and take up residence in the house as soon as it is inhabited. Usually one particular object of furniture or one particular place can be the breeding place for these parasites. He said we must not only fumigate the house but endeavour to find the offending source.

Inch by inch we searched that house. He was a delightful companion, making the whole thing seem like a detective adventure. We had sent all the refugees out of their rooms, and only The Giant, baleful and threatening, could be seen marching up and down in the square. At last after several rooms had yielded nothing we came to a room in which there was a most beautiful painted screen. As I have said before, all the furniture in these houses had been given by Chelsea residents for the refugees. This screen was very old and had padded silk painted panels. It was Chinese, and I would have loved to possess it. After all the chairs and beds had been examined as well as the wall-paper and the rugs, I was admiring the screen when the officer from the Health Department said, 'Now – I wonder if that isn't the culprit?' He took a penknife and slit one of the padded panels – he slit it carefully with a regard for its beauty. I was horrified that it had to be cut at all. But with a cry of triumph he said, 'Got 'em. Look! Look!' and showed me the horrible nest of the biters!

'Will it have to be destroyed?' I asked him. 'Probably. It may be possible to fumigate it and get rid of them completely – but it would be better to burn it. We'll have to see.' The house was sealed while the fumigation went on. We had had trouble with the refugees, who had been told to take what they needed for the day and to spend the time at the canteen until they went to the shelter. By the next morning the house would be clear again. I was very sorry for them. It was, as they said, a horrible thing to have happened to refugees in our country, but it couldn't be helped.

Next day the house was examined again by the sanitary squad. They had decided not to return the screen. It seemed a shame that such a beautiful object should have been the home of such low parasites, but as the sanitary officer said, maybe even bugs can appreciate beauty! Mrs Freeth had known at once what the red lumps were when the women had stood showing me their arms, but she had been too diplomatic to say so.

The bites disappeared with the lotion and the bugs with the fumigation – and the refugees returned to the house, but with the unanimous request that they all be moved to another house because they knew that bugs never disappeared and they had no confidence in the fumigating van. The Town Hall said this was not possible and that as the house was now clear of the bugs, they must remain. Opinion of our British cleanliness had had a severe set-back.

Suzanne was consoling over this incident, and also amusing. By now I had got into the habit of dropping in to the Royal Hospital very frequently. I would find Suzanne in the kitchen busy with meals or chores. I loved going there and often Maurice would take me and show me something lovely in the old building, or point out an aspect of it which I had not known. It seemed to me that to live in that graceful elegant place with its ghosts and shadows of its long past history must be very satisfying. I always took from it some kind of peace which was absent anywhere else – and yet the Royal Hospital had already had some eight HE bombs on it, and on the night of October 16th had had no less than three unexploded bombs on the Infirmary and the old men had had to be evacuated. Connie Oades, as warden, had told me how she had had to go and help get the old men into their wheel-chairs to be moved. Some of them were very ill, but all were reluctant to leave. They were soldiers, they insisted, their place was to stay put! Soldiers did not run away. But the bombs had to be moved too – and might explode. The old men had to go.

One of them would not get into his wheel-chair and Connie played a game of peep-bo with him for he was senile and enjoyed childhood games – and thus she got him into the chair and they were all lined up. Only then did she discover that they were all still in their night-shirts and rightly indignant about it! One evening when incendiaries were falling and Richard and I had been dining with the Fitzgeralds we saw Maurice walking about trailing yards of hosepipe, and in the strange light, with his gas mask on for protection from the fumes, he looked like some prehistoric creature with an inordinate length of tail. Creeping behind him just to see that he was all right was Elizabeth in Suzanne's French tin hat! Richard and I had dined with them in the lovely dining-room looking out over the Thames, with exquisite old branched candlesticks lit on the enormous family table, and then, the raid becoming unpleasantly localized, Maurice and Richard had gone out to deal with incendiaries while the dessert waited.

Suzanne's mother, now permanently bed-ridden but looking beautiful in her lace cap with lavender ribbons, would hold court amongst her pillows. When the awful droning of the raiders rose to a shrill roar overhead and the horrible endless swooshing of a bomb started she would hold a beautiful rosary in her frail old hands and as the noise increased so did the volume of her Aves and Hail Marys. She was always anxious as to the whereabouts of each member of the family during these nightly ordeals and knew that her son-in-law was invariably patrolling the grounds no matter how heavy the raid.

CHAPTER SEVENTEEN

JENNY WAS DELIGHTED at hearing from foreign news sources of Dutch underground movements which were hampering the Nazis in their control of the people and causing them endless trouble and annoyance. They refused to salute Nazi officers and pushed many into the canals at night. The first movement to be formed, known as the Nederlandsche Unie, did not believe in the liberation of Holland or the re-establishment of the House of Orange. For this reason Dr Colijn, the Prime Minister, had withdrawn from it. I had met Dr Colijn when living in Holland, and had painted one of his little granddaughters, and I remembered the thrill with which I had seen a Vermeer painting hanging in his beautiful house in The Hague. He was a delightful man, and his sincerity and stern adherence to what he considered to be right had struck me most forcibly. I wondered how an English friend of mine, widow of a famous Dutch Professor who belonged to this university circle, was faring under the hated Seyss-Inquart and his henchmen? How would they behave to the British-born wives in Holland, Norway, Belgium, and Germany? Would they be as well-treated as the German wives of Englishmen here? I doubted it.

General de Gaulle was rapidly gathering ground. He had returned from French Equatorial Africa where he had reorganized the administration there and also in the Cameroons. He broadcast a strong condemnation of the Vichy Government. The French, he said, were being relentlessly deprived of all social liberty. He was sure that the passion for freedom which had inspired Jeanne d'Arc, and Clemenceau, would lead to the deliverance of France. The Free French were to be seen all over London now, and I sometimes went to help in their canteen – this being a delightful change from the sordid chores which seemed daily to fall to me. In spite of their misfortunes the French were gay – wonderful company, wonderfully adaptable. I loved those evenings working there. They sang, danced, and almost brought the roof down – the noise of the Blitz was often completely drowned by the noise of the Free French.

There was still a lot of fun in London in spite of the black-out – or perhaps because of it – and all the canteens and pubs sounded to the roaring of 'Roll Out the Barrel' and the 'Lambeth Walk' and 'Run, Rabbit, Run'. At the beginning of the war there had been a song which had caught on like wild-fire. It had a rollicking catchy tune – and words which took the public fancy. But since Dunkirk and the fall of France we never heard or sang it any more. It was 'We're going to hang out our Washing on the Siegfried Line' – the Siegfried Line had proved stronger than the Maginot one.

Dr Pennell was excited because Mr Nehru had been imprisoned on November 5th for inflammatory speeches calculated to hinder the war effort, and she remarked drily that the day of his arrest had been well chosen as it was Guy Fawkes Day! His sister, Mrs Pandit, was also conducting a campaign against India helping in the war. Both of these people I had met in India, and had visited Mrs Pandit in her home in Lucknow. She was very charming and intelligent, and to an artist so absolutely beautiful that I had a great admiration for her and hoped that she would not imitate her brother and be incarcerated.

The frequent visits of friends of other nationalities were a welcome relief from the petty annoyances of the somewhat drab work we were all doing. Lotuh Kuo, my lovely Chinese friend, had often some exciting and thrilling bit of news from China to tell us. Just now she and her husband were adopting two war orphans, victims of Japanese aggression – just as Carla and Francesca were victims of the Nazis.

But I think it was Asta Lange who had the most exciting story of all for us. She had many Norwegian friends in London and belonged to a circle of women who worked for Norwegian Servicemen. She told us how a huge sum of gold had been whisked away from under the Nazis' noses and conveyed to the coast by relays of children on sledges. These magnificent children had saved this gold from being seized by the occupying Germans simply by sitting on it. The sledges were heaped with furs and skins for warmth, and under these was the gold. The children sat on the gold bars without giving the slightest indication of their precious burden. They got it safely to the coast where it was shipped, almost under the eyes of the Germans, on to a fishing vessel, and brought at great risk to England. We loved this story – when Asta told it on a Sunday morning while we were all drinking our beer, which was becoming scarcer and scarcer.

We often dined at the Café Royal and also at the Royal Court Hotel in Sloane Square. When on my return from the Far East I had been moving in to Cheyne Place I had stayed there and Mr

Wilde, the Manager, had been most kind and helpful. He had been for many years in Egypt and as both Richard and I knew Cairo and Alexandria we always had plenty to talk about. We sometimes remarked on the large amount of glass in the dining-room, the walls of which were almost covered with mirror-glass, giving the illusion of very great space. The hotel had a deep strongly reinforced air-raid shelter for its residents of which Mr Wilde was justly proud. He himself was always in evidence on noisy evenings when the bombs were near, reassuring the guests.

On the night of November 12th we had dined there rather early and the sirens had sounded while we were having dinner. Richard had to go on fire-duty at the Ministry and I had left him at the entrance to Sloane Square Station and hurried home in case I was called. It was not my evening for duty but several nurses had colds and I had said I would be available if needed. I had hardly reached home when a terrific thud shook the road, but I could see nothing. The wardens were out, and there was activity in the sky and the barrage was pretty heavy, but the great thud had not been located immediately.

About half past ten the telephone rang and someone called me to go at once to the Royal Court Hotel. The line was very bad, almost impossible to hear, and it was with difficulty that I had got the message at all. As I had only just left the hotel I presumed that I had left something valuable behind there. I rang the FAP and said that I had just been called by someone to go to the hotel, and to my astonishment the VAD who answered the telephone said, 'Yes, Mobile Unit has just gone there.'

The square presented an amazing sight – two great flaming jets guarded the pit which had once been the station. The bomb had severed the gas main. The firemen shouted to me as I tried to pick my way across to the Royal Court Hotel, and the newly built station had just disappeared into the depth below. They were already bringing out the first dead and injured and carrying those requiring immediate treatment into the hotel.

Dr and Mrs Phillips were at work in charge of the Mobile Unit. Mr Wilde and the staff were splendid. Table napkins, towels, blankets, and rugs all appeared as we laid the injured down in the lounge and hall. It was a pretty grim business – and again the appalling dirt was the most striking thing. It was evident that getting the bodies out was going to take all that night and many more. The bomb had fallen as a train was leaving the station, and the rear carriage was caught directly – the remainder of the train was shot by the blast almost to South Kensington station. This incident was most ghastly as regards the holocaust of human flesh. Identification was almost impossible – and bodies were put together roughly on to stretchers and some of them taken into nearby houses to be pieced together later somehow. George Evans was working down on the station. The worst casualties were the Underground staff who had been in the canteen on the station when the bomb fell. There were fourteen men, one conductress, and two attendants in the canteen. By the following Saturday – the bomb having fallen on the Tuesday previously – there had been thirty-eight stretchers of human flesh pieced together – but George Evans told me that there were still seventeen people to be accounted for. Countless dustbins and what we called 'bundles' of pieces of human flesh had been retrieved as well – so awful was the carnage and blood that two gallons of disinfectant had to be used. The body of the conductress had disintegrated, only one small female piece found as evidence of her having been in the canteen, as she was known to have been, at the time the bomb fell.

When helping with the first essential aid to those being placed in ambulances for hospital the very things of which that doctor had warned us from his Spanish war experiences were abundantly apparent. In the hotel we used anything at hand to staunch blood and clean dirt off the injured until they could be properly attended to in hospital. Sterilization in any form was out of the question. Our Mobile doctor and unit were absolutely splendid – as were the hotel staff working with them. When I went home exhausted after Mr Wilde had given us all a stiff drink the thing which I most needed was a bath. I was filthy, blood and dirt were over all my clothes – as they had been on the casualties. The dirt, indeed, was the most noticeable thing about almost all casualties. What one needed for the sufferers before the extent of their injuries could be assessed was a hot shower – and this was the one thing which no FAP could provide. We just had to wash off the dirt using swabs and basins of water, but in most cases the clothes of those who had been in an 'incident' were useless afterwards and had to be removed immediately because of filth. The smell of explosions was very pungent, and one that stuck in the nostrils afterwards. The dust and plaster smelt too, an ancient timeless smell of civilization.

In Sloane Square there had been a terrifying smell of gas. All round it buildings were damaged and the square strewn with wreckage and glass. Only the ultra-modern newly designed Peter Jones building stood proudly without a pane of its acres of glass broken. This was explained by the caving in of the station itself so that the blast went up the Underground tunnel and the actual explosion was muffled. Mr Wilde told me that it was not such a tremendous thud as one would have expected. At first they did not realize that it was so near, and the cries of those below on the station were muffled too by the debris which had descended on them from above.

After this incident there was again a call for volunteers for the mortuary to help piece bodies together. There was one woman, a local resident, doing magnificent work on the bodies. She was a delightful person – I can remember her vividly, but not, alas, her name. She was not a nurse, and, after all, the last service to the dead is part of a nurse's training, but she was doing this, she told me, as an offering to those brave transport personnel who had carried on all through the Blitz and lost their lives in the canteen on the station.

I was accustomed to the task by now but never lost my violent revulsion, just as it never lost its grim horror. The wardens hated it too, for it was part of their everyday duties to pick up the pieces of their fellow-men and women after the raids. The police, they told me, would not do this, nor would they help move bodies. Connie had experience of this when it was her job to move a man's heavy body outside a house in Burton Court. A chair leg had been driven right through him. The dead man's family would have had to step over his body welded to the chair when they emerged. She was not strong enough to move it herself, but two policemen refused absolutely to help her. I should have thought that some dead were less unpleasant than the drunks they had to move.

On the Sunday after this Mr Rock Carling came to lunch and walked with us in Battersea Park. He was interested in all I could tell him of the Sloane Square casualties, and when I said that his last long talk with me about such things had made my small part in it much easier he was very pleased and told me a lot about some of the incidents which he had recently investigated as Consultant to Administration to Civil Defence and the Ministry of Health. He had already been bombed in eleven cities. In the terrible fire on the docks the Isle of Dogs suffered terribly. Immediately afterwards he had to inspect the FAPs there. One of them, in charge of a large elderly East-End lady, had everything in such perfect order that he was astonished. He said to her, 'Look here, I can always find something to criticize in a FAP if I want to. I don't believe your needles are sharp.' 'You can take a look at 'em,' she retorted. They were the sharpest he had come across and he asked her how she got them like it. 'I've got a friend who's a watchmaker who looks after 'em for me,' she said. The idea spread from this and soon all over the country the surgeons' needles were looked after by watchmakers.

Some of the things he had discovered were fascinating. In one naval yard he found the ammunition stored right up against a timber yard. In another place he found large stores of war gases in exposed tanks which, if hit by a bomb, would have spread poison gas all over the country. In the making of camouflage piles of old car tyres were burned for smoke screens, and in one place this was being done right up against the water supply of a city. Richard often accompanied him and Colonel Bateman on some of these investigations, as he also did to the mortuaries. 'Rockie', as I always called him, was so absolutely sick of seeing mortuaries that he refused to visit any more. He agreed with me that it was a pity that we did not disintegrate as the burial service said 'earth to earth, dust to dust, ashes to ashes' without any flesh and blood to have to be dealt with by our fellow-men.

Rockie liked to discuss painting and painters – he loved looking at my work and asking me about it. I have found that doctors and surgeons in all countries have this appreciation and love of art and are amongst the greatest patrons of it. My very first commission had been from a young surgeon whose wife wanted him painted in his robes soon after he qualified, and he paid me for it in instalments.

With the onset of real winter and the early fall of darkness – it was suddenly bitterly cold – the nightly trek to the shelters assumed a grim aspect. Many left their bedding and rugs on their bunks – but the shelters were often damp, and although there were wardens in charge it was not always possible for someone to be on duty all day and there were dishonest people ready to steal and re-sell blankets and pillows, just as there were ghouls to be seen picking away at the ruins of houses from which it was forbidden to even the owners to remove their own possessions. Sometimes the things left lying about in rain and wind were just asking to be stolen; it was quite common to see them still there after several weeks if they were in a place inaccessible to the passer-by.

Not all the men who were employed to do the salvage work were above looting from the houses on which they were working, judging from the weekly reports of court cases for this crime. There were a great many more than one would have thought. Commodities were scarce and it was a temptation to see things which could be used left rotting in the inclement weather. All goods salvaged from ruins had to be taken to places set aside for them by the borough from which they had to be claimed by the owner or heirs. By now there were many ruined houses, many great gaping holes between rows of badly damaged ones, and whole devastated areas over which no guard of any kind was kept. As darkness fell earlier so the sirens sounded earlier every night and life became one scramble to get things done before the warning sounded its mournful curfew.

One little Belgian boy in a house in Royal Avenue had been very unwell for some weeks. He had intermittent fever and a cough, he was losing weight and had no energy or appetite. Dr Thompson asked me to take him to a well-known children's specialist at the Victoria Hospital. The specialist, after examining him, asked me if I could keep a very careful chart of the boy's temperature for the next two weeks during which time he was to stay in bed.

This was no easy task and I explained that the family were housed on the top floor of the house and went regularly to a shelter every night. I doubted if they would agree to the boy staying in bed or to staying with him. It was impossible to take him into the hospital – only one ward was kept open now – and that was for emergencies. If, as the specialist suspected, the child was threatened with tuberculosis, then he could send him to hospital in Windsor – but until he was fairly certain there was no chance of getting him into hospital.

It was a difficult task to get Madame C to understand that her son was threatened with a serious illness. She was certain that all that was the matter was constipation, from which the whole family suffered, made worse, she said, by the shelters having no proper sanitation. The specialist told me to impress on her that it was the child's chest which was the danger, not his bowels. She was a very talkative woman and, once started on the subject of constipation, it was almost impossible to get her to stop. I promised to try to get the boy kept in bed and to make the chart at the times requested. Madame C had three other children and a husband who was extremely affected by the Blitz. This was understandable as the family had experienced machine-gunning and bombing on their trek from Belgium, but it was his fear which affected the wife and children, who would not have minded the Blitz so much otherwise. As I had feared, Monsieur C would not hear of Raymond staying in bed in the house; he must go to the shelter. I argued with him and was finally obliged to warn the father that his son had suspected tuberculosis and that taking him to a damp shelter when he already had a fever was highly dangerous and could result in serious trouble.

The child himself had told me that he wanted to stay in bed, that he felt tired, he only wanted to sleep and sleep. I tried to persuade the family on the ground floor of the house to change rooms so that the boy would at least not be on the top floor, but no one liked top floors since the Blitz had started.

I think it was during some of those many visits to Raymond to make that chart that I first began to know real fear. Up to that time I had not really minded the Blitz at all. I had just married, and we were very happy, although the occasions when we were both together were increasingly rare. Richard was frequently away on tour for the Ministry, and I was often on night duty, but the bombs seemed only a macabre background to our personal life, and the fear that either of us would be a victim of the Blitz was a remote thought – but it was one which now began recurringly to enter my head. Richard had told me that when they had to 'go over the top' in the 1914-18 war it never occurred to the individual that he would be killed – the next man, or the one behind him perhaps, but not *him*. I suppose the same feeling made us all able to get on with our various occupations. It was, in a way, like entering for a lottery: out of millions of houses only a very small percentage got destroyed in each raid. When I told Richard that I was beginning to be afraid, that I worried sometimes when he was away, that was the argument he used to reassure me. 'It's one house in a million which is hit,' he said. Nevertheless, when watching at night by the bedside of this little boy, his mother having gone in exhaustion to the shelter, I was often afraid alone there on the top floor of that empty house in deserted Royal Avenue. The child needed frequent reassurance, being feverish and apprehensive at each fearful whoosh and whistle of a bomb. The succeeding explosions caused him to bury his small face in the pillow and his hot little hands would grip mine in an agony of suspense.

I used to play a game going to and from these nightly vigils. I would run down the dark avenue and as each bomb fell I would count it as one more orange for Nell Gwynne. Sometimes her orange basket was quite full before I reached Raymond, who liked to play the game with me, I having told him an interminable story about the orange girl and the King. Sometimes I took Vicki with me. She was indifferent to gunfire and bombs and lay quite happily in the bed with the child. Out in the open I never felt nervous, the spectacle in the sky was too exciting, the beauty of the searchlight patterns too diverting for fear. It was when under a roof that I was the victim of these stirrings of apprehension.

One very bad night when a bomb had fallen in Royal Avenue very near the house, Raymond said to me, 'Marraine, are you frightened?' I hesitated. Should I admit that I *was* or should I lie? Which? Before I could answer he said, 'I am very frightened indeed – shall I say my prayers to Our Lady for both of us?...I've got my rosary here...' I agreed thankfully, and he murmured the prayers, telling the beads round as the planes circled as if he were following their death wish and fighting it. So had Suzanne's mother done, her frail ivory hands making exactly the same movements. When the terrific crash came which shook the house and we heard the ensuing clattering of tiles and glass Raymond took my hand and pressed it in anguish between his small hot ones...but he did not falter in his prayers. When silence came – and we were still there – he put down the rosary and said, 'I said one for Vicki too. I'm sure Our Lady likes dogs, aren't you?'

At last the chart was complete and the specialist, satisfied that his suspicions were justified, asked me to bring Raymond's parents to see him as the boy would have to go out of London to a hospital in Windsor.

This was easily decided, but to persuade the parents was quite another matter. The child himself was quite willing to go – he wanted to get well and he didn't like being left to sleep in the house during the Blitz while the rest of his family were in the shelter.

It took hours of argument before they agreed to talk it over and let me know the next day. Raymond had to go almost at once as there was a vacant bed waiting for him. We did not get much notice when the actual day came. The parents had finally agreed to let him go after being told that they could visit him on Sundays. Madame C was upset that she was not allowed to go with him, but she was, I found, chiefly upset because she had administered a laxative to the boy and was worried about its having effect on the journey. Having reassured her that this could be dealt with, she was very good about his going. There was another child travelling in the ambulance with Raymond and one of the nurses from the Victoria Hospital came with us.

I missed Raymond very much, he was a darling little boy, but it was lovely to feel that he was in the country air, and in comparative peace compared with Chelsea, and there was no denying those nightly visits had weighed heavily on me. If I left him with his mother alone in that house I could not sleep myself and had, sooner or later, got up and gone round to see that they were all right. He settled in very quickly at the hospital and, like Catherine, was learning English, and wrote me some delightful little letters.

The suspicion and spite of some refugees against their fellows were a headache to us. Suspicion, as in Ruth's case, seemed to be one of the qualities born of fear and uncertainty. There were constant complaints of light signals being made from the windows of some refugee or other. Deputations of refugees had come several times about an unfortunate widower who occupied a room on the top floor of a house in St Leonard's Terrace. They said that during the raids this man signalled the Luftwaffe by a series of flashes done in some code or other. These accusations grew so insistent that the police came to hear of them. One day a member of the CID whom I had met already in connexion with the refugees, came to see me about the matter. I had not myself seen the signals – but was obliged to admit that a great many of the refugees were emphatic that Monsieur D, a most mild and amiable man, was a spy. He kept apart, they said, he did not mix with the other refugees. He was secretive and did not sleep in a shelter. Why not? What did he stay up there for – there must be some good reason. He was a spy and signalled the raiders. I liked Monsieur D, perhaps because he was that much different and because he never complained about anything. I told the Inspector all I could about him, and his file was carefully studied again. There was nothing against him – anyhow nothing known against him.

Two days later the same CID officer came again. They had put a watch on the house – it seemed that there *were* peculiar lights from the window of Monsieur D's room. They were going to keep watch the following night and if the same movements were observed they would come and fetch me in a police car so that I could accompany them to confront him. Would I hold myself ready if they came?

I was very excited about this – my instinct was to go at once to Monsieur D and warn him, but this I was told expressly not to do. I agreed to go after the CID officer had told Richard about their plan. The next evening was extremely dark, and shortly before midnight a police car came for me. A constable had been on watch, and Monsieur D was signalling again. 'Come and see for yourself,' said the police.

We drove to St Leonard's Terrace and parked the car under some trees in Burton Court. 'We have to investigate this because the man's window is, as the complainants said, directly opposite the balloon site,' I was told. It was – that was obvious.

We sat there with the Blitz for entertainment and listened to the gun-fire and the planes. Suddenly the police officer next to me said, '*Now!* Look at his window.' I looked. There were certainly some queer quick streaks of yellow light shooting across the window. In the pitch blackness of the November night they appeared startlingly noticeable. We watched for a minute or so and then the inspector opened the door of the car. 'Is the house unlocked?' he asked me. It was – all the refugee houses were left unlocked at night because of firebombs. 'You go up first,' said the Inspector. 'We don't want to scare the man – it may have some absolutely innocent explanation, but in any case he must be warned that he is infringing the black-out regulations.' There was such a noise from the anti-aircraft barrage that our footsteps on the stairs must have passed unnoticed. All the rooms on the landings were closed, and as all electric-light bulbs had been removed, we used our hooded torches to find the way. I knew the room well, having often visited Monsieur D in it. He had been in bed with a heavy cold for a few days and Mrs Freeth had cooked his meals and I had carried them up to him.

When we all stood outside the door we could hear voices. Monsieur D was not alone – and clearly not in bed. I had been told to tap on the door and at the same time open it so as not to give him time to hide anything. I did not like doing this – but had to obey instructions. Accordingly, at a signal from the police, I tapped sharply on the door, saying, 'Monsieur D, Monsieur D...' and opened it.

Monsieur D was in his shirt and socks – he appeared flabbergasted at my intrusion. At first he did not see the police behind me...'Marraine...' he faltered, staring open-mouthed at me. In his hand was a torch. It looked bad. But by the light of mine I had seen something else – a bare leg emerging from under the iron bedstead in the corner. Not a man's leg – a white, shapely, feminine one. I said to the terrified man, 'Who have you got under the bed? *Quick*, tell me.' He faltered, stammered, and finally said, 'Someone you wouldn't know, Marraine.' I went over to the bed and shone my torch under it. Monsieur D was wrong. There was a squeal of protest, but the face revealed had so much merriment in it and at the same time such pleading that I stood against the bed so that the legs were no longer visible. I addressed myself to Monsieur D, telling him of the accusations against him. He was open-mouthed with astonishment. Him signalling? *Him?* Why he'd kill anyone with his bare hands if he found them signalling to those Boche swine. I cut him short. 'I know what you are doing – I know *her*,' I said, 'but what are you doing with that torch, that's what the police want to know? Your morals are your own affair – but lights in the black-out are *theirs*!' He looked down sheepishly at the unguarded torch in his hand. 'It's her stockings,' he said reluctantly. 'She's lost her stockings...you know how scarce stockings are, Marraine. I had to look for them. I can't put the lights on as the windows are not blacked out – I was hunting with the torch. I have to undress by it every night. I keep it down, it can't possibly show from the window.'

The inspector said now, 'What explanation does he give? Who is under the bed?' 'He has a woman under the bed. He says she went under it when she heard me tap at the door. She's lost her stockings – he was looking for them with the torch. That explains those queer streaks of light we saw. He says that he undresses by it every night.' The inspector went over to the bed and looked underneath. Without a word he came back to Monsieur D. 'Tell him that this is a police warning about infringing the black-out,' he said. 'Make it stern. Tell him if it happens again he'll be fined – he could be imprisoned.' At the same time he bent and picked up a silk stocking and handed it without a word to the frightened man. 'I'll see if I can get you some black-out curtains tomorrow,' I promised him. He caught hold of my arm and began a long excited apology for the predicament in which we had found him.

The police were already going down the stairs again and said they would wait for me below. 'Get the lady dressed,' I advised him; 'it's bitterly cold up here, and here's the other stocking!' I picked it up from where the beam of my torch had caught it. 'Why didn't you hang a blanket over the window?' I asked him. 'But, Marraine,' he stammered, 'we did think of it – but it's so cold – as you said just now – we needed the blanket on the bed!'

I said good-night, ran downstairs and collapsed with laughter in the police car. The lady was as well known to them, I was told, as she was to me. The raids and the black-out were conducive to her trade but not to the amenities associated with it. We sat in that car and laughed and laughed at the story of poor Monsieur D and the stockings. I promised to see to his blackout, and was driven home, the police all still chuckling.

Next morning Monsieur D arrived to make his apologies. 'You must understand, Marraine, that I am deeply ashamed that you should find me in such a predicament, but after all I am a lone man. She is a good girl – she does not charge me much. She knows that I am on Public Relief.' All the refugees were on Public Relief, and it was this remark of Monsieur D's which so amused Richard. It had been my duty to take many of the refugees to the Relieving Officer so that they could draw a weekly allowance. He wondered what officialdom would think of this use of its money.

We had another midnight adventure with the police a few nights later – but this one was less amusing. One of the very noisiest raids which we had ever had was on. We had not gone to bed because we had been putting out incendiaries – now almost a nightly task which, as Richard said, at least gave us some exercise and a lot of fun. We were just going to bed when there was a violent knocking at the front door. When we opened it a Special Constable almost fell in. He appeared in such a state of collapse that we helped him into the room, which was now a sort of bed-sitter. He was in a pitiable state – weeping, shuddering, and groaning. I thought he was suffering from a shock of some kind. We gave him a drink but when I was going to give him another one Richard stopped me and told me in French that he thought the man was already drunk. He had collapsed on to our bed and lay there shivering and moaning. It was impossible to get anything coherent out of him. We saw that he did not come from Chelsea and asked him which was his beat. Time went on and the Blitz went on – but we wanted to get some sleep ourselves and here was this stranger lying inert on our bed.

Richard tried to rouse him and when it was unsuccessful he looked in his pocket for his police identification. When he found it he saw that he was miles off his beat. What was he doing in Chelsea? Richard was very tired, he said he had no intention of sharing the bed with a policeman, we should get him on his feet and turn him out again. I would not agree to this as he seemed to be ill from fright already and the inferno going on all round could only make him worse – besides, what chance would he have of taking cover? Richard said a Special Constable should not take cover – he was on duty in the Blitz to help others. It was after midnight and he decided to telephone the police station to which the man was attached.

I got the man to drink some coffee and he seemed better after it, but quite unable to realize where he was, how he got there, or what he was supposed to be doing. While Richard was telephoning I went to get some more coffee because it seemed to be reviving him. When I returned from the kitchen the front door was open and the Special had disappeared! When Richard came down from the studio he joined me in the search. He had vanished as suddenly as he had appeared. After waiting some time we went to bed.

About three o'clock in the morning we were awakened by loud peals of the bell. There were two police cars outside. The station had sent to collect its lost Special but we could not tell them where he was, and after we gave them a very guarded account so as not to injure the poor fugitive they departed with a lot of noise. We had just got to sleep again when more loud peals at the bell woke us. Two more police cars had arrived to collect the missing man! I was glad that he had gone – maybe the coffee had pulled him together. He did not seem to know what had happened to him. It was almost dawn by the time that the second lot of police left us and so I made some breakfast and we got up and went out to see how the raid was getting on.

CHAPTER EIGHTEEN

OUR FRIENDS Eve and Moley were in trouble at this period of the Blitz. Their flat had been badly damaged by bomb blast and was unsafe, and Eve had to enter University College Hospital for a major operation. She had barely emerged from the anaesthetic when Maples's enormous store, which adjoins the hospital, was bombed and became a raging furnace. The patients were wheeled in their beds into the corridors, packed closely together.

The firemen were fighting heroically on the blazing Maples fire but from the corridor window the glare of the flames was reflected and was terrifying to the helpless patients, who knew that the flare was a target for the Luftwaffe, which was dropping high explosives into it. Eve was not frightened; like the others she was quite calm until one of the patients panicked. Suddenly the panic spread like lightning all down the closely packed beds. 'We've got to get out of here! We'll all be trapped like rats. Get us out! Get us out!' a man began screaming – and others took up his cry, 'Get us out of here!' and now Eve was really frightened – not so much of the fire but of the panic.

A huge smoke-grimed fireman came pushing his way down the corridor between the beds – they were fighting the fire from the hospital as from all sides. He took in the situation immediately from Eve's face. Pausing by her bed he said, indicating the screaming panic-maker, 'Shall I knock him out for you?' and in a few moments he had restored confidence and wheeled Eve's bed to the window so that she could watch the firemen at work on the fire which, in ferocity and size, made an unforgettable sight. There is something horribly stimulating and exciting in a big fire – and even there, unable to move and in great danger from its proximity, she could but marvel at its beauty. I had seen several terrible fires in Chelsea since the beginning of the Blitz and they never failed to give me a horrible thrill with their blend of terror and sheer terrifying beauty. I had watched the magnificent work of the firemen and was equally thrilled by their superb bravery.

Next morning Eve had to be taken by ambulance to the country. Moley travelled with her. All the way across London and its outskirts the vehicle bumped violently over the firemen's hoses still blocking the streets as they fought the smouldering fires before nightfall. Each bump was an agony to the patient, who feared that the recently inserted stitches would give way. In order to distract her mind from her discomfort and pain, Moley described to her a series of beautiful country houses which they were passing. He is an authority on certain periods of English architecture and made his descriptions so real in minute details of their setting, style, and period that Eve could visualize each one. It was only when they reached their destination that she realized that he could not see a thing from his seat in the ambulance!

At the end of November reports of war damage were published in the Press. We Londoners had not been able to avoid seeing the ruins of some of our most beloved buildings – but to the provincial people the report was news – just as reports of their losses were news to us. Censorship was strictly enforced, and the deaths of our friends from enemy action were not allowed to be published in the newspapers until fourteen days after the event. St James's, Piccadilly, that lovely church familiar to every visitor as well as every Londoner, had been demolished, Notre Dame de la France in Leicester Square had been totally wrecked, the Carlton and the Savoy Hotels damaged, as was Greenwich Observatory. My sister had written to me about the damage in Bristol and the loss of so many lovely buildings there, now the public knew that the University Great Hall, the Elizabethan St Peter's Hospital, the famous Dutch House, the Old Crown Court in the Guildhall were all destroyed, and the lovely old Temple Church completely wrecked.

America was sending gifts from Red Cross and charitable organizations. My sister, working in Bristol, was receiving great cases of blankets and clothing for the bombed-out people. Margerie Scott had now extended her already wide activities all over Canada, whence a steady stream of parcels was pouring in. She had been heard in her broadcasts by a huge organization called Beta Sigma Phi, an international sorority, and their International HQ in Kansas City wrote to her and asked her to become an honorary member. She agreed, not knowing exactly what it involved, and they began sending her thousands and thousands of dollars to buy mobile units, to equip an air-raid shelter under a dramatic club for young people which she ran in Elm Park Gardens, in fact money to provide for all kinds of things which war-time Britain could not find. Many old bombed-out people in Cheyne Hospital received beautiful blankets and warm coats and jerseys from these wonderfully generous people in Canada and America. The children all received toys and clothes – Margerie Scott was indeed the real Father Christmas in Chelsea. (These organizations kept up their stream of gifts until after the end of the war and formed Margerie Scott Clubs all over Canada.)

In the desert of Libya the battle against the Italians was proceeding with great violence, but our air raids on Germany had been somewhat slackened owing to the weather, as had theirs on us; and our bombers visited Naples, that lovely bay which no imagination of mine could connect with such things as war and air raids, but which now held cruisers and destroyers that had to be eliminated.

In Chelsea we were still having bombs, and on the morning of December 8th, after a noisy night, I was due for day duty at the FAP and arriving there early in the morning was greeted by Peggy, immaculate as usual, who said, 'Come and see our visitor who arrived early this morning – but take off your shoes first. You might wake him up.' I thought that she meant that a child casualty had been brought in during the Blitz of the previous night – but no! It was no baby but a large UXB sitting in the surgery!!

We peeped round the door, which Peggy opened very cautiously. There it was, in the small room, an uninvited guest waiting to be removed like all gate-crashers! There was intense excitement at the FAP, which had been ordered to evacuate. Everyone was creeping about in stockinged feet. Sister-in-charge wanted all equipment and drugs removed from the cupboard before we had to evacuate. She said that each of us could make one trip past the bomb to the cupboard and carry all we could. This we did in our stockinged feet, scarcely daring to breathe. The young officer from the Bomb Disposal Squad had told me that UXBs were not nearly as dangerous as people imagined. They seldom went off, he said, and, as Sister insisted when one VAD demurred, if the thing had crashed through five floors after striking the roof and landing with a terrific impact on the surgery floor why should it go off when we 'walked delicately like Agag in the sight of the Lord' round it?

But there was one UXB which had gone off eight hours after being dropped. It had fallen in a house in Sydney Street on October 16th. Eight hours after the occupants had all been evacuated the bomb exploded and took a complete slice out of the house as if it had been cut with a knife as a cake is. The walls each side were exposed, displaying the rooms, and on a landing hung a little boy's hat and coat, forlorn and pathetic.

I could not help thinking of this as I crept round in my turn to rescue Sister's precious equipment, but I was consoled by what the young officer had told me. 'If it goes off and you're near it you won't know a thing.' But all the same I couldn't help wondering if this wasn't perhaps the bomb with my name on it!

We had to evacuate our post for several days and the whole road was roped off and barred to traffic until the disposal squad's arrival. They were kept so busy now that this took time. This was the first unexploded bomb I had seen at such close quarters, and somehow it didn't seem to have any connexion with the violence caused by explosion. It just looked like an ugly snout-nosed greenish-grey torpedo with small horns coming out of it. Our post had to be closed and we were all detailed to hospitals until the bomb had been removed.

The same night a bomb had fallen in Tedworth Square and caused consternation amongst the refugees who lived in the houses there. Smith Street and Wellington Square had also had bombs and all these were in the immediate vicinity. Many of the refugees who had been separated from their acquaintances and friends on arrival in England had by now got into touch with them. Some of them were quite near in London, and every few days one or another of them would excitedly bring me letters from various London boroughs. It seemed that we were lucky in Chelsea, having not so far lost one of our refugees. Quite a number of Belgians had been killed in October in an air raid when sheltering in Bounds Green underground station. Each Belgian who told me about it enlarged the number of casualties, but certainly it was over a dozen – probably fifteen – including several known to the Chelsea ones.

The bomb in Smith Street made a huge crater in the road and I asked a man who worked in the local pub there if he had heard anything of it. He said, '*Heard?* Well, not exactly heard. It was like this. I've got a cat, and hearing the raid on, I come out to look for 'm, see? I calls Puss, Puss – and this ruddy great thing comes down. I couldn't hear nothing for some time! and all me clothes was blown off me. But the cat – he come back as large as life waving 'is tail as pleased as punch!'

On the 20th we had quite heavy day raids again on London, and I sat with Carla's letter before me. In two days she would be breaking up – could she come up just for the actual Christmas, please, *please*? she wrote. Well, I just couldn't take the risk and decided to telephone the nuns to break it gently to her. But that evening Madeleine, a charming young French refugee, was taken suddenly ill. Her mother came round to fetch me, and in the excitement of getting her to hospital – for she had bronchial pneumonia – I forgot about Carla. Madeleine was terribly ill; she had been poorly for days but had said nothing as she did not want to worry her mother. Dr Thompson took her into St Luke's at once and gave her the new drug M and B. He was so delighted with the results that he telephoned me to come the next afternoon and see his patient. Madeleine, who had been taken away in an ambulance, blue in the face and breathing in harsh, ugly, rasping spasms, was sitting up in bed looking pink and pretty again with all the taut strained lines gone from her young face. Beside her sat her mother wreathed in smiles – she just couldn't do enough for the nurse and the young doctor who had miraculously restored her only daughter. Every time one of them passed the bed she caught at their hands and kissed them – they were embarrassed but I think rather touched.

When I got home from this satisfactory outcome I saw a small figure sitting patiently on a suitcase on the doorstep inside the archway. It was Carla.

She had apparently saved up her pocket money, got one of the day girls to buy her a ticket and simply joined the school party going to the London train. When she saw me she flung herself at me in a storm of tears. What could I do but tell her she could stay?

Just before Christmas the raids on Bristol became even greater in magnitude. My sister, Gerry, had been in touch with me all through our bad weeks of Blitz and telephoned me every day to ask if I were all right – lately I had been telephoning her. Bristol had suffered terribly. She sent me her comments on the splendid behaviour of the Bristolians during some appalling nights. Her husband was a doctor and on constant call, and she herself was working full-time in Civil Defence.

On October 20th, during a terrible air attack on Bristol, Kumari's brother, Indi, was killed flying with the Nizam of Hyderabad's Squadron, which was helping to defend the town. The squadron gained glory in history by shooting down sixty-four out of the hundred enemy planes destroyed in the huge-scale attack on

Bristol. But Indi, an eager, intrepid, and skilled pilot, was one of those whose planes were shot down after he had destroyed several German planes in fierce dog-fights.

Kumari came to tell me of his death. She was so quiet and restrained in her grief that it was agonizing to look at the tragic beauty of her small face. She had adored her brother – and he was the only son. Her parents had two more daughters but Indi alone would have carried on the family name. He had loved the life with the RAF, she said, he had been supremely happy – and she knew that he had died happy – because he was defending the country he loved. I could not accept her attitude. Whenever some lovely young life had been sacrificed I felt only fury – and despair. Sometimes when I awoke in the night I would think of all the young lives being lost all over the battle areas – and in every country. In Holland, France, Belgium, Poland, and Norway they were dying every day for their country – being sent to monstrous prison camps because they would not bow to the Nazi heel – and every day there were RAF men being killed in these endless air battles, or 'failing to return' as the BBC put it in their bulletins, and all those who were being lost at sea. Kumari did not see it as I did. 'Why do you all fear death and regret it so much?' she asked. 'Surely if you are Christians and know that you are going on to eternal life you should welcome it.' Kumari was a Hindu and knew that her present life was but a small cycle in the reincarnations of the soul until she attained eternal rest with the Brahma. She accepted Indi's death as his destiny – that his incarnation on this earth had been ruthlessly, and to my mind needlessly, cut short by war did not upset her. She grieved for the loss of her beloved brother – but she did not grieve because he was *dead.* 'He is reincarnated, that is all,' she said. 'He is to get a decoration. His wing-commander wrote to me. Father will be very proud of him.'

I admired her attitude enormously. I had completed a sketch of Indi in his uniform and this I gave her now. She was delighted with it and asked if she might send it to her father. I looked at it again before she took it away. He was a wonderful-looking boy – with the proud straight features seen often in Hyderabad, which was his home. He had had a most endearing personality and I had loved his society. I could not look at the sketch without pain – but Kumari, tearless and composed, regarded the drawing critically. 'It is a very good likeness,' she said quietly, 'Father will be delighted to have it.'

It was a quiet Christmas but it was a happy one for Carla, who was radiant. On Christmas Day the King broadcast from Sandringham. He spoke first to the children, to all those separated by war from their parents, to those in Canada, Australia, New Zealand, and South Africa. There were many of these, for the evacuation scheme had gone on in spite of the tragedy of the *City of Benares*. To the older people he said, 'In the last Great War the flower of our youth was destroyed and the rest of the people saw but little of the battle. This time we are all in the front line and in danger together, and I know that the older among us are proud that it should be so. Remember this, if war brings separation it brings new unity also, the unity which comes from common perils and common sufferings willingly shared. To be good comrades and good neighbours in trouble is one of the finest opportunities of the civilian population...'

He finished with a warning that the difficulties and dangers still to come should not be underrated but that we might look forward to a happier New Year from the successes which our fighting men and their Allies won at heavy odds by land, air, and sea.

In the afternoon we had a party in the studio for Carla and the refugee children. Larry and Cecil gave away presents, dressed up as Father Christmases – the children were thrilled to have two of them, one from the Continent and one from Britain, we told them. The costumes had been dug up somewhere in the Town Hall and cleaned and renovated by Kathleen. Earlier, on Christmas Eve, Suzanne had received all the refugees who cared to go, in her drawing-room in the Royal Hospital where a noble Christmas tree was set in the windows: they had refreshments and sang carols. It was a lovely ceremony in a lovely room, but it was nostalgic too – for almost all the refugees were remembering other Christmases in their own countries, and on December 14th all Belgian males in the 1925 to 1941 class had been called to the colours in the Belgian Army in England. There were quite a number of lads about to be sixteen – it seemed terribly young to have to fight. (Our own youngsters of sixteen and seventeen were having a very difficult time. Either they were too old to be evacuated or were already out at work and had no spare cash. They had in many cases to fend for themselves, their mothers having evacuated and their fathers being in the Forces. They did splendid work helping out the ARP Services as messengers and extras, and Margerie Scott was one of those who occupied themselves with their welfare. From her eloquent radio appeals she had already received large sums of money to found dramatic clubs in reinforced basements for them so that they could find some form of light relief from the dreariness of their lives.) We dispersed before actual black-out for fear of an Alert. But there was no Alert! Apparently the Germans, in spite of Hitler, still loved their *Heilige Abend* too much to leave their bases to bomb us.

Richard and I had a late party to celebrate the first Christmas of our married life. We had asked all the guests to bring their night-clothes – it was quite common now when invited out for dinner to take pyjamas and toilet-bags – and were prepared to squeeze them all into the hall or the shelter. But the hours went on and no sirens interrupted our party – it was a bomb-free night everywhere. Nevertheless I decided to send Carla back on the morning of the 27th. She had had a wonderful few days, been thoroughly spoiled by Larry and Richard, by Mrs Freeth, and by us all. She wanted me to take her back – she had left without permission and I had telephoned the agitated nuns at the convent school. They were not angry with the child – they were understanding and kind women, and knew that Carla's sense of insecurity and of not belonging anywhere made it vital that she found the affection she craved.

She gave me one small insight of how she was suffering at school. We were passing Shawfield Street where some of the Demolition Squad were still clearing the dangerous ruins and, as we passed one of them, a huge beefy red-faced fellow, who before the war had been a builder's labourer, saw Vicki and shouted, 'Heil Miss Hitler! Heil!' and they all raised their hands in mock Nazi salute at Vicki. I was used to this – in fact it had become a standard joke and all my friends now called my Dachshund 'Miss Hitler'. I waved at the men and laughed. But the effect on Carla was startling. She ran like a whirlwind over to the group of men and attacked the beefy one, Smasher, with her fists. 'How dare you, how dare you! You bullies! You beasts!' she screamed and her small face was contorted with fury. The men were flabbergasted; too taken aback to say a word they just stood staring at their huge comrade being attacked by this bundle of fury. It took quite a feat of strength to dislodge her and calm her down. 'He's *mean*! *Mean!*' she kept crying. 'It's not my fault, it's not my fault. I wish I were dead!' I was as puzzled as the men were – that she should resent the nickname I understood – but this was out of all reason. I apologized for her and led her weeping away from them. Afterwards it came out that the girls at school all called *her* 'Miss Hitler'.

The peace of Christmas was shattered by an appalling fire raid on London on the 29th. German machines dropped shower after shower of incendiaries on the City. It was a Sunday night and offices and buildings were for the most part unattended, and the Fire Service and ARP, who did heroic work in fighting the fires, had difficulty in getting into many of the blazing premises.

The terrifying glow in the sky could be seen all up the river, and it was so light in Chelsea that one could almost see to read in the streets. Fire bombs fell in our area too, but they were easily dealt with, while the blaze in the City went on all night – a target for bombs from the Luftwaffe who had set it alight. Every Fire Service in the Metropolitan area was called in to help and they fought the flames with epic courage. But in spite of Government appeals so many commercial buildings were locked against burglars and so many of the City's historic churches locked also that the flames got a firm hold before anything could be done. The Thames was at its lowest tide, as it had several times been when we had needed water in Chelsea, and some of the pumps had been rendered useless when the mains had been severed. In one of our Chelsea fire raids the water mains had been burst so that the fire-points were useless and the Thames was so low that there was only mud, while in the streets the water from the severed mains near the Embankment was deep enough for a boat to float on and for cars to be half-submerged in it.

We got more news of this terrible fire raid than of almost any calamity hitherto – for it was impossible to keep a catastrophe of such dimensions from the public. The raid lasted only two hours, the firemen told us next day; obviously the Germans intended returning with fresh loads of incendiaries – but for some reason they did not do so. The sky was a bright orange-red – as it is soon after sunrise – indeed it gave the feeling of a sunny dawn in the night. We went up on to our flat roof, which was pretty high and gave a splendid view over London, and it was awful – although beautiful, a brilliant blood-red – the kind of sky in which Turner would have delighted. All I could think of were the words of the round, 'London's burning, London's burning. Fire, fire. Fetch water, fetch water, or all will be lost', and thousands must have felt as furiously angry at the sight and at their inability to do anything about it.

The Press told us quite quickly this time about the appalling destruction and vast areas of burnt-out buildings, and later we heard about the danger which St Paul's Cathedral had been in – ringed by fire, but not locked and unattended like all those other City churches – and so it was saved. The Cathedral had a splendid fire-watching team led by the Dean, and at great personal risk they fought the fires with water from tanks and storage baths which they had had the foresight to keep ready. It is difficult to explain the feelings which such a terrible spectacle caused in us all. So it must have been in the Great Fire of London – the citizens, much less well-equipped for fire fighting then, must have stood and watched with similar rage, fear, and that sense of helpless frustration which anyone watching the death of a beloved friend and unable to help must feel. Many firemen lost their lives – and many had their eyesight damaged. There were not so many casualties amongst the residents because the City is not a residential area – but even so there were too many, and when we heard the number of historic and much-loved buildings which had perished the fury of everyone was fanned anew. The Guildhall, over five hundred years old, was badly damaged. St Bride's Fleet Street, the newspapers' church, St Lawrence Jewry, Christ Church, Greyfriars, St Andrew by the Wardrobe were some of the Wren churches which were hit. The Central Criminal Court, Dr Johnson's house, the Society of Apothecaries, Trinity House, the Coopers' and Saddlers', the Barbers' Hall, and many other world-famous City landmarks had vanished or been severely damaged.

The Lord Mayor of London, Sir George Wilkinson, said of the Londoners this night, when he was walking in the City, 'In the face of destruction they carried on as though engaged on everyday peace-time occupations. Young and old they passed on their way through the City calmly as though no unusual conditions existed.' He called the British 'truly an incalculable and unshakable race' and paid high tribute to the Fire and Police Services' magnificent work, which was still unflagging at the end of the long night.

It was several days later that we heard that the continuation of this devastating attack was only prevented by the sudden changing of the weather over Northern France, so that the German bombers could not leave their bases. The public's comment was, that, as in the days of Drake's encounter with the Spanish Armada, God had intervened now, as then, to help England by changing the weather!

The immediate result of this catastrophe was the bringing in of the Fire-watching Bill by Mr Herbert Morrison on December 31st, by which fire watching was made compulsory for every house, office, factory, and shop. Some of the City fires went on smouldering for days, and the New Year's Honours List was dwarfed in the Press by details of the full magnitude of the calamity, which cast gloom over us all. The Fire-watching Bill made little difference to us in Chelsea where we had been formed in fire-fighting parties for months, but it did mean that the owners of large buildings and factories had to take some kind of responsibility for fire-guarding them instead of leaving it all to volunteers. I was thankful that I had not given way to Carla's entreaties to stay and had sent her back immediately afterwards. The spectacle of a Chelsea mother with two dazed small boys emerging from a shelter and pointing out to them the orange sky as 'That's the City burning – you look *now, Ken, so you won't forget what the Germans did*,' was indicative of its effect on the boy, who replied apprehensively, 'They won't burn Chelsea, will they, Mum?' Having been brought up from their peaceful country evacuation home to Chelsea for Christmas it was obvious from their faces that their fear was lest Mum should burn too!

The New Year was seen in quietly by Richard and me at the Café Royal but quite riotously in many West End night-clubs and cafés, which were crowded. From all the pubs and the wardens' posts there were also sounds of jollification and singing. The Belgians were happy because there was strong resistance in Belgium to the Nazi Occupation, again chiefly amongst the students in the universities and schoolboys. They now had their own French/Flemish newspaper printed in London and were getting news in it from neutral sources of how their country was faring. So hostile were the students of Brussels University that a German Commissioner was installed to participate in its running and it was not to be closed as in the last war, but Belgian professors were to lecture in Germany while German ones were to be appointed in Liege, Ghent, and Brussels.

On the 3rd we had a sharp night air raid and incendiaries were dropped in an attempt to set fire to the City again, but this time there were plenty of fire spotters and fire guards and the bombs were promptly dealt with. The All Clear went before midnight and there was very little damage. Other parts of Britain were now receiving the Luftwaffe's attention, especially Bristol and Plymouth, and in the middle of the month Plymouth had one of the worst fire raids it had yet experienced.

Jennie, who had spent most of Christmas with us, was furious because those Dutch Nazis who had betrayed Holland had been put in charge of the Dutch radio, which was not a state one but was composed of four privately owned companies. On every front there seemed to be fighting – the war between China and Japan was still dragging on – and General Chiang Kai-shek made a broadcast saying that 1941 would he a decisive year for China.

British preparations for the assault on Tobruk were being made by the RAF, who were bombing it heavily, and in the Sudan fighting was continuous. South African troops supported by Abyssinians had occupied El Bardu, while Rhodesian aircraft were attacking East Africa and British, Indian, and Sudanese troops were pursuing the retreating Italians. The Belgians were told by M Camille Gutt, the Belgian Minister of Finance in London, that Belgian-Congolese troops were already operating with British and Sudanese ones in the Sudan and that further contingents would be sent to the War Zones.

During the first part of the month we experienced some short, sharp, day-light raids on London. They came to be known as 'hit and run' raids. The planes usually came in low cloud, flying at a great height, and, suddenly emerging, would swoop down, drop their bombs, and make off, pursued by Spitfires. They caused quite a lot of damage, and sometimes a bomb would drop before the sirens sounded or we would hear the plane and the swoosh of a bomb simultaneously with the sirens.

The capture of Tobruk was completed by nightfall of the 22nd, the assault of Bardia having been led by the Australians, and helped by some Free French troops who played an important part in the victory in which some 20,000 prisoners were taken. We began to get accustomed to pictures in the Press of great masses of miserable, exhausted-looking prisoners behind barbed-wire compounds. Some of them looked thankful to be out of the fighting.

When the Emperor of Abyssinia, Haile Selassie, crossed the frontier from the Sudan into his kingdom at the head of his troops after five years of exile there was great exultation, and he personally planted the red, green, and gold flag on Abyssinian soil as part of a solemn religious ceremony. He was the first exiled monarch to be restored to his throne since the outbreak of war – it must have given hope to those others being given the hospitality of our land.

At the end of January an unexploded bomb fell in Tedworth Square, fortunately in the gardens, but the refugees in the several houses near had to be evacuated and go to a Rest Centre in the day and change their shelters at night. They did not like this, although the nearness of the bomb had shaken them! They, like thousands of Londoners, had become accustomed to their own bunk or space in their own shelter – they regarded it as part of their home. The wardens and I had a lot of trouble calming them down and settling them into other shelters until the bomb had been removed.

The Giant had become rather silent and morose, and had almost ceased his pranks and practical jokes. I was sorry to see him so gloomy – and this, the second bomb very close to the shelter he and his family used, depressed him further. He felt that the course of the war was not hopeful – and was doubtful of the outcome. He shook his head gloomily, and I was thankful when another house in Royal Avenue offered him hospitality until the bomb had been removed – had he been in a Rest Centre there might have been trouble. Almost as soon as the UXB had been removed by the REs another one fell and this time exploded in the square on February 8th.

It was most unfortunate, and the refugees were again firmly convinced that either there was a spy amongst them who signalled or that the Luftwaffe knew that they were all in Chelsea.

The two power stations, Battersea and Lots Road, were the real targets, and the hit-and-run raids proved this – for the planes came astonishingly low and near to them. The bombs would fall in the river again and again, without harming either the power stations or the bridges across the Thames. After every raid we would look up and there were the great chimneys still intact, belching out smoke, and the bridges still spanning the river.

Wardens were being cut down – and it was rumoured that in March they would be further reduced in number. Now that there were intervals between the raids ungrateful people forgot their need of them and began making remarks that the wardens and the AFS personnel did nothing but play darts and cards, and sit about or lie about sleeping, just as they had done in the phoney war.

Having more free time now I began going to some concerts with Larry. He loved music and whenever he could get off from his duties he would come with me. I had a portable gramophone which had travelled all over the Far East with me, and Larry was always giving me records of the music we heard at the concerts. I had a wonderful collection of classical and jazz music. From China and Japan and India I had brought back a collection of records of music of those countries, and these never failed to fascinate him. He was a dreamy, rather sensitive person and it seemed extraordinary to me that he had volunteered for the Canadian Army as he had done. But he had ideals – and he was willing to fight for them although the idea of war was repugnant to him. When I used to tell him of the horrors left behind after a heavy raid, and of the grim task which fell to the wardens and nurses, he would look at me and say that to do such work I must have the same ideals as he had, but I couldn't honestly say that I had. I hated anything to do with war and violence and cruelty – that was all.

It was now almost impossible to sketch anywhere – and absolutely forbidden to make drawings of the bomb-damaged buildings without a Ministry of Works permit. Every drawing had to be passed by them and was stamped by them on the back as having been permitted but not for reproduction. After Rex Whistler had told me to apply for such a permit I did some drawings of the blitzed houses in Chelsea, and I also began a large portrait of Richard. Elliot Hodgkin had married and moved away from the Royal Hospital Road, and I missed seeing him at work. Ethel Walker was in Robin Hood's Bay. She had twice come to see me and had invited me down there to stay. She had also persuaded me to put her portrait of me down in the basement with the other paintings I had recently bought. She was quite sure, she said, that eventually all the houses near the river would be damaged.

Leon's visits to London were mostly to argue with the Ministry for which he was working. Artists do not take kindly to red tape – and the camouflage unit were finding themselves entangled with it. He would often come along the Royal Hospital Road and call in at No 33 on the way. It was always a joy to see him; like Rex Whistler he brought some original and absolutely fascinating new idea to everything in which he was interested.

Anne and Cecil were going out together more and more. Anne worked very hard for a firm engaged on war-work, and during the heavy Blitz she had never missed or shirked the perilous journeys to and from the City – nor had she ever showed any sign of fear whatsoever, nor any desire to avoid the firewatching duties for which she had volunteered. She had a great many friends but they had been scattered by the war and she turned more and more to Cecil, who was very attracted to her, Larry told me. At Christmas I had noticed them together several times when I was walking on the Embankment.

On a very cold Sunday in February we had built up a huge fire in the studio because we had guests coming that evening and it was bitterly cold, with a north-east wind. The flames blazed up and it threw out such a comforting heat that, both sleepy after a good lunch, we were dozing when Mrs Freeth came up excitedly saying that she thought the chimney was on fire. We went out into the Royal Hospital Road – there was no doubt about it. Flames were coming from it, and a great ugly belch of smoke was fouling the air. It was a double offence to have a chimney on fire during the war, and when the flames became worse we reluctantly telephoned the Fire Brigade. They arrived promptly in full force with fire engines and pumps and invaded the house. The mess was appalling as they turned their hoses down the chimney from the flat roof where Kathleen and I had tried to make a garden. All the water and soot poured into the studio, great clouds of black smoke belched over the carpets, the chairs, and the walls. The boots of the firemen soaked the stair carpets and the parquet floors before they were satisfied that the fire was out and the danger gone.

They appeared to enjoy it thoroughly – as, indeed, I did too. Afterwards Richard produced some wonderful old port which Mr Ferebee had had in store, and all the firemen sat down with us in the dining-room-cum-bedroom, which was the only place not soaking wet, and sipped port, and told us about some of their Blitz experiences. They were fine men, and the fire engines a gorgeous sight, and neighbours all dropped in to ask if we had had a daylight fire bomb, although there had been no Alert! When they had gone, cheerful and not at all censorious, Mrs Freeth and I set to work to clear up the mess. No matter what period of the war it was I always seemed to be clearing up dirt of some kind. Professor Tonks [formerly Slade Professor at London University] had always described dirty colour as colour in the wrong place – so I suppose dirt could be defined as matter in the wrong place, as was the mess made by firemen's boots, floods of water, and soot.

We got our local sweep, Tony Smith [he later won the George Cross for bravery during the Blitz], to come and sweep the chimney after this but, as he said, it was a case of locking the door after the horse had flown – the chimney had burnt itself out. Tony was a great character, inclined to be melancholy at times. He was doing splendid work in heavy rescue and was valued for his complete disregard of danger. He chided us for having left the chimney for so long without sweeping and said we were fortunate that it had happened in day-light and not after black-out. 'You'd have copped it all right then,' he chuckled. Tony was an extremely skilled sweep and as he never made any mess himself during the operation, the appalling mess which our negligence had cost us amused him very much. Mrs Freeth and I appreciated Tony, but owing to his Civil Defence duties it was not always easy to obtain his services.

It was interesting to notice how completely the Belgian women were under the domination of their husbands. Those women who, in turn, had to do the cooking in the canteen took it as a very serious matter. How serious I didn't realize until a Sunday morning in February when Mrs Freeth and I were in the kitchen and two of them, Madame R, a very nice woman, and Madame B, the wife of little Monsieur B who was a Civil Servant, came round in great distress. They had decided to make raspberry jelly for the Sunday lunch, and the jelly had not jelled. They had made it the previous evening as they had been told by the ladies who helped them with the menus, but when they had arrived at the canteen this morning there were great bowls of red liquid – and no jelly. The store cupboards were locked up for it was Sunday, the shops shut – what could they do? Madame R, who was extremely conscientious, was in tears. The men would be furious, absolutely furious! They loved their food – and the Sunday lunch was always a special one. What would they do when they found plates of red soup instead of jelly? 'I know what I'd do,' said Mrs Freeth, 'I'd tell them if they didn't like it they could do the other thing!'

The terror of the poor women amazed us. The Giant, they said, would throw his plate at them as he had twice done already with his food when it hadn't pleased him. Had we any gelatine? We hadn't. I debated whether or not I should wake up Mr Ferebee or his pretty wife but it seemed a shame – Sunday was the only one day on which they could sleep late because they both did their share of fire-watching.

We asked Kathleen. She had none either. It was Mrs Freeth who looked through the cupboards and said, 'We've lots of semolina – why not use that to thicken it? Cook it up again with some semolina.' It sounded revolting, but Mrs Freeth gave them a huge packet and instructions to put the whole lot into the jelly, and stir it well while cooking. Their terror had upset us all – we couldn't imagine English husbands making such a fuss if a dish went wrong. Next day the two women arrived to thank us for our suggestion. The pudding had apparently been the success of the month's menus. They had all loved it and had asked to have it again. Both women were in high favour for having created a new dish!

CHAPTER NINETEEN

THERE HAD BEEN almost five weeks' lull in the bombing and life was becoming more normal. We had time to take a look at ourselves again and to begin to repair some of the ravages. Women went to have their hair permed – perming had fallen off a lot during the Blitz for no one fancied being caught in a raid when fastened securely to the waving machine. In the bright sunshine which heralded spring the clothes which had seen us through some terrible nights had an exhausted, stale look – as had our faces. Older men had been required to register on January 29th – those who were between thirty-seven and forty. The following day Hitler had made a bombastic Sport-Palast speech railing violently against England and asserting his innocence of guilt for the war which he insisted had been thrust upon him. His harsh, boasting voice was almost demented. General Milch, Inspector General of Luftwaffe, broadcasting two days later, was in marked contrast with a serious, quiet warning to the Germans that the British would not be beaten as easily as the Belgians, Poles, and Norwegians. The British, he told them, had proved in 1918 that as a Germanic race, they were 'fighters like the Germans'. On January 26th Wendell Wilkie had arrived on a visit to Britain in the Yankee Clipper to study war conditions. He was taken round bomb damage all over London and to shelters in the heart of the City, and at the conclusion he said, 'It was wonderful. Of all the people I talked to not one was depressed or down-hearted and I talked to dozens of them. I chatted and shook hands with them and did not hear one word of complaint. It was very moving...I am a pretty hard-boiled egg but sometimes I turned my head away overcome with emotion.' He broadcast to Germany at the end of the German language bulletin, telling them that although he was of pure German descent he loathed and detested aggression and tyranny and that his feelings were shared by the overwhelming majority of his fellow-countrymen of German descent, and that the German Americans rejected and hated the aggression and lust for power of the present German Government.

About this time I received a letter from refugees in an internment camp. Alas, although I had so glibly assured Ruth that concentration camps did not exist in Britain the recent disclosures of Sir Waldron Smithers about conditions at Hyton Camp had shaken me, as it had him and thousands of others. This letter contained the news that the writer and his wife, who had been ruthlessly separated and put into different camps, as had all enemy aliens regardless of whether or not they were refugees or supporters of the present regime in their countries, were now happily united with their children in a camp in the Isle of Wight. All their comments on the camps in which they had been living since their internment had been heavily scored out by the censor.

With the long lull in the Blitz there had been time to go to the theatres. Several of them were open again, and one or two had never closed. The lunch-hour ballet, like the lunch-hour concerts, had taken the fancy of the Londoners – especially the Chelsea ones. Both the Ambassadors and the Arts theatres were running lunch-hour ballet. At the New Theatre the Sadlers Wells were giving magnificent performances – short and cheap. Here I spent wonderful lunch hours watching Margot Fonteyn, Frederick Ashton, and Robert Helpmann dancing in a constantly varied programme including *The Prospect Before Us*, *The Wise Virgins*, *Lac des Cygnes*, and *Les Rendezvous* for the modest price of a stall seat for 1*s* 6*d*. At the Arts Prudence Hyman (whose sister worked in our Chelsea canteen), Walter Gore, Harold Turner, Molly Lake, and Helene Wolska delighted us with other ballets, while at the Ambassadors Peggy van Praagh and Sally Gilmour and other talented dancers offered us still further ballet for only 1s a stall.

The spring was coming! And it was a commentary to me on that 'incalculable and unshakable race, the British', that *The Times* could still publish a whole-page photograph of snowdrops or anemones growing wild in our countryside and give up a considerable piece of its now precious paper to a letter on 'Road Deaths of Toads'. In what other country would you expect to find these included with such wonderful news as the surrender of Benghazi? The splendid advance of our troops in Libya had been absorbing most of our attention for some time, and the names of places hitherto unheard of by many had become household words as their fate swung from one side to the other in the fierce battles for their capture, Bardia, Tobruk, Benghazi, and now Karen, the gateway to Eritrea, was being fought for. Kingdom after kingdom was falling and monarch after monarch seeking refuge in other lands. King Carol had fled Rumania, the Regent Paul had abdicated from Yugoslavia and the young King Peter assumed power – in Greece the fighting was bitter, as it was in Italy and Libya. So bewildering a revolution in history was the endless chain of events, so fluid the state of any country engaged or drawn into the war that it was impossible for us to follow its course – the small amount of censored information released to us put each new calamity or triumph into false perspective. I had a map which Richard gave me on which to follow the course of the war, but its front widened so rapidly that to keep up with it was hopeless; nevertheless our own small bomb incidents tended to assume tremendous importance unless some effort was made to take a wider view.

When I told the Belgians that the RAF had bombed Ostend and that the Navy had bombarded it, reducing the industrial area to a mass of flames, they took it very badly. 'But the British can't bomb *us* – we're their Allies – we're not German just because the Germans have occupied us,' they cried indignantly. They did not believe me until they read it in their own Flemish newspaper.

Whenever there was a lull – even for a few nights – in the Blitz the wardens said that the raid which broke that lull was invariably a terrible one. It was as if Hitler understood that when a thing has to be endured continuously it becomes an accepted everyday fact, whereas when there are gaps it reappears with redoubled horror. Courage, keyed-up, can break when no longer needed, and all the ARP Services were agreed that after a lull everything was twice as hard to bear, while some wardens told me they had to force themselves to take up their dangerous tasks.

While we were having a rest from the Blitz in London the provinces were receiving the Luftwaffe's attention. My sisters told me that whenever they were being raided they were at least thankful that London was probably having no Alerts and vice versa. We telephoned one another every morning after a heavy Blitz. Each town thought that no other town suffered anything like as much as it did.

Our London holiday from bombs was shattered by a heavy raid on the night of March 8th, a date which became known everywhere as the Café de Paris night. I first heard of the Café de Paris tragedy from my friend Kay Kelly, a lovely actress who had joined the FANYs early on in the war and was now driving Mr Hore Belisha. He had a friend in Tite Street, just round the corner from Cheyne Place, and when Kay drove him there she would come in to the studio for a cup of coffee and a chat. He would then telephone her when he was ready to leave Tire Street. Kay came in on the morning of March 9th and told me that one of her friends had been going to the Café de Paris the previous night but had suddenly had a premonition not to go. The party which she had been asked to join had gone -- and three of them were dead. She had brought a beautiful clock for me to keep for her – she could not have it in barracks, and wanted it kept going; it had been given her by Ian Hay, in whose play *The Midshipmaid* she had been acting just before war broke out. I looked at her now, trim and neat in her FANY uniform, and thought how beautiful she was and how lucky Mr Hore Belisha was to have such a good driver who was also quite ravishing to the eyes!

She had already heard some of the details of the Café de Paris bomb – and when Richard came in that night I heard more. It had been a bad night in Chelsea too, and we had had several bombs, including another UXB in Ranelagh Gardens, and another in Chelsea Bridge Road; others in Sloane Street, Basil Mansions, and the Pimlico area had exploded and we had casualties in the FAP. The most horrible wounds to deal with were caused by glass – and we spent hours picking out minute glass splinters. One of the incentives to wearing thicker footwear was the masses of glass invariably lying in the streets after bombing. Sometimes the houses from which the glass had fallen were some distance from the bomb, while those quite near it had still their glass intact; there was no knowing what blast would do – its effects were extraordinarily varied.

Kay was very shaken over the Café de Paris – she often went there, and so did we. It was said to be absolutely safe because it was fairly deep underground. The details were pretty horrible and the public had seen a good deal more of it than they usually saw of bomb incidents, because apparently the ARP Services had not got there at all quickly, and the dead had all been laid out on the pavements. At the FAP one of the girls knew more – and told us how, when coming out of another café in Coventry Street, she saw the crowd, and the bodies being brought out – there were eighty-four dead.

Afterwards Rockie told us that there was to be an inquiry into the whole business of why the ARP Services had been so long in arriving. Although the ARP was under the local authorities, if there was evidence of negligence or confusion in dealing with incidents the Home Office had the right to intervene and if necessary to put in a Controller of ARP Services. This had already been done in one or two boroughs. But it was easy to criticize; it had been a terrible night – and there had been widespread damage. Sometimes if the Blitz was very noisy it was extremely difficult for the telephonists in the wardens' posts to get through or to make themselves heard when they had to report an incident. The very fact that only accredited telephonists could do this, made it even more difficult in a very heavy raid. The Café de Paris story became a classic among the stories of the Blitz for the magnificent behaviour of the guests involved in the horrible nightmare of darkness, death, and destruction which followed the explosion of the bomb right on the dance floor. It also put some people off *going* to night-clubs and cafés for a time; but not for long – most of them still had the Kismet theory, that if you were going you would go anyhow – wherever you might chance to be.

The war was long, and looked as if it would be longer – the Blitz cast gloom and its grim evidence in ruins which had to be passed continuously made us long for a party – for a bit of fun. 'Let's go *out*!' we would suddenly decide – and after the long freedom from the sirens we were all getting bolder and bolder about cinemas, theatres, and night-clubs – in all of which we had been earnestly asked not to assemble. The German raids were becoming spasmodic, not continuous now, it was no longer the thing to talk about bombs. Bombs were out! And whenever anyone began a story of what had happened to him or her or their friends in an incident we would sigh, 'Oh God, not *another* bomb story!' so that the Café de Paris incident with its band playing 'Oh Johnnie, Oh Johnnie, Oh' when the bomb fell amongst the dancers, came as a distinct shock. A reminder that Hitler had not finished!

In spite of the comparative lull now in the air raids, Germany was boasting that she was preparing her big spring offensive. We had been bombing Berlin intensively and our troops were advancing towards Addis Ababa. The real reason for the German fury was the Lend-Lease Bill which became law on March 11th, Roosevelt stated bluntly that the aim of the USA was all-out aid for the victory of the Allies. Threats of retaliation by the torpedoing of American ships carrying arms were loud and furious, the *Volkischer Beobachtung* wrote, 'Germany is now preparing to cause the final defeat of England and determined to have a formidable Day of Judgement not only on Churchill and his followers but on the

British nation. We will bring to England a revolution of blood and tears which as a punishment will reduce the British population to degradation and poverty.'

This was as blunt as were President Roosevelt's words. I don't think it frightened anybody because we had the absolute conviction now that Churchill would lead us safely to victory. It was innate in all of us – after all, hadn't we all been taught in our history books that Britain always came out on top? I had met people on the Continent and in India who said that we British were a most conceited and arrogant race – that we behaved as if we were superior beings. Well, that might be so – but if we had those qualities they stood us in good stead now. For no one took any notice of the flood of threats from Germany. We took much more notice of the fact that cheese was to be rationed. It had long been the one thing we could fall back on now that almost everything else was doled out in one or two ounces per head per week. At the end of March we were to be allotted one ounce of cheese per week – good-bye to Mrs Freeth's cheese omelettes, and surely the next thing to go would be eggs. When our butter ration had been suddenly increased from two to four ounces temporarily because of an unexpected supply it had seemed too good to be true. I was beginning to get tired very easily – as we all were – and it was not to be wondered at on the rations on which we had to do a hard day's work. Lord Woolton might tell us continually that people all ate too much meat and that potatoes were good for us – but there was not much danger of having too much meat when the ration was 1s 2d. worth a week.

March 23rd was a Day of National Prayer, ordered by the King. I went to Chelsea Old Church with a turn-out of the Red Cross. Since having had to pick up and fit together the pieces of my fellow-men, women, and children, I was not sure about prayer – a nagging doubt was at work in me – but I loved Chelsea Old Church, More's church we often called it, and Richard had been christened in it. There was a Parade of the Chelsea Sea Cadet Corps and Chelsea Air Training Corps. There were about sixty lads in each unit; their fine, keen young faces and their smart trim appearance made a most poignant impression on me as I looked at them in the light from the lovely windows of the Old Church. If the war went on much longer – and Churchill had just warned us that it would – then many of these boys would soon be wearing Naval and Air Force uniforms. The vicar, the Rev R Sadleir, who was Chaplain to the ATC, conducted the service, and afterwards the cadets were inspected. The little garden at the rear of the church was full of spring flowers just coming out. The Embankment was quite crowded with spectators and the parents of the boys on parade. I wandered round the church after the service, showing it to Larry, who had accompanied me.

The Rev Sadleir was the leader of a fire party for watching this famous church and they used his study on the first floor of Petyt House as a fire post. He had arranged tiers of bunks at one end of the room so that the watchers could sleep when not on duty. The fire watchers were very proud of their comfortable post and very proud of their leader, the vicar. Larry spoke to many of the cadets afterwards. I have never known a young man more interested in and attracted to children and adolescents – he loved them and had already asked if he could be godfather to my baby, which was to be born in September. At the very end of March Mr Herbert Morrison in a broadcast gave us a warning about the possibility of the use of gas by the Germans. 'Have your gas masks ready,' he warned us.

This resulted in some practices in the FAP with our gas-masks on and it was a most eerie feeling seeing our fellow VADs in such hideous guise. We also went to a fresh spate of lectures on gas. One listener told the lecturer that she had discovered that by wearing her gas mask while peeling onions she avoided the usual weeping from their irritation of the eyes. Before the lecturer could comment every woman present had already shouted, 'Where did you get the onions?' for they were as scarce as gold and the most wonderful present I had received recently had been two enormous onions in a box from my sister in Bristol.

The problem of occupying the refugees was one to which we were all giving thought. Apparently they were not yet considered sufficiently screened for munition work. One or two of their own Civil Servants were already working with the Belgian Government now set up in Eaton Square, and these men were slowly beginning to assume some kind of responsibility for the others. Most of the houses in which they were living had gardens at the rear and Suzanne and I thought that it would be a good idea if they could cultivate these gardens and grow themselves some vegetables. The Committee thought it an excellent plan, and Margerie Scott, as usual, found gardening implements for them. The question was, however, how to divide up the small gardens so that each family living in the house should get an equal share. This was so delicate a task that some of the Town Hall officials had to be asked to do it. The gardens were divided, seeds and plants arrived with forks, spades, shovels and picks and rakes. The refugees were delighted and all got to work on their plots. Alas – it seemed that the division was not satisfactory to their ideas of fair shares. I got complaints but ignored them. I had not divided the gardens, I told them, why blame me?

One Sunday morning in March an apologetic policeman appeared, begging me to come at once as the refugees were fighting and he wanted them to be warned that if they would not desist he would have no choice but to arrest them. One of the old Pensioners who was having his Sunday beer with us offered to come round at once and help. 'I'll give 'em fighting,' said the old man, who was over eighty, 'I'll soon show 'em.' In his scarlet coat and his row of medals, which included those of four wars, and with his white moustache bristling, he meant what he said. I promised to send the policeman back for him should we need help.

We arrived in Tedworth Square to find an amazing spectacle on this quiet Sunday morning. In the back garden of the house where The Giant lived (I had feared it as soon as the policeman came) he and two other men were fighting savagely with the picks and forks provided for cultivating the soil. Their womenfolk were watching and encouraging them with excited exhortations...all except Madame R, who had come over from another house to try to stop the combatants. Two of the smaller men were warding off The Giant. With their backs to the wall of the garden they were parrying, with spades, his attacks with a huge garden fork, and at the same time endeavouring to get a thrust in at him whenever possible. Monsieur C's face was cut and blood was streaming from it, Monsieur B's hand was bleeding, and all three combatants had filthy faces from wiping their wounds after having been digging. The women fell upon me, as with the policeman I endeavoured to make myself heard. The Giant shamefacedly lowered his fork as soon as he saw me. 'It's not my fault, Marraine – it's no good your blaming me. This P here, he took more than half a metre of my plot while I was in the shelter last night. Yes, Marraine, he and that C there, moved the pegs and the string put there by the gentleman from the Town Hall while I was in the shelter during the raid. They thought I wouldn't see. But I saw – as soon as I got back from Mass this morning I saw that the pegs and string had been moved. I challenged them – and *why them*? Because they were late in coming into the shelter last night. Yes, *very late*. And I know that they're no braver than the rest of us and would only stay during a raid for something important. My plot! That's what was important to them. Stealing it! *Thieves! Thieves!*' He shouted loudly, raising the fork again. 'Stop it!' I told him sharply. 'If you don't stop this fight the police will have to arrest you. We don't allow fighting here! You know that already. You have made trouble before – and the police know you for it. Put down that fork.' 'I will if those thieves will put down their spades,' he cried. 'Let them put them down first.' '*No. You all put them down,*' I shouted, in Flemish, while the policeman shouted in stentorian tones, 'Put those implements down – in the name of the law!'

Very reluctantly they laid the things down and the policeman gathered them up. I said to him, 'Shall we take them round to my place? They can have them back when this business is settled.' He collected the remainder of the gardening tools into a heap. The Giant looked up dismayed as a child deprived of his toys. 'But, Marraine,' he wailed, 'no more work on the garden to-day? It's *Sunday* – everyone gardens on Sundays.'

But there was the problem of the plot and its having been moved. The women reluctantly agreed that it *had* been moved. But the two men stoutly denied having moved it. Why were they late in going to the shelter? I asked them. It had been Saturday, they had drawn their Public Relief money on the Friday, they had gone to a pub for a drink. They were just beginning to pluck up courage to enter pubs. They missed their wine and cognac, they said. They had met an Englishman who had stood them both drinks. He knew Ostend well and had been to Dunkirk and they had got on fine. Did they know his name? I asked them! Yes, they did. They took out a crumpled piece of paper. Written on it was the name of Tom Baynes, whose boat had been to Dunkirk.

'It's no good,' I told The Giant. 'They have an alibi. Whoever did it, it wasn't them.' Both their wives confirmed that they had come to the shelter smelling of drink, and both had told their wives of their new acquaintance.

The Giant was not satisfied. 'Listen,' I said. 'I'll put it back to where it used to be. Will that satisfy you?' 'No,' he shouted. He wanted to know which person amongst them was a thief. He was not accustomed to living with thieves, would I ask the police to investigate? The police had something better to do than investigate such petty things, I retorted. Probably someone had done it for a joke. I translated a long and impressive speech by the policeman about law and order and that such incidents could only lengthen and not shorten the period until they could all be employed in the war effort. Although they could not understand him, his stern voice and face were enough without the translation. They were frightened and abashed, and the two with cuts followed me sheepishly to No 33 to have their wounds dressed while the representative of law and order led the way with the gardening things.

Our guests were highly amused at my bringing back two patients, but the Chelsea Pensioners were scandalized. 'Don't they reverence the Sabbath in their country?' one demanded. 'Fighting on a Sunday morning!' 'They've been to Mass,' I said. 'Shocking!' exploded the grand old man. 'Supposing we were to come out of Church Parade and start fighting over our allotments! We've got 'em, you know. We can all have a bit if we want it. Got to help the war effort! My two patients, bound up and disinfected, were given some beer and, sheepish and apologetic, took leave of us for the canteen in St Leonard's Terrace.

There were two young girls who were much on my mind now that my hours of duty were somewhat less. One was Catherine, who was terribly unhappy still, and the other was Anne.

Catherine was shunned by many of the refugees, who felt that her place was with her baby. She was still anaemic and frail after her illness, and I began teaching her English apart from the class. I saw that her fanatical insistence on joining one of the Women's Services was something implanted very deeply and that I had no right to dissuade her from it. Whenever she saw Kay Kelly in her smart uniform she would become melancholy and brooding. Kay's sister Vi was now in the WAAF, having sent her little daughter to America to relatives and I asked her if it would be possible to get Catherine into that Service. She said that it might take time, but that they wanted more recruits and Catherine's knowledge of Flemish might be useful. She could also type as she had had to do her former employer's business letters and keep his accounts. I told her that if she would work hard at her English and concentrate on getting her health improved as Dr Pennell wanted her to, then she might have a chance of getting into one of the Services.

She had not been to visit Francesca once – and when I asked her why not she replied that she just didn't feel she could go there. I wrote to the nursery and was told that Francesca was well and growing splendidly – that she was a lovely child and they couldn't understand why her mother did not take any interest in her. The fact that Catherine did not want to visit her baby infuriated the women refugees. She was unnatural, they said.

Anne, on the other hand, looked very happy and she had that vital look which is inseparable from love. She was, she told me, madly in love with Cecil and he with her. I thought it was lovely – they were both very young, very good-looking, and very attractive. What, then, was the trouble? I asked Anne, when she came in one evening after telephoning me. It was Mother, she said. Kathleen, apparently, was opposed to their marriage. She did not think they were suited – and she wanted Anne to wait. Cecil, with the same impatience as the other Canadians, to see some real *action*, was certain that very soon his unit would be sent overseas and he wanted to marry before he went. She asked me to talk to Kathleen. Her mother, she said, would listen to me although I was so much younger than she was. When did they want to get married? I asked. Quite soon – in fact almost immediately. Cecil could get a special licence – they both lived in Chelsea, there would be no residential qualification trouble. They wanted to be married at *once*.

Anne was over twenty-one – legally Kathleen could not prevent her marriage – but the two had always been very close, partly because Kathleen had long been widowed, and partly because Anne had always shared the responsibility of Penty with her mother. We were in a dilemma over it. I felt that I was not capable of giving advice or trying to influence either party. Richard felt the same way but was inclined to agree with Kathleen that to wait would be wiser. He reminded me when I pressed the young lovers' cause that we knew absolutely nothing about Cecil. I have always thought that we can really know little about anyone – only what they choose to show us and that is not always their true side, so what difference did it make? They were in love – and I felt for them. *We* were very happy, why shouldn't they be?

We talked to Kathleen that evening. She was terribly upset. She couldn't tell us why she felt that it would be a mistake, but she did feel it. She was Irish, and she had frequent intuitions which were infallible. I did not laugh at such things – I had them myself – and they were often right. But whereas she had one that the marriage would be a tragedy mine was that it would be a success. The change in Anne was wonderful. She was gay, always laughing and teasing Cecil, her blue eyes literally dancing with mischief, her whole demeanour was one of happiness and of the fact that she was loved and wanted. Cecil was less demonstrative – but he was terribly in love and impatient to marry her.

Kathleen, after much discussion, said that there was nothing she could do. Anne had never gone against her wishes before – but Kathleen felt that she would do so now. She wanted Cecil and she was going to marry him. We had a long talk with her about everything – and about Penty, whose future was an ever-increasing anxiety to Kathleen. I think Kathleen felt that Anne should do much better for herself. Cecil had no money except his pay, and Anne, who earned a good salary in the City, had been used to comfort, if not luxury. But Cecil was very young, and was the type who would get on. Canada is the land of opportunity – surely after the war he would not lack chances? The thing which swayed me and which had struck me forcibly all through the Blitz was the bond between these two people. You could call it sex or you could call it love – it was that indefinable something which is the strongest and most lovely of all human emotions. I had seen it all through the horrible tragedies of the war – this love which mattered so much more than the Blitz or the bombs showed me that the annihilation of the body was of no importance. I had seen a couple locked together during the most terrible bombing, absolutely oblivious of anything except each other. I had seen husbands and wives united after thinking that one was dead and their meeting had been too poignant to watch. The love of mothers for their missing children was equally – perhaps more – moving because of its unselfishness, but it did not have the terrible urgency or indefinable insistence of that other love. I saw this now between those two, Cecil and Anne, and who were we to deny it them? I was far nearer to them in age than I was to Kathleen and I pleaded for them.

Anne and Cecil were married in the middle of March at the Chelsea Registrar's Office. Richard and I gave them a small wedding luncheon at the Royal Court Hotel. Mr Wilde worked wonders, producing not only white flowers for the table and silver horseshoes for each of us, but a small white wedding cake with a wonderful sugar and silver Cupid on it. Kathleen and I gave up our sugar and fat ration so that this could be made. Cecil was shy, but his best man, a friend from the Canadian RASC, was a man of the world and soon put him at his ease. Anne looked lovely in a blue dress and tiny hat. She was radiant. I had never seen her look prettier. Kathleen put a good face on it, and the party was a great success. We drank to the young couple's health in champagne and Mr Wilde added some of his own as a gift to the war-time wedding. Cecil talked of taking Anne to Canada when the war was over – she was excited at the idea. Kathleen was upset. I liked Cecil – he was shy with women and not at his ease in company – but as he had spent a great deal of his life in the frozen North as a trapper this was not to be wondered at. He was an orphan, he told us – and had gone to Canada as a child. We gathered that he had had a lonely but not unhappy life. The best man was a delightful person. He told me that Cecil was very popular in the regiment, that he had a lot of friends. We had asked him to invite some of them to lunch – but he had only wanted this one special friend – and Anne had not wanted any of her girl friends. So we were a small party – but a very gay one. Anne and Cecil went away for a couple of days – Cecil had no leave until April when they planned a proper honeymoon. When they had left Kathleen came back with us and stayed for the evening. She was terribly upset – she was not happy about the marriage and I wondered if we had done right in approving it. But, as Richard said, what was the use of her objecting? Anne was over twenty-one and would have married him anyway.

'You're going to have a baby. It's not all pleasure having children,' Kathleen said to me. 'You have to give up so much for them – but they are reluctant to give up anything for you.' I tried to comfort her by saying that Anne looked so radiant but she burst into tears and said she felt already that she was in their way. The flat was her home – but the young ones seemed to have taken it over completely and it was no longer hers. She didn't know if she would be able to continue to live with them there. But where else would she go? And that she did not want to live alone was obvious. We encouraged her to talk about her business, which was doing very promisingly. She became enthusiastic at once. She had all sorts of plans for it – if only the war would end and the restrictions on everything be lifted she felt that she could spread her wings and soar. There was no limit to her ideas and plans. Kathleen was really gifted in designing clothes – her creations had that something which marked them from the ordinary everyday garment. No matter how simple a dress or coat she made – it had distinction. The Blitz had become so much less frequent and violent that there was a spate of entertaining now that it was no longer such a problem to get home in the black-out.

As I knew now that I was going to have a baby in the autumn, Betty Compton sent me to her gynaecologist, who told me that he did not consider me very robust and that he would prefer me to give up some of my work, and this I agreed to do at the end of April. He also said that he would not confine me in London – he was adamant and, remembering Catherine's ordeal, I understood his reasons. We were delighted at the prospect of a baby, and decided immediately that our home would not be large enough and I must set about finding a larger one. Spring was well on the way, the raids were lessening, life began to look radiant.

On the 17th Richard left the Ministry of Home Security and was appointed Director of the Home Division of the Ministry of Information. I was glad for him as it meant promotion, but sorry otherwise. This Ministry had become a source of much satire and amusement to the public – and somehow I mistrusted it as much as the public did. The Ministry of Home Security had something reassuring in its very title although doubtless it suffered from the inevitable anomalies and red tape as did all the other war-time ministries.

At this time all women, married or single, were required to register for war work. The decision to use and direct women in the war-drive upset many people, who said that even in Germany women were still absolutely free to help in the war effort or to tend their families; but most of us felt that this was only right and were glad to be regarded as equally liable as men for the defence of our country.

There were so many damaged houses now in Chelsea, and so many requisitioned ones, that to find a new home suitable for a family was not easy, but after much search I had found one just around the corner in Tite Street which seemed to answer the purpose. It was a delightful modern house with a small garden, and had plenty of large airy rooms. The owners were in the country, but the agents said that there would be no difficulty in renting it on a long lease with a possibility of buying it if we wished. Kathleen and Mrs Freeth both approved it, and Kay, who inspected it with me while Mr Hore Belisha was visiting his friend only a few houses away, thought it was a wonderful find. I was thankful for her that the Blitz had quietened down recently. Mr Hore Belisha was a most considerate and charming person, but he had a cottage on Wimbledon Common and Kay often had to drive through the heavy Blitz when taking him there or returning with the car. Like our ambulance drivers she simply took it all as part of the job.

CHAPTER TWENTY

IN APRIL it really seemed that the worst of the winter's horrors could be forgotten. Everywhere in their gardens or allotments people were digging and sowing seeds. Even the smallest amount of food grown helped. The refugees, now that the question of their garden plots had been settled satisfactorily, were very happy raking and sowing and many of them were planting potatoes. The trees, probably because we now had time to look at them, seemed especially lovely this year, the flowering ones laden with blossom. In the little physics garden in Swan Walk everything was budding and shooting. The gardener allowed me to take Vicki in there. The gate had to be kept unlocked now because of raids, and this small, fascinating place full of rare herbs and strange medicinal plants was a great joy to me. In the grounds of the Royal Hospital I met Asta Lange and Peer Gynt again. He still loved Vicki as much as ever. The Norwegians were having a terrible time under the Germans, who were helped by the Norwegian Nazis, known as the Hirdmen. The children, Asta told me, used to go and stand outside the Royal Palace and shout, 'Long live the King and Queen. Down with Quisling,' and were brutally treated by the Hirdmen and the German Nazis. They didn't care – they went on doing it. The Hirdmen had formed a Nazi regiment and their marching song began, 'In serried ranks, we march through London's streets.' This amused Asta very much. 'Let them come and try it!' she scoffed. So great were the disturbances caused by the Resistance in Norway that Himmler, chief of Nazi police, had to go there to try to quell the insurrection. Asta's family were all in Norway, but she was undaunted – the war could only end in victory and the end of the criminals who were behaving so brutally to her fellow countrymen.

Easter was early that year, Good Friday being on April 11th. The week-end was cold, there had been snow and sleet although the spring was so advanced. I had at last given in to the pleadings of my young niece to be allowed to come and stay with us in Chelsea. I also gave in to Carla's entreaties. Ruth was still in the mental hospital – she was, in fact, no better. Carla was beginning to feel the need of a home of some kind and I agreed that she should come for ten days. Ruth still appeared to have no recollection of Carla – or of her sons in Germany. Her mind was a blank as regards her former life. I had had letters from some friends of hers offering to help with Carla – but not to have her with them. They felt that a child would be too much of a responsibility in war-time. What they offered was money – but this I did not accept. What if they should want it back from Ruth at some future date? No, I had accepted Carla as my responsibility and she was passionately attached to me now.

My niece, known as Bobbie, although her name was Nora, arrived in high spirits from her boarding-school in Dorchester. She was delighted to be in London. Carla arrived, equally gay. Both were growing into very pretty girls, both blonde and blue-eyed. I took them to buy clothes and was urged by Richard to get some for myself. But if I were going to have a baby what would be the use?

When a few days later the rationing of clothing was announced I understood his having pressed me to do this, but I was very indignant that he had not told me the real reason for his advice – it seemed to me to be carrying governmental caution too far.

On Easter Sunday we had an Easter egg-hunt for the refugee children. We hid the eggs in the gardens of each house and at a signal they had to hunt for them. Larry had supplied a great many of the eggs and thoroughly enjoyed the fun in giving the children, now able to talk to him in English, some clues as to whether or not they were 'hot' or 'cold'.

Sweets were not yet rationed, although very scarce, but there were plenty of chocolate eggs at a price, and Richard gave me the very biggest one I had ever had. Carla's and Bobbie's were almost as huge. We had given great pleasure to old Granny of Paradise Walk by giving her an Easter egg. She was quite overcome with delight when the two girls, who liked to go and pet the horse Beauty and take her tit-bits, presented her with it. Beauty was still very frightened and restive in heavy raids – but since the lull she had become much easier to manage. The old couple loved her, and she was their first thought when the sirens sounded.

Granny was still hoping that they would get the old-age pension – she had spoken to me about this many times. Richard told me that they should swear an affidavit as to the place and dates of their births to the best of their ability. I took Granny to my solicitors and this was done the week before Easter. The documents lay in my desk and immediately after Easter I intended taking them to the Town Hall to see what could be done. The fruit and vegetable trade was diminishing rapidly now that the war curtailed imports and transport was difficult. They felt that their living would soon be taken from them and what would they do then, at their age, asked Granny? Her husband still drove most mornings to Covent Garden in Richard's overcoat, but sometimes he came back with almost nothing. Food for the horse was becoming very difficult too, and altogether life was very hard for the old couple and their lodger.

Anne and Cecil had gone away for their honeymoon. They were both able to add the Easter holiday on to some leave so that they had over a fortnight. They went to the Midlands, where Anne had friends, for part of the time. Kathleen was alone and spent a lot of time with us.

On Easter Saturday A P Herbert, whose work I had always liked, and whom I had met with Leon and Mary Underwood, gave us a delightful Postscript in a broadcast. He called it, 'Let's be Gay!' It exactly suited our mood of spring after winter, and the lull after the storm of the Blitz. I know I liked it so much that I wrote it down for the two girls. It began:

> Let's be gay. It's Easter Day –
> And Spring, at last, is on its way.
> It's Hitler's habit in the Spring
> To do some dark disgusting thing,
> But you and I may still decline
> To sign on Hitler's dotty line.
> Let's be gay. It is the Spring
> And even postscripts have to sing.

The last verse went:

> Let us be gay because we've got
> The finest leader of the lot.
> Let us be gay because we see
> The breed is what it used to be,
> Let us be gay because we know
> That Franklin Roosevelt won't let go
> And in the war of Night and Day
> The English-speakers lead the way.

I thought APH had caught the feeling of us all wonderfully. The news that America was going all out to help us *had* made a difference in our outlook, Larry was jubilant but he was not satisfied

– he wanted the United States to come right out in the open and join the Allies in actual war. There were other volunteers with the Canadians who were Americans like him, and in the ARP we had several working with us – nurses, fire-watchers, and wardens doing voluntary shifts.

Yes, we all felt cheerful! The winter, which had been grim, was over. Every day the sun became a little stronger, and life a little brighter. In this mood we decided to give a really big cocktail party on Easter Sunday, as we had not had one since our marriage. Bank holidays had been abolished since the war, everyone had to work on the Monday. We had a very gay party, in marked contrast to the one I had had in that fateful June of last year. There were a number of schoolgirls and boys in London for their holidays and I asked several of them for Carla and Bobbie. They looked after the cocktail snacks and were a great success. Larry had brought some of the Canadians, including Anne's and Cecil's best man. Many colleagues of Richard's from the Ministries came, and many of my colleagues from the FAP and the Control Centre, all the Fitzgerald family from the Royal Hospital, Asta and Jennie, Kumari, and Dr Pennell – and, to my great joy, Marianne Ducroix, happy and assured now that the French were helping magnificently in the Libyan campaign. It was a lovely party! and it seemed in some way for me to have a special significance. I was very happy that we were going to have a child – and feeling wonderfully fit. All my family, especially my mother, were delighted, and had already begun sending me small garments for the baby.

During the evening Carla and Bobbie gave Vicki a whole glass of sherry. She loved it so much that they gave her another one before I could prevent them. Poor Miss Hitler was very drunk! She could not stand up properly, but rolled about in a helpless, ridiculous way. Afterwards she undoubtedly had a hang-over and would not look at alcohol but turned her face away resolutely whenever a glass of any kind was offered her. I saw Carla off on the Monday; she did not want to go. She was an affectionate child and cried bitterly at leaving me, but she had been invited to a school-friend's for the remainder of the holidays and I felt that for her own sake she must make friends and learn to stand on her own feet. I promised her that by next holidays we would have moved to the house in Tite Street and that there would always be a room for her there. My sister telephoned the next morning and said that Bobbie must return. The child pleaded with me to stay – but my sister, who told me afterwards that she had the strangest presentiment of disaster, was adamant about her immediate return. That evening we were all playing about in the studio with Vicki and a ball, and Richard was tipping his chair backwards as he caught it from Bobbie. I had yielded to persuasion and had moved the Green Cat from the window on to a low table. As Richard tilted backwards, his foot caught the table and tipped it over. The Green Cat fell on to the carpet. It was a thick carpet but one of his pointed ears was knocked off and broken into several pieces.

I made an abominable fuss about it. I was terribly upset – not only because the Cat was so beautiful, but because it had been impressed on me that he was the Guardian of the Home and must be kept intact and inviolate. Richard was very apologetic but he was rightly annoyed at the fuss I made. He said it could be repaired so cleverly that no one would know. He also reminded me that many people had lost everything in the bombing. I put the damaged Cat back in the window – it did not seem to matter now.

With Bobbie and Carla gone I felt quite desolate, and so did Mrs Freeth. Larry brought me a blue rabbit for the baby which he said would be a boy – we put this beside the damaged Cat to console him. It was Wednesday, April 16th, and a lovely warm day – so warm that it seemed that summer had arrived without any proper spring.

In the afternoon I went to visit some of the refugees. They were very excited; two of the men had gone to join their boats in Brixham, and there was a prospect of others getting employment soon. They were also digging and planting potatoes in their small plots. For once there was not a single complaint – they were full of the same gay feeling as I was.

Vicki had been trying to get out all day to Peer Gynt, who had escaped from Asta and was sitting hopefully in the middle of the Royal Hospital Road watching our windows and our front door – the spring and biology had affected them too. At lunchtime a policeman had rung the bell and asked if it were my dog in the road as it was obstructing the traffic which had to go all round it. I explained about Vicki being the object of his attentions and we chased him off. When I went out in the afternoon with her we were relieved to find that he had gone home.

Anne and Cecil returned from their honeymoon about six o'clock. Kathleen came to wait with me for their arrival. I had saved a bottle of champagne for them. I had had a postcard from them both – so had Larry.

Anne came in, impetuous and gay, and flung herself upon us. She looked radiant. I held her away from me and said, 'Well, how was it?' She hugged me, and said, 'Wonderful! *Wonderful!*' and her glowing face was all the evidence I needed. Richard came home and we drank their health and future happiness and they insisted on drinking to the baby we were expecting. We stood there, Larry, Cecil, and Richard, all well over six feet tall, and Kathleen, Anne, and I, and drank to everything – to Victory, to Canada, to America, to them, to Kathleen, and to us. Then the honeymooners went upstairs to unpack and Kathleen stayed with us for a while. When I looked at her I saw that she was weeping bitterly. She could not get accustomed to Anne being married to Cecil. But I thought that she would have felt the same way at first about any man who married Anne and that she would soon get over it. But she was sad – and we couldn't cheer her up as we usually could. She had financial worries, she said, and they kept her awake. She worried about Penty too. She seemed to have a presentiment that death was not far away for she asked me suddenly if I would become a trustee and guardian to Penty. I hesitated – already I had Catherine and Francesca and Carla – and now my own baby was on the way. I felt it would not be fair to Richard to burden him with any more responsibilities – although I intended to shoulder mine quite independently.

She said, 'All right, let's leave it for a few days. I know you'll do what you can for her if anything happens to me.' I said, 'Nothing is going to happen to you, have another drink.'

We discussed the financial troubles – and told her we could help her. She went away much happier, and kissed me very warmly.

It was too late to start cooking. I had sent Mrs Freeth home. She had not wanted to go, but I thought she had been working too hard and I made her go. Richard suggested that we went out for dinner. We would go and see Madame Caletta, who had been carrying on the restaurant very successfully since her husband's death. We talked with Madame Caletta about the sunshine, the quieter nights, the war, and everything in general and we had a very enjoyable dinner. It had been quite light when we entered the restaurant, but when we came out it was quite dark. As we walked home enjoying the warm air to our astonishment the sirens went – first in the distance those eerie mournful howls and then nearer until they blasted the still air in full fury. It was five minutes past nine.

Almost immediately there was the sickening roar of a great drove of planes which increased and increased so that we knew that there must be hundreds of them. The guns opened up at once – a terrific barrage, so loud that it was difficult to speak, and huge flares – different to any which we had seen – were being dropped.

I was wearing a black afternoon dress and Richard had said to me, 'You never wear your pearls now, they'll lose their colour if you don't wear them,' and so I had put them on for the first time since the Blitz.

The raid became heavier and heavier after we reached home. The wardens were all out – we had met Nonie Iredale-Smith and George Evans and several others hurrying on their bicycles. And sitting in the road, oblivious to the noise of guns, was the faithful Peer Gynt. I tried unsuccessfully to send him home. I was no longer on duty. Betty Compton had said that the refugees took up enough of my time and as the raids were lessening I should do as our gynecologist wished and take things more easily. It seemed strange not to rush to change into my uniform and report at the FAP or at the Control Centre. We left the studio and went downstairs to the dining-room in which we still slept when the raid became even more heavy. As it intensified and more and more planes came over I telephoned Kathleen and asked her if she were not going to take shelter over the road in the basement of her little shop. She said she was tired and felt like sleeping in her own bed. Her bedroom, like Anne's and Cecil's, was right under the roof. I don't know why I begged her so strongly to come downstairs, offering her a bed in the hall, which we considered the safest place as it had one wall of ferro-concrete and the others were very thick. Richard added his arguments to mine in vain. I asked about Anne and Cecil. 'What d'you expect?' she said. 'They've gone to bed.'

Anne came to the telephone herself; she sounded as if she were in a dilemma. It was quite clear that she did not like the raid – the noise must have been even more deafening up there and with the terrific barrage it would have been quite possible for shell-caps to penetrate the roof. Cecil settled the matter. He quite obviously took the receiver from her, speaking to me himself. 'Have a heart,' he said laughingly. 'It's still our honeymoon – we've got two more days.' 'You can have our bed,' I said, 'if you'll only come down. Richard says it's a terribly heavy raid and that there are droves of German planes. Do come down – anyhow for a while.' 'Sure we'll come down,' he said jokingly. 'Don't worry. *We'll come down with the rubble.'*

We had never experienced such a night – bombs seemed to rain down – and in the intervals of their explosions which tonight were the loudest and longest we could remember we could hear the guns in the planes as the fighters chased them. The sky was alight with flares, searchlights, and exploding shells – it was a magnificent but appalling sight! The fires which we could see were terrifying – the largest, in the direction of Victoria, was enormous and appeared to be increasing. Behind us, much nearer, there was a terrible blaze in the direction of Burton Court. Wardens kept running by and we heard the revving up of engines from the auxiliary fire-station a few doors down at No 21. We were keeping a sharp look-out for incendiaries and there seemed to be no watchers about at all. About twenty past eleven we decided to settle down and read for a time. Neither of us felt like going to bed – it was far too noisy and exciting. A warden raced by shouting, and suddenly we heard a shout of 'Lights, lights' from the street. Richard wondered if the recent near explosions had caused the black-out curtains to shift in the studio and he said, 'I'll run up and have a look.'

He had scarcely gone when the lights all went out. There was a strange quiet – a dead hush, and prickles of terror went up my spine as a rustling, crackling, endless sound as of ripping, tearing paper began. I did not know what it was, and I screamed to Richard, *'Come down, come down!'* Before I could hear whether or not he was coming down the stairs, things began to drop – great masses fell – great crashes sounded all round me. I had flung myself down by the bed hiding Vicki under my stomach, trying thus to save her and the coming baby from harm. I buried my face in the eiderdown of the bed as the rain of debris went on falling for what seemed ages...ages...The bed was covered and so was I – I could scarcely breathe – things fell all round my head – some of it almost choked me as the stuff, whatever it was, reached my neck and my mouth.

At last there was a comparative silence and with great difficulty I raised my head and shook it free of heavy, choking, dusty stuff. An arm had fallen round my neck – a warm, living arm, and for one moment I thought that Richard had entered in the darkness and was holding me, but when very, very cautiously, I raised my hand to it, I found that it was a woman's bare arm with two rings on the third finger and it stopped short in a sticky mess. I shook myself free of it. Vicki, who had behaved absolutely perfectly, keeping so still that she could have been dead, became excited now as she smelt the blood. I screamed again, *'Richard, Richard'*, and to my astonishment he answered quite near me. 'Where are you?' I cried – more things had begun falling. 'At the bottom of the stairs,' he said.

'Keep there. Keep still – there are more things falling,' I cried and buried my head again as more debris fell all round me. At last it appeared to have stopped. I raised my head again – I could see the sky and the searchlights and I knew that the whole of the three upper stories of the house had gone. 'We've been hit,' I said. *'One in a million!'* and the only feeling I was conscious of was furious anger.

It was pitch dark – too dangerous to move without some idea of what the position was. I had had my torch in my hand but the blast had thrown it from me. 'Light a match,' I said. 'What about gas?' asked Richard. 'Can't smell any yet – be quick,' I said. He lit several matches, standing, as I saw by their light, in the entrance to the room. There were no ceilings, nothing above me as I crouched there. The front of the room had blown out – but the wall nearest to the one where I was crouching, the ferro-concrete one, was still there, as was the one to the hall. By the light of the matches I saw something more terrifying than the arm which was now partially covered with debris – the light lathes from the ceiling had all fallen down across me – so that their weight had not hurt me at all – but balanced on them were huge blocks and lumps of masonry. If I moved they might all crash down. 'Don't come any nearer,' I shouted to Richard. He said, 'Keep still – I'm going to try and get out – the front door is twisted and jammed.'

I had seen where my best exit passage lay when Richard had lit the matches for me and while he was trying to shift the broken door I began wriggling very, very carefully and cautiously along the floor. It was not easy – for I was not as slim as normally, and I had Vicki. It was so perilous that I thought of loosing her and letting her find her own way out. Had she not behaved so wonderfully I would have been obliged to leave her – for the thought uppermost of anything else in my mind was to save my baby. The baby, hitherto a nebulous dream of the future, now became urgently real and my only thought was of it. I shouted again and again – for if only the heavy rescue would come, as they had always promised me they would if I were buried, I would not have to face this perilous crawl – but no sound came from the streets.

I have never been brave at doing dangerous things – I can only do them if I do them very quickly. As children we used to go fishing with my father in Devonshire, and had to cross some of the deep streams bridged only by a tree trunk – not even a flat one. My father always walked straight over without looking to left or right. This, he told me, was the only way. Sometimes I would not cross and he would simply leave me behind until I did.

There were constant terrific explosions and things fell each time there was a fresh thud. If I did not get out soon some of those huge blocks were bound to fall on me. I shouted again, 'Help, help,' and so did Richard. The sounds echoed in the darkness and then far away I heard a woman's voice calling...'They're coming...they'll come...' and it died away and we didn't know if it was to us they would come, because from the thuds and whooshes and violent explosions all round they must have been pretty busy.

'I've got the door open enough to squeeze through,' Richard called. 'Don't light any more matches, I can smell gas,' I warned him. I could not see him – nor he me. 'I'm going to try and crawl through this space to the door,' I said, and I began doing it immediately. I remembered what Tapper told me, *Test it first, tap it gently!* and his warning, 'Don't go scrabbling at anything in case it all comes down on you.' Very slowly and cautiously I squeezed my way along the tiny tunnel under the hanging lathes, on which were balanced the concrete blocks which I had only caught sight of for a split second in the light of the matches. It seemed a life-time. There were two awful moments when my shoulders brushed something and there was a fall of stuff again – and then I was at the door and Richard had caught me and pulled me carefully up. We stood there for a minute clinging together.

'Anne's dead – her arm is in there,' I said.

'I'm afraid they're all dead – the whole stories have gone,' he said. 'D'you think you can walk?'

We now had to squeeze through the jammed door, which he had managed to shift a little. I begged him not to put his weight on it again in case there was another collapse of what was left standing. It was almost impossible to get out because of the piled-up glass in the entrance to the flats under the archway. I had to climb and even so I could feel the glass cutting my legs. At the back of the archway there was a solid mass of debris – and above it nothing remained of the Marshmans' flat – just this great pile of rubble. I rushed at it crying frantically, 'Kathleen, Kathleen! Cecil! Cecil!' but there wasn't a sound.

Above the garage the flat where the landlord's chauffeur lived looked pretty badly damaged. I shouted for him – and he answered from the shelter, the entrance to which was blocked by another great mound of debris. 'We can't get at you,' I screamed. 'We'll tell them to come – the house has gone.' But there was no answer to this, and none to my further halloos. We climbed out finally over the broken glass to the Royal Hospital Road. A great fire was blazing in the direction of the Elms Garage behind Paradise Walk and the whole street was piled several feet high with glass and rubble. In the sky the light from fires was brilliant, it looked like Blake's pictures of Hell.

On a pile of glass in the middle of the road sat Peer Gynt, who had been courting Vicki all day. He was in the very spot where he had been when the policeman had complained that all the traffic had to go round him.

When he saw me come out carrying her, he leaped from his pile of glass and saluted her with joyous barks and whines. He had sat there through all that appalling Blitz, and would not leave her now.

The Ferebees were, we knew, in the basement under the shop, but the whole shop was wrecked and we ran to the entrance and shouted again and again. The fire behind their premises was appalling. We shouted and banged on the ruined door to try to get some reply from them. The whole scene was so like the vision I had had of it after the doctor from the Spanish war's lecture that it was incredible. Fires blazed on every side, great masses of brickwork and masonry kept falling and falling, crashing into the already huge mounds, and the smell was like Guy Fawkes night.

There was not a warden, not a soul about – it looked like a dead place – not a sign of life from anywhere and yet we knew that in many of the houses people were down in their basements unconscious of the horrors above them. I looked down at my legs – they felt cold – and saw that I had no dress below the thighs. It, and my slip, had vanished; the top of the black dress was quite whole

– but the skirt was gone. The whole of it felt wet and sticky – and I knew it was the blood from Anne's arm.

I went back resolutely under the archway in spite of Richard's protests and shouted again and again but there wasn't a sound. In the mass of glass under the archway I saw something which looked like a garment – white – and I thought I could wrap it round my bare thighs, but it was caught firmly and I could not get it. 'Come along – the whole place is going to collapse!' cried Richard as another tremendous thud shook the road, and I had barely got back under the archway before another avalanche of what had once been No 31 fell on to the remains of No 33. It was horrible!

And then I saw Nonie dashing towards us. 'They're all trapped – all of them – the Marshmans – the Ferebees – the Evans, do something quickly!' I cried.

'Get to a shelter somewhere – there's more coming down! They're coming – they'll be here very soon – you can't do anything!' she cried and continued on her urgent errand. In the telephone box at the top of Tite Street a badly wounded warden was trying to get through. 'God, what a night!' he gasped. He was bleeding profusely but would not let me help him in the street. 'Let's go to the FAP,' I said to Richard. 'It's only a second from here.' 'Go there,' shouted the warden. 'They'll be glad of help.'

We were just turning down Tite Street when we saw two parachutes floating down in the direction of the river. 'Lie down! Lie down!' screamed the warden. We flung ourselves down – but it was not pleasant to lie on glass. After what seemed a lifetime there followed two long dull roars and then an appalling explosion. The fires in Burton Court were mounting high in the sky and against them Blossom the balloon stood out in brilliant relief, and at the bottom of Paradise Walk there was a tremendous red glare.

I did not want to go to the FAP. *Anne, Anne*, I kept thinking. Could one live with one's arm ripped off at the shoulder? *Was she alive, and Kathleen? What of her?* She had told me she had a stray kitten in the bed with her when I had telephoned. Like me she loved animals, and had adopted this small homeless creature because she missed her dogs, which were still in the country.

But Richard pulled me firmly by the arm now. 'There's nothing you can do – only the heavy rescue can get through those piles of masonry and bricks,' and he steered me firmly into the heavily sandbagged FAP. Here the scene was indescribable. There had been a bomb so near that it had severed the water mains and damaged the place itself, and they had no means of sterilizing. The roof, which had been damaged on a previous occasion, had a sort of canvas overhead. Stretchers lay all over the floor awaiting ambulances and casualties were everywhere, humped on benches, huddled on chairs, lying on the floor. We walked in and I bumped into Peggy. She stared at me obviously without recognition. 'Peggy,' I said, 'our house has gone – I think everyone else is dead.' And then she knew me. She put down her tray and took me upstairs. She found me an overall and a cloak.

'The AFS Station has been hit – that's only a few doors from you,' she said. 'It's one hell of a night. There are people trapped everywhere and we're full of homeless as well as casualties.'

'We're homeless,' I said. 'The whole of our piece of the Royal Hospital Road has gone.' 'Are you hurt?' she asked, still looking at me as if I were a ghost. I said I was all right and we went downstairs to the surgery where the casualties were being attended to. Suddenly my legs gave way, and I sat down on a bench next to an old woman wearing a straw hat. Waves of terror came over me – each resounding crash of the bombs which were raining down sent fresh waves of awful sickening fear over me. I was *terrified* now, and I knew that this was really craven fear – such as I had never known. I wanted the ground to open and swallow me up – to hide me from this fearful terror from the skies – it was a disgusting, degrading, nauseating feeling – my body was still wet with Anne's blood – I was literally petrified with terror. 'Where is Richard?' I cried suddenly to Peggy, for I knew that he had gone back to try to do something about the others still under those great mounds and the fear was partly for him – and the baby. She finished dressing a wound and said, 'I think you'd better let the doctor see you – you look terrible.' I said, 'I'm frightened – horribly frightened – *I'm sick with fear* – it's nothing else.' She took my hands and held them tight. 'Come,' she said. In the crowded passage we bumped into Richard. To me he looked ghastly pale. 'It's no use,' he said. 'But the Ferebees are all right and so are the Evans – they're only trapped – but there is no sign of life from what was our house.'

'Don't go out again. *Don't!*' I cried and I clung to him for a minute – the world kept rocking round – and then the stretcher-bearers said to him, 'Could you come and help us – we're overwhelmed.'

'Drink this first,' said Peggy, appearing with a small glass. Richard swallowed the drink – and vanished into the noise of the streets with the stretcher-bearers. Peggy brought me a glass and told me to drink. It was brandy – hot and fiery as I swallowed it. What I wanted was water – my throat and mouth were full of dust and filth, but the brandy pulled me together. I went to a table on which was a bowl for scrubbing up and washed the filth from my hands. All over the floor were casualties and stretchers, for every ambulance was out. Lots of the Canadians who were billeted over the garage behind were in with cuts and wounds from glass – some had burns. Sister-in-charge said, 'Come along, you can start here,' and I took my place with the other VADs who were flooded out with waiting casualties and more and more arriving.

For one moment I felt I couldn't do it. How could I dress wounds, pick out glass, bandage and clean up when Kathleen, Cecil, and perhaps even Anne were still alive lying under that weight of debris? A wave of acute terror swept over me again as another huge bomb fell – it sounded as if it were just down on the Embankment. We knew from a warden who came in that one of the parachutes we had seen had landed on the Infirmary of the Royal Hospital and that there were over forty old Pensioners and nurses trapped there. I looked at Sister-in-charge – calm, placid, and authoritative – and then at Dr Lendal Tweed, unperturbable as she attended to each case, and the words of the Sister at that first hospital I had worked in came back to me, and I put Anne, Cecil, and Kathleen and all of them out of my mind and concentrated on what was before me, waiting to be done. At once the sickening fear left me, and suddenly I was quite steady again. The terror had only lasted a few minutes – but it had humiliated me, and was the most degrading experience I had ever known. With Peggy, Joyce, Doreen, and others whom I knew and had always worked with, I fell into line.

Horror piled upon horror as each fresh batch of homeless or walking casualties came in with news of calamities. The fires were terrifying – and more than the one fire station had been put out of action. I did not see Richard again except for brief glimpses of him when he came in bearing one end of a heavy stretcher or going out with a light empty one.

We worked at the lines of grey-faced, patient, huddled people. We made tea for them under great difficulties, we boiled our precious store of water for some kind of sterilization, although the casualties, like me, were filthy. At about two o'clock there was a brief lull and we thought for one glorious moment that the raid was over and that the All Clear would be going very shortly. But almost immediately there was a fresh wave of planes and a new rain of bombs and the guns opened up again in a deafening barrage. I found myself about to deal with the old woman in the straw hat who had been next to me on the bench. 'Where are you hurt?' I asked her. She put both hands up to the straw hat and clutched it firmly. 'It's me 'ead,' she said. 'It's got a bit of something on it – it's cut and I found me 'at so I jammed it on quick.' And then I saw that there were bloodstains all down her neck. 'Take off your hat,' I said very gently. But she would not. She seemed afraid to uncover her head. Very gently I lifted it when at last she allowed me to do so. Part of the top of her scalp was gone – and for one second the whole room spun round again. She was talking quite rationally. I took a large dressing and laid it gently over the top of her head and took her over to Dr Lendal Tweed. She examined her briefly and Sister put on a dressing, then they nodded in the direction of the stretcher-cases for hospital. The old woman put the hat firmly on top of the dressing. She was very cold, she told me. I fetched a blanket and wrapped it round her. Dr Lendal Tweed called me back. 'I heard you've been bombed?' she said, looking at my curious attire. 'Come here. Are you all right?' 'The baby's jumping,' I said. 'It's frightening – a most queer feeling.' She felt my pulse and said, 'You're fine. What d'you expect it to do? It's time it jumped – it's quite normal.'

The gruelling night went on – Peggy was terribly kind, whenever she had a free moment she came to me, as did Sister. But I was all right – it had been just those split seconds of terror – and the agonizing fear for the baby. I went occasionally to see Vicki, who was being nursed in turn by the casualties. She seemed to give them some comfort. The stretcher-bearers told me at intervals that her suitor was still outside the FAP and that no amount of bombs or guns had any effect on his ardour!

That it was our worst night yet was on everybody's lips – and when news came in that the Old Church had gone it seemed the climax to the mounting horrors. The Old Church – I thought of it on that Sunday of March 23rd with all those Sea and ATC Cadets in it – with the daffodils coming out around More's and Hans Sloane's tombs. 'It's a pile of dust,' one of the stretcher-bearers said. 'The whole of that bit – all Petyt Place seems to have disappeared – and the fire-watchers with it!'

Soon after we digested this it was quiet – and at long last the welcome distant sirens sounded far away – then nearer – and then loudly our own from the Albert Bridge proclaimed that the raid was over.

CHAPTER TWENTY-ONE

THE ALL CLEAR had sounded at five minutes to five; it had been one of the longest raids we had known – all but eight hours. In the cold pale morning light we surveyed the appalling havoc of what had been our small colony in the Royal Hospital Road. How we had ever emerged from the mess that had been our home seemed incredible – it was one huge pile of rubble, and more had fallen since we had left it. Farther up the road, at the ruined AFS Station, the heavy rescue appeared to be digging. The Ferebees' shop was shattered but we had been told that they were all right – safe in their basement. The basement of Kathleen's little shop was still intact – we went over in the hopes that perhaps she, at least, had changed her mind and slept there. The door was broken and open – but the basement was empty. We shouted again and again to ask the Ferebees if they knew anything of her fate – but there was only silence – it seemed a dead, desolated street now, with great masses and mounds which had been our house – and the three adjoining it but close at hand a blackbird was singing gloriously.

Picking our way across the piles of glass was perilous, and when I saw in the mass something which looked like a garment and found it was a very old camel-hair coat of mine I fell upon it as if it were the most valuable mink. It was indescribably filthy – but it was a coat, an old friend, and as far as I could see we had no material possessions left in the world. My dress had been blasted off below the hips and I had only an overall – the coat was warm and the early morning air struck chill. Richard would not let me stay to grabble for more treasures but hurried me along to the Royal Hospital. It was terribly difficult to get along because of the glass and debris, and the evidence of last night's damage was apparent everywhere – windows were out, tiles lay in pieces with the bricks, but in the grey light we scarcely noticed it – the hose pipes trailed all across the front entrances and courtyards of the Royal Hospital and we could hear activity somewhere but could see no signs of it as we approached the Fitzgeralds' apartments. The door was wide open and no one came when we rang the bell. As always, we just went in. There was no one in the large hall or in the drawing-room and library. 'They'll be down in the kitchen,' I said, for I knew that Maurice, at least, would be up, he would have been in the thick of the previous night's bombing with Captain Lockley.

We went down into the great kitchen. They were all there – and at our entrance stood looking at us in amazement as if we were ghosts. Then Suzanne caught me in her arms and embraced me and they all began talking excitedly. 'We heard that your house had had a direct hit,' cried Suzanne, 'and we sent Elizabeth as soon as the All Clear sounded to ask about you. She came back looking terrible – a little white-faced ghost. At first she couldn't say a word, and when we impatiently questioned her about you she said, "There is no house – they are all dead."' And they had wept – for Richard and me – and for the baby about which they had all been so glad. When we appeared so quietly and unexpectedly in their kitchen it was as if we had been resurrected – for they had mourned us as dead – as many people were to do.

How they welcomed us! I can never forget their warmth and kindness that morning and their joy that we were alive. They had had a terrible night – as had most of Chelsea. The parachute mines had been dropped in pairs all along the river – and one had landed on the Infirmary, as we had been told. Maurice and Captain Townsend were still out with the heavy rescue who were still digging for the bodies of those killed. So far thirteen had been brought out and had been laid in the chapel – amongst them the oldest of the Pensioners, Rattray, who was a hundred years old and had been in the sick bay for a slight indisposition.

The one thing I wanted was a bath – and there was no water anywhere. My body was saturated with Anne's blood. When I caught sight of myself in a mirror I understood why Peggy had stared at me without recognition the previous night. My hair was white. At first I thought that it had turned white as fiction tells us can happen from great shock or grief, but my face was white too – streaked like a clown's – and closer examination showed me that my entire head and hair were white from the plaster and dust which had buried me. Suzanne lent me a stiff brush and it was a relief to find that when I was brushed my hair was still its normal colour!

Just enough water remained in the tank for me to have an apology for a bath. I think it did more harm than good for the water was stained red almost at once when I started washing myself and I felt even more dirty. Peggy had lent me a nurse's dress and this I put on now. What remained of my black dress was saturated in blood, and the pearls which I had been wearing had broken and fallen to my waist and had been held there by my belt. They were now red, not white, and I washed them in the bath and knew that I could never bear to wear them again.

Suzanne made us have some breakfast – and to my surprise I managed to eat a little – but Richard could not. He looked curiously mechanical, like a robot – as if he were living in a dream and performing everyday actions as a puppet does. I felt the same, detached from my body. When my face smiled, or my mouth opened to speak or eat, I felt that it wasn't part of me, and I could hear myself saying, 'Now I'm smiling, now I'm eating, now I'm drinking.' I thought he must feel the same way. Afterwards I found that he was suffering from concussion and that this detached feeling must have been far more marked for him.

He left me to try to rest while he went back to see if there was any news of Anne and Cecil and Kathleen. I tried to rest – but it was impossible. The Infirmary had suffered terrible damage from the parachute mine – and they did not as yet know how many casualties they had – but there were many injured as well as the dead.

Maurice confirmed that the Old Church had been completely demolished by another parachute mine and that the fire-watching party had perished in it with the exception of one member of it. A German plane had been brought down in Kensington High Street and a German pilot had parachuted over the Old Church and had given himself up to David Thomas. The Elms Garage above which the Canadians had billets had been set on fire by a high explosive bomb and the fearful blaze which we had seen on emerging from our wrecked home was from here. I was immediately uneasy about Larry, who had recently been given a billet in a house just there – I had the strangest feeling that he was in danger. There had been a number of Canadian casualties in the FAP, some of them badly burned. There was a strange dead stillness everywhere after the night's appalling havoc, as if the very earth had received a shock and was as numb as its inhabitants from the night's savagery.

I was anxious to get back to the site of No 33 to meet Mrs Freeth so that she would not get a shock. But having been up all night she had arrived early and, unfortunately, like Elizabeth, she had been told that we were dead. It was wonderful to see her face when she saw me picking my way over the heaps of glass with Vicki tucked under my arm. She was overjoyed – but the shock was too much for her and her small delicate face was absolutely colourless and I thought that she was going to faint. Telling her that had she been sleeping in her usual place in the kitchen she would have been killed instantly was no consolation to her for the loss of our home and friends.

Mr Ferebee came out of what remained of the shop – the contents of which were strewn all over the road. He seemed terribly upset. He took my hands very quietly and said that they had just taken my husband's body to the mortuary. 'No, No,' I told him, Richard was alive and well. But where was he now? Had he been poking about in the ruins and got caught in another fall of masonry? But as I stood there asking after all the neighbours with Mr Ferebee, whose wife and daughter Joan were both unhurt, Richard came down Tite Street. He had been to identify Cecil's body. They had not yet found Kathleen or Anne.

I took Mrs Freeth back to the Royal Hospital for a cup of tea – she was terribly pale and shocked, and on the way I called in at the FAP. They were still receiving a few late casualties, and still dealing with stretcher and ambulance cases as people were released from being trapped. A Canadian whom I knew was coming into the post as I was leaving. He told me that they had a lot of injured Canadians – and that Larry was just being brought out from the house in which he had been sleeping recently, 'He's pretty far gone,' he said, 'he was trapped under heavy stuff for hours.' I ran down Tite Street with him, leaving Mrs Freeth and Vicki to wait. Larry was quite conscious as he lay there on the pavement awaiting a stretcher party. He smiled as I bent down and knelt on the pavement beside him. 'You'll have to find another godfather for junior,' he said in a whisper, then he gave a sigh – just as if he were very tired after the long night, and was falling asleep.

When I went back to the site of No 33 later, heavy rescue were already digging. Two of the diggers were friends of mine. When they saw me they downed spades and rushed up. 'We've just told a lady you're dead,' they cried and, dirty as they were, hugged me and Vicki. 'Miss Hitler's safe! Good for her! We were digging for you, Miss Hitler.' They handed her round, one to another. I asked about the lady who had come asking for me – I feared it was Jennie who had been coming to lunch and might have turned up early – as indeed she had. It was a lady with a bunch of flowers and a box of chocolates, they said. She appeared faint when she saw the appalling mass of ruins, and had asked them if they knew what had happened to me. The large dirty man holding Vicki said apologetically, 'I said, "If she's a young woman we've just dug up her arm" – you see we was digging in the front part of what was your home – so naturally I thought it was your arm. Well, when she heard that she went all faint again. We hadn't much water to spare, as you know the main's gone – but I gave her a few splashes. And then Mrs Freeth here come up and tells her you was all right and in the Royal Hospital, so off she goes to telephone you – in that call box there – ' he pointed to the box in which we had seen the wounded warden last night. 'And when she gets in there there's blood all over the place and bits of flesh – so she passes right out.'

I asked them what they were digging further for. 'The baby,' said one tough man, holding up a tiny woollen sock and what had once been the blue rabbit. 'There must have been a baby staying here last night.' 'No,' I said. 'No. The baby's still here! It's not born yet.' The man holding Vicki came over to me. 'There's lots of little things here in the dirt,' he said sadly, 'they're all spoiled.' They were covered with a strange blackish, sticky mess.

I had caught sight of that piece of white stuff I had seen in the pile of bricks the previous night. I started climbing up the pile. 'Hi! I'll get it for you,' said the man. 'It's part of the parachute – that's what this little lot was – a bloody parachute mine! Here you are – it'll make some new clothes in place of all these!' and he handed me a huge piece of heavy white silk. It was a wonderful find and I took it gratefully. 'There was a bloody German come down in one of them over Chelsea Old Church last night,' he said. 'One of my mates has just told us about it.'

'And the Old Lombard Restaurant's gone – still digging for the trapped there,' said another. From Chris and Denise in the Control Room I heard that the list of incidents was formidably long and that it had been Chelsea's very worst night. So overwhelmed with catastrophes were the ARP and Fire Services that for a short time there had been chaos resulting from the six parachute mines, many heavy high-explosive bombs, and showers of incendiaries hurled on the small borough. The Mutual Aid plan by which neighbouring boroughs helped one another could not be operated because Kensington was equally hard-pressed with heavy incidents.

Standing there by the great heap which had been our home without possessing even a pocket handkerchief gave me an extraordinary feeling of freedom mingled with awe. Yesterday it had been a lovely home filled with choice and beautiful objects. Like all the others round it, it had vanished in a few seconds, truly 'gone with the wind'. I understood a little then of how some of the bombed-out and refugees must have felt, but strangely enough I didn't mind at all. I had already learned that home is to be with the person you love, and hadn't I been wonderfully blessed in having Richard, the expected baby, and even Vicki all saved? As I turned over some of the rubble looking for even a chip of the Green Cat I thought of the Second Commandment, for, like the huge carpets, the heavy furniture, and easels, he had simply disintegrated into dust.

Some hundred feet away I found my portable gramophone almost buried in debris. It was full of small bits of concrete and smelled of gunpowder. There was a record on the disc and when I started the machine the gay, clear tune of 'Oh Johnnie, Oh Johnnie, Oh' floated out amongst all that devastation. I took the record and smashed it. That fateful song which had heralded the violent death of so many dancers at the Café de Paris had been one of Anne's favourites.

A terrible aching emptiness, a feeling of acute helplessness and futility, came over me as I surveyed the appalling devastation of our little 'colony'. It all seemed so senseless. I had overheard a small boy say to his mother when passing Shawfield Street – still an area of desolation – 'But who done it, Mum?' And when she replied that the German airmen were responsible the child had said, 'When I'm grown up I'll be able to smash up houses – you don't let me break anything, you punish me if I do.'

I could still hear the teasing, laughing voice of Cecil on the telephone the previous night as he had said, 'Sure we'll come down. We'll come down with the rubble!' And just then the telephone in the ruins of our home began ringing loudly and insistently. It seemed extraordinary that it could still be in working order and yet completely inaccessible buried in that heap. I knew that it must be my sister telephoning as usual to know if we were all right.

When I turned away from the diggers and the site there stood Catherine and a crowd of refugees. They were gazing at the huge mounds which represented the place where they had always been able to come with their troubles – silent and red-eyed they gathered round me, overcome with the magnitude of the devastation around them. The Giant, gruff and furious, embraced me openly with tears streaming down his face. I thought, how strange that he can cry – I would so love to find some relief in tears – but not one would come. I could not weep – but my throat ached and ached; and I thought why is it that we British all go about in a calamity or tragedy with stiff upper lips and poker faces while these people can weep and cry and laugh and release their feelings as they ought to do?

Catherine, white-faced and silent, did not cry either, but the misery in her eyes was eloquent. 'Where will you go, Marraine? What shall you do now?' They gathered excitedly round Mrs Freeth and we told them about Kathleen, Anne, Larry, and Cecil, whom they had all known. I said that there was the house in Tite Street – negotiations were completed for that. I saw them look at one another and then Catherine said, 'It's been terribly damaged – you won't be able to live there.' She came and said urgently, 'You could come to my room – and there's another empty one in the house – won't you come and stay there?' I said I was going to some relatives for a few nights because it seemed that I might be going to lose the baby – after that I would come back and see them all, and that if they needed anything they could go to Suzanne. Catherine's mute misery was heart-rending. I went over to her and told her that I would try to find a house where she could come to us and have Francesca with her, and she looked despairingly at me when I said good-bye. It was melancholy leaving them all standing there in the ruins, and I felt as though I were the Old Woman who lived in a Shoe having to leave her large family.

But there was nothing sentimental or melancholy about old Granny from Paradise Walk. When I turned to leave the refugees, there she stood, arms akimbo, surveying the heap which had once been my home. 'Are they all gone?' she demanded. I thought she meant Kathleen, Anne, and Cecil. I nodded, not able to speak. 'It's cruel bad luck after all the trouble we went to,' she said. 'What trouble?' I asked, puzzled. 'Why, going to the lawyers and all that swearing, it'll all be wasted. Have you looked in that heap there?' And then I realized that she was speaking of the papers which were to help prove the dates of her and her husband's births – that was the only thing which interested her.

Later in the day I went to identify Kathleen. She looked quite peaceful with the kitten still in her arms. Someone would later have to perform on Anne's broken body that last task which I had done for so many of my fellow citizens.

I had no clothes – nor had Richard – and clothes were rationed. I went to the Assistance Office to which the Town Hall sent me. There were long queues of draggled and desolate-looking people waiting for clothes coupons because they had been bombed-out. At the Town Hall Margerie Scott had been very sweet and had given me a slip of paper with details of the total destruction of my home and possessions. A charming man looked at me and said, 'You'll want new ration books and everything, won't you?' Margerie Scott had obviously stated in her note that I was pregnant. He gave me coupons for the expected baby too. I was wearing the dirty old camel-hair coat and a scarf was tied round my head to hide the filthy state of my hair. My legs were cut and scratched and my stockings in tatters. He looked me up and down and said with a charming smile, 'I'd better give you some money, hadn't I?' and into my ungloved hand he put thirty pounds in notes. I had never been given money without having to earn it and I must have looked surprised, for he said, 'It's all right – it'll come off your War Damage claim, it's not charity.'

There was a little woman from Dovehouse Street sitting huddled on a bench awaiting her turn. Dovehouse Street had had a parachute mine on it and the Chelsea Hospital for Women had dealt with many casualties. Suddenly her control gave way and she began screaming in a frenzy of grief...'He's gone...He's gone and I'm all alone and no home – nothing. No one wants me...Why didn't I go with him, it's cruel, it's cruel, cruel. *Why? Why?*' Her anguish was terrible.

In the appalled silence with which officialdom treats such out-bursts – almost as if she had said or done something obscene – a sleek, well-dressed clergyman standing there whom I had never seen in Chelsea went up to her and told her sternly to desist – that what had happened was God's will and that she must accept it and thank Him for her own deliverance from death. She looked at him in dazed misery as if he spoke a foreign language and began screaming again even more wildly. 'God! There's no God! There's only Hitler and the Devil!' When he began remonstrating with her again in an intolerably unctuous voice I went over to her and rocked her as one does a child in pain. Slowly she became quiet and her violence gave way to bitter sobbing. 'She must accept it – not resent it in this bitter spirit,' he said to me. 'Acceptance of God's will is part of the Christian faith.' I looked at his well-kept hands, at his beautifully tended nails, and I thought of the Reverend Arrowsmith and his curate digging frantically with their bare hands in the rubble, of the Reverend Newsom sitting night after night on a hard bench sharing with his parishioners the perils of the Blitz, and then of the vicar of the Old Church, the Reverend Sadleir, fighting the incendiaries and looking after his fire parties so wonderfully – and now his church was gone. I thought of how Kathleen and Anne were dead – and Penty, who could never earn her own living or care for herself, was still alive – of Cecil and Larry who had volunteered to come from so far to help Britain in her need – and I said nothing. It did not seem to me that there was anything to say.

When she was quieter I took the woman to the canteen and made her drink some tea and swallow some aspirin and bromide. 'God?' she kept saying. 'There's no God! There's no God. If there is he's a devil!' The anguish was giving way to a bitter resignation. Her home had been demolished as mine had been, and she would have to go to a Rest Centre until she decided what to do. This seemed to her terrible – to her a Rest Centre was a kind of Poor-House! Her husband had been killed – he had been her life, her all. She had loved him. 'He was no beauty,' she kept telling me, 'but he suited me all right – and he never hurt a creature in his life. Why should he be blown to pieces?' Why indeed? Why? Hers was the question to which there is no answer except perhaps that of the well-meaning clergyman.

It was difficult to leave the little woman, who asked pathetically if she could not come with me out of London, but I did not dare to take her, as the relatives who had agreed to receive us for a few days had not been very pleased at the prospect of having us. I left her with the WVS, who said they would get her fixed up somewhere and would help her to get some clothes.

Suzanne came with me to buy the necessities we both urgently needed and then Richard and I were driven out of London. It was not easy to drive anywhere – the streets were blocked by great mounds of fallen masonry, glass, and debris. All along the Embankment the firemen's hoses lay across the wide street and houses sprawled with the vitals and bones spread out. The Old Lombard Restaurant had been almost demolished and men were digging on it as we passed. The top stories of Cheyne Hospital appeared to have been badly damaged, but as we came to the Old Church we stopped appalled, and got out of the car. I had heard about the horror of the night there – but its reality surpassed imagination. One great mound of dust was all that was left of the lovely little church – and men were digging all over it! The sun shone on the gap where Petyt Place had been – removed as if with giant tongs. The vicar was safe – but the entire fire-watching party, including seventeen-year-old schoolboy Michael Hodge, home for the holidays, had all perished with the exception of one member.

All up Old Church Street there were smoking ruins and masses of glass and debris sprawled everywhere. A heavy acrid smell lingered in the air in spite of the breeze from the river – the smell we had come to identify with Blitz.

We had heard that Dr Castillo had again done heroic work during the night, and amongst his casualties in Old Church Street had been a sixteen-year-old girl, Emma Chandler, trapped in the ruins of her home, with whom he had stayed for hours giving her morphia and talking to her until she was freed – to die soon afterwards, as the old woman in the straw hat had done.

I could not bear to leave Chelsea even for the few nights which the doctors insisted were necessary if I wanted my baby to be born safely; and to leave her thus with gaping wounds, smouldering burns, and her mortuaries crowded made it more poignant. The dust was still rising from the great mounds of rubble – it looked like smoke – and through its film the daffodils in More's little garden which had surrounded the church were dancing gaily.

Kathleen, Anne, and Cecil were buried with full military honours by the Canadian authorities in a joint grave in Kensal Green Cemetery. It was a most moving ceremony, and many of Cecil's unit of the Canadian Army Service Corps were present – including all his officers. There are other graves with the simple stone and the maple leaf on it, round them – the Canadians who died in the 1914-18 war – but for civilians to be honoured by the maple leaf and the 'Pro Patria' is unique. The authorities had intended Cecil to be buried with Larry at Woking with the Canadian casualties of the current war, but Kathleen's relatives wanted the family together, and after some trouble this was arranged. On the stone Cecil's name and military number are followed by these words, 'Also his wife, Anne, and her mother, Kathleen Marshman, were killed by enemy action at the same time. Pro Patria.'

It seemed to me right that they should all be honoured in this way – it symbolized for me all those men and women, many of them civilians, who were taking part in the battle of London and linked them with the Army.

As soon as I was allowed I began helping Kathleen's sister-in-law, May Sargent, in salvaging what we could for the benefit of the only remaining member of the family, Penty, still in the country with the friends in whose guardianship she had been left. There was little to salvage – and the search through the filthy, evil-smelling, dusty mess of salvage from the various sites was heart-rending. All the objects, garments, and remnants of once valued household goods which had been found by the demolition men had been stored in requisitioned houses by the borough. Strangely enough, although the Marshman's flat had been above ours, and had completely vanished in the explosion, we did find a few small things which Kathleen had loved. We arrived one day at the desolate mound of rubble to find the diggers having their mid-morning tea on the pavement. They were sitting on a beautiful Persian rug and drinking their tea from an old silver tea-pot which Kathleen had used every afternoon. May asked them rather sarcastically when they would be finished with the tea-pot as she wanted to claim it but, unabashed, they replied that it made such good tea that they had got quite accustomed to it! Together she and I visited the dreary rooms set aside for housing salvaged goods. Incredibly filthy, smelling of explosives and the strange smell which can be only described as 'Blitz', it was a sordid and melancholy task. There was absolutely nothing found which was usable from our home – the only small things salvaged had been got out the day after the bombing by young Paul Fitzgerald who, unknown to anyone, and in spite of the appalling danger, had crawled in and retrieved a few toilet articles of mine from the damaged dressing-table.

There were many stories of the night of April 16th – already known as 'the Wednesday'. The German parachutist had actually landed almost on the church and had given himself up to the wardens, who were at first at a loss to know what to do with him. There had been parachute mines on Cheyne Walk, Cranmer Court, the Old Church, and our one on Cheyne Place, as well as the Royal Hospital Infirmary, Dovehouse Street, and Sutton Dwellings, and high-explosive bombs on the Elms Garage, Post E in Cale Street, Chelsea Square, and many off the Embankment, as well as hundreds of incendiaries. There had been a very large number of casualties and terrible damage. Several firemen had been killed and many wardens injured, and Roger Crewdson had been killed at his post.

Maurice, not knowing what to do with the thirteen dead from the badly damaged Infirmary, had laid them in the Chapel, whereupon it had been suggested to him that the Chapel had been desecrated and would have to be reconsecrated. He had immediately got in touch with the highest Church authority on this point and he was delighted with the reply – that there was no precedent for this as no record existed of its having been done in the case of Thomas a Becket!

Mr Graham Kerr had spent the most dangerous night of the Blitz guarding a tree which had been hurled across the Embankment road by an explosion – later he was joined by an oil bomb! In spite of this he stuck the whole appalling night out in the open there, holding a red lantern for the ARP Services for which Nonie Iredale-Smith was doing an equally dangerous task by trying to keep the thoroughfare clear. George Evans had had to rope off our part of the Royal Hospital Road because of the devastation and had some trouble with a Naval officer who had been badly shocked and had all the lights of his car full on. When another car approached with a Naval officer in it George was ready and, still smarting from his recent encounter, he said, 'You can b— well get to the other side of that barrier – that's what it's there for!' The Naval officer, a short sturdy man with rows of ribbons and much gold braid, obeyed immediately and got back into the car. He drove straight to the Town Hall, and complimented them on their wardens – and left £5 as a gift for Post K. The Naval officer was Evans of the Broke, Regional Commissioner for London!

All over London there were similar stories of 'the Wednesday' and the savage and indiscriminate bombing of that night was being boasted of by the Germans.

The war news at this time seemed particularly depressing to me, probably because I was suffering from the loss of so many friends. Richard was extremely busy at the Ministry, and away frequently on tour. Relatives and friends deprived of any help in the home and many of them engaged on war work were very kind but I began hunting at once for a house.

Our troops were withdrawing from Greece and the Germans had occupied Larissa, Thermopylae, and Thebes and were rapidly advancing on Athens, the Greek army having capitulated in Epirus and Macedonia. Fighting was still violent at Tobruk where we had repulsed the Germans, and the RAF were bombing Cologne, Hamburg, Kiel, and Wilhelmshaven heavily. Plymouth was still being heavily attacked by the Luftwaffe, my mother wrote me.

In the evacuation of our troops from Greece we had lost several vessels, including HMS *Diamond* and *Wryneck*. All the time I was hunting vainly for some kind of home the news from Greece was bad – until finally the Germans entered Athens and completed their occupation of the Greek mainland.

On May 4th Hitler addressed the Reichstag in the Kroll Opera House. Again he tried to shift the guilt for the war on to England. 'All my attempts to make an understanding for a lasting friendly collaboration with England failed,' he said, 'owing to a small clique which refused every German offer and wanted war by all means.' He ranted on in his usual vein about Jewish capitalists and England's guilt and concluded with the statement that 'In this Jewish capitalist age, the National Socialist State stands out as a solid monument to common sense. It will survive for a thousand years.'

I read this in the *Manchester Guardian* and wondered just why he should have chosen a thousand years – why not two thousand? Or why not settle it for eternity while he was about it? To listen to his ravings, as I often did, was to receive the very proof that he, at any rate, could not last, such maniacal outpourings proclaiming his own doom. Nevertheless, it was depressing to listen to the thunderous applause with which his every utterance was greeted. How different was a speech by Mr Churchill on May 7th, giving the position of affairs in the Middle East and the distribution of our forces there. Again he repeated, 'I have never promised you anything but blood, tears, toil, and sweat to which I will now add our fair share of mistakes, shortcomings, and disappointments, and also that this may go on for a very long time, at the end of which I believe that there will be complete, absolute, and final victory.' He went on to give us a grave warning about the Battle of the Atlantic not being over.

It was strange but the British seemed to flower on 'the blood, tears, toil, and sweat' while the Germans only bloomed in the sun of Hitler's extravagant utterances. I had seen my friends in the height of the Blitz battling amongst those four things promised by Mr Churchill, and in my much-travelled life I have never been more thrilled and amazed by their heroism. The quietest and most unexpected people seemed endowed with the courage of lions and the endurance of steel. Tireless and undaunted, they knew no thought of self as they faced fearful odds in the battle to save their fellow-men and their borough from the destruction from the skies.

Chelsea's last heavy raid of the eight months' Blitz came on May 10/11th. There had been bad incidents on the Saturday following 'the Wednesday', but it was on May 11th, when the Houses of Parliament were hit, that Chelsea suffered most. The Red Cross and St John's did magnificent work on both these occasions and were warmly praised, with the whole ARP Services. On May 11th a heavy bomb fell through the operating theatre of St Luke's Hospital, killing two doctors and several nurses and wrecking two wards, the radiography and kitchen departments, and most of the reception halls as well as the doctors' quarters. The hospital had to be closed for the simple reason that it could no longer be run.

Dr Richard Symes Thompson was one of the doctors killed by the bomb. The death of this unusual and brilliant young man was a personal as well as a public loss. He had taken great interest in the refugees and had been a real friend. He had shown great skill in new methods of treating burns, of which we had many in the Blitz. It was he who had been so kind over David, Madeleine, and little Raymond.

Thousands of incendiaries were showered on Chelsea during the raid of May 11th and many high-explosive bombs fell in the river. Work was hampered by a blazing barge loaded with paper outside Phillips Mills and the air was thick with little pieces of black charred paper like a black snowstorm. The acrid smell of burning paper was quite overpowering and suffocating to the firemen and wardens fighting the blaze. The shower of charred paper like a flickering curtain silhouetted against the flames was an eerie and unforgettable spectacle.

The closing of St Luke's Hospital, combined with the loss of more friends both in the RAF and at sea, was for me another landmark in the war, but although we did not know it at the time, May 11th was to mark the end of the eight months' Blitz on London. Three years were to elapse before Chelsea's foundations were to be shaken by an 'incident' (February 23rd, 1944), the magnitude of which was to make all the preceding ones seem small. Incident No 757 in the Control Room file became known as a classic and was called the 'Guinness' one. As with all other incidents, the triumph for the wardens, especially Post C, after eight days, tracing of its seventy-five dead and many more injured who were to succumb later, lay in the last words on the Control file: 'Untraced, Nil.'

In June we found an old house about twenty-five miles from Chelsea at Claygate near Esher, and here we stayed until it was severely damaged by a flying bomb, and we returned to Chelsea. The house next to the church at Claygate was large, if not comfortable, and it had a rambling old-world garden. There was room for Catherine and Francesca, for Carla and for our coming baby, and for the many refugees who came to visit us there. It was astonishing how quickly they found their way from Waterloo and arrived full of troubles, as usual. To my surprise and delight the Welsh Guards were later stationed at Esher and I found Rex Whistler billeted on the very next house to ours with, as he remarked chuckling, 'only the church between us'. It was from here that he left with his unit for Normandy on D Day, to be killed almost instantly.

Our little colony in the Royal Hospital Road was sadly changed and depleted. The Ferebees had been obliged to move to another shop because of the complete wrecking of the one there. All our former neighbours were either dead or had moved away because of the devastation. It was too painful to return to that immediate neighbourhood even had we been able to find a house there. Only the Royal Hospital remained as beautiful as ever; in spite of its formidable list of bombs and severe damage its lovely facade was unchanged, and the kindness of the Fitzgerald family made it home to me whenever I went on my regular visits to the refugees. It was the very first place in London to which I took my son, John, born in an air raid, and a fine sturdy baby in spite of all the gloomy prognoses. He had no more faithful nurse and 'baby sitter' than Miss Hitler, whose maternal instincts found an outlet in guarding him.

Later, in the autumn, I went with May Sargent to meet Penty, Kathleen's younger daughter, at a London station. I was told that she had never mentioned her mother or her sister. It is difficult to know what is going on in the minds of normal people, but in those who are different – over whose minds a double veil is drawn – it is impossible. I don't know how much Penty actually realized. I was told that she did not appear to have understood anything of what had happened to her home and family; but when she saw me a great trembling came over her, and for a time she could not say anything. Then she said, in the quick, slight, hesitating speech which was hers, 'How's the Green Cat?'

THE END

The following photographs did not appear in the original edition of *A Chelsea Concerto*. They are published now courtesy of John Parker, Frances Faviell's son.

1. The remains of Cheyne Walk, after the air raid described in Chapter XX

2. Richard Parker, Frances Faviell and Vicki, early 1940's

FURROWED MIDDLEBROW

Printed in Great Britain
by Amazon